Francesco Bartolomeo Conti

His Life and Music

Hermine Weigel Williams

Ashgate

Aldershot • Brookfield USA • Singapore • Sydney

Published by

Ashgate Publishing Limited
Gower House, Croft Road,
Aldershot, Hampshire GU11 3HR
Great Britain

Ashgate Publishing Company
Old Post Road,
Brookfield, Vermont 05036–9704
USA

Ashgate website: http://www.ashgate.com

ISBN 1–85928–388–8

British Library Cataloguing-in-Publication Data
Williams, Hermine Weigel
     Francesco Bartolomeo Conti: His Life and Music
     1. Conti, Francesco Bartolomeo, 1682-1732. 2. Composers—Italy—Biography.
     3. Composers—Austria—Vienna—Biography. 4. Music—Austria—Vienna—
     18th century—History and criticism. I. Title.
     780.9'2

US Library of Congress Cataloging-in-Publication Data
Williams, Hermine Weigel.
     Francesco Bartolomeo Conti: His Life and Music
        p.   cm.   An expanded and rev. version of the author's thesis (Ph.D.)
     Colombia University, 1964.
     Includes bibliographical references (p.) and index (hbk).
     1. Conti, Francesco. 1682-1732. 2. Music—Austria–Vienna—18th century—
     History and criticism. I. Title.
     ML410.C7533W55   1999   99-31629
     782'.0092—dc21   CIP

This volume is printed on acid free paper.

Printed and bound in Great Britain by MPG Books Ltd, Bodmin, Cornwall

Francesco Bartolomeo Conti

His Life and Music

For Jay, and my children

Jay III, Lynn Marie, Amédée Daryl, and Ruth Christine

Contents

List of examples

List of tables

Auditorium of the Hoftheater, Vienna, designed by Francesco Galli-Bibiena.
Engraving by Johann Andreas Pfeffel and Christian Engelbrecht, c. 1704.
(Reproduced with permission of the Deutsches Theatermuseum, Munich.)

Introduction

At the beginning of the eighteenth century, three composers dominated the musical life of the Habsburg court in Vienna – Johann Josef Fux (1660-1741), Antonio Caldara (1670-1736), and Francesco Bartolomeo Conti (1682-1732). While Fux and Caldara have been the focus of numerous studies, with representative scores published in facsimile and modern editions, the third member of this trio has received relatively little attention.[1]

Historical perspective

The very first study of Conti's life and works was a dissertation written by Josef Schneider in 1902 for the University of Vienna. Less than a third of that study, however, is devoted to a discussion of biographical materials and musical style. Instead, the major portion of the dissertation presents a thematic catalogue of the operas, oratorios, and cantatas. For each work cited, Schneider has provided the scoring and opening line of text of every aria, duet, and chorus.[2] In Georg Reichert's dissertation of 1935 on the history of the early eighteenth-century Viennese mass, also written for the University of Vienna, one can find a description and illustrated examples of two of Conti's masses.[3] Nothing else of any significance appeared from 1935 until the 1960s, except the biographical entry in *Die Musik in Geschichte und Gegenwart* by Bernhard Paumgartner, who described Conti as possibly being one of the most musically gifted of all the Viennese opera composers of his generation.[4] In 1963 Wulf Arlt published an extensive study of Conti's earliest extant opera, *Il trionfo dell'amicizia e dell' amore*, and in 1967 Stefan Kunze included a discussion of *Don Chischiotte in Sierra Morena* in his informative essay on the *buffo* librettos based upon the Don Quixote story.[5]

My interest in Conti as both a composer and a performer spans more than four decades. It began with the writing of a dissertation on his life and operas

(1964), continued with the publication of several of his instrumental *sinfonie* and a preliminary thematic index of his major secular and sacred dramatic works (1983), and eventually broadened into an essay which summarized his sacred music (1984).[6] More recently I have expanded my investigation to include the cantatas and intermezzos. This volume therefore represents a collation of past and current research which presumably provides a more composite picture of Conti's dual role as performer and composer and places into proper perspective his contribution to the history of the Austro-Italian Baroque era. The present study offers an opportunity to correct errors of judgment and fact set forth in my own writings cited above as well as in those recently published by others that have touched upon Conti's career in relation to Fux, Caldara, and Pietro Pariati. No attempt has been made to provide detailed information about the music composed by Francesco's son, Ignazio Conti. That aspect of the Conti saga will be explored at a later date. Similarly, the preparation of an updated thematic catalogue of the works of both Francesco and Ignazio Conti has been deferred until an analysis of watermarks and copyists can be more fully researched.[7]

The organization of this book

The present study makes available to a wider audience material first presented in my dissertation. To this has been added my subsequent research on Conti's life and compositions, substantially expanding the perimeters of the dissertation which was limited to secular dramatic works. The book is divided into two parts. The first treats the biographical aspects of Conti's career; the second focuses on the librettists, the performing musicians, and the music. The text is illustrated with a limited number of examples, supplementing those found in appendix III of my dissertation and in *The Symphony 1720-1840*, Series B, volume II (devoted to a representative sampling of overtures by Italians in Vienna), the latter containing nine complete *sinfonie* by Conti.

Acknowledgements

The material set forth in this study is based primarily on sources located in Vienna. I am indebted to Dr Günter Broschel, together with the current and past directors and staff of the Musiksammlung of the Österreichische

Nationalbibiliothek who have graciously responded promptly to my every request for access to their extensive collection of manuscripts. Dr. Otto Biba of the Gesellschaft der Musikfreunde and the archivist of the Schottenstift were most helpful in making their respective manuscript collections available for my research. I am also indebted to the staff of the Stadtarchiv, Staatsarchiv, Universitätsbibliothek, and the Finanz- und Hokammerarchiv, where court documents, financial records, testaments and other personal papers, and copies of the *Wienerisches Diarium* were consulted.

I gratefully acknowledge the help received from the directors and staff of libraries outside Vienna who supplied me with microfilms and photocopies of Conti's manuscripts or provided information about their archival holdings. These libraries include: Stift Herzogenburg, Herzogenburg; Department of Manuscripts, the British Library, London; Deutsche Staatsbibliothek, Berlin; Biblioteca musicale G. B. Martini, Bologna; Staats- und Universitätsbilbiothek, Hamburg; Mecklenburgische Landesbiblitothek, Schwerin; Library of Congress, Washington, DC; Biblioteca Nazionale Central and Archivio di Stato, Florence; Uppsala Universitetsbibliotek, Upssala; Universitäts- und Landesbibliothek, Münster; Meininger Museen, Musikgeschichte Archiv, Meiningen; Archiv města Brna, Brno; Sächsische Landesbibliothek, Dresden; Hessische Landes- und Hochschulbibliothek, Darmstadt; and the Osborn Collection in the Beinecke Rare Book and Manuscript Library, Yale University, New Haven, CT.

I owe special thanks to a number of people who helped me during the course of writing this book. First and foremost, I want to extend special thanks to my friend and colleague, Brian W. Pritchard, of the University of Canterbury, Christchurch, New Zealand, who was ever willing and eager to respond to my numerous queries, especially those that related to sacred music performed in the Hofkapelle. His extensive knowledge of the music Antonio Caldara wrote for the imperial court proved to be an invaluable source of information. My thanks go also to Dr Wolfgang Payrich, Dr Inga Johansson, Dr Jürgen Neubacher, Dr Herta Müller, Dr Albert Ernst, Dr František Novák, Dr Rosalia Manno Tolu, Dr Urte Härtwig, Dr Giovanna Gronda, Dr Joachim Schlichte, Brian Moll, and the staff of the Burke Library of Hamilton College.

Permission to use excerpts for the musical examples was requested from the following: Schottenstift, Vienna: example 12.1-7; Sächsische Landesbibliothek, Dresden: examples 7.1a-d, 12.8a-b; Musiksammlung der Österreichischen Nationalbibliothek, Vienna: examples 8.2, 9.1-8, 10.1-5, 11.1-8; The Beinecke

Rare Book and Manuscript Library, New Haven, CT: example 8.1; and Deutsche Staatsbibliothek, Berlin: examples 8.3-4.

I am indebted to Christopher Marshall of Auckland, New Zealand, who graciously offered to format the musical examples for this book. Last, but not least, I wish to thank my husband, Jay, who has helped in whatever way he could to foster an environment conducive to research and writing.

Hermine Weigel Williams
Clinton, New York, June 1999

Notes

1 In addition to pre-1970 studies by Ludwig Ritter von Köchel, John Henry van der Meer, and Ursula Kirkendale, among others, there are two recently published volumes of in-depth essays on the music composed by Caldara and Fux: Brian W. Pritchard, ed., *Antonio Caldara, Essays on His Life and Times* (London, 1987) and Harry White, ed., *Johann Josef Fux and the Music of the Austro-Italian Baroque* (London, 1992).

2 Josef Schneider, 'Francesco Conti als dramatischer Componist' (diss., University of Vienna, 1902).

3 Georg Reichert, *Zur Geschichte der Wiener Messenkomponist in der ersten Hälfte des 18. Jahrhunderts* (diss., University of Vienna, 1935).

4 Bernhard Paumgartner, 'Conti', *Die Musik in der Geschichte und Gegenwart* (1952), II, 1640-43. An illustration accompanying this entry reportedly shows the opening folio of the overture to *Don Chisciotte in Sierra in Morena* (1719), but it bears no relationship to Conti's original overture. For a discussion of this problem, see chapter seven.

5 Wulf Arlt, 'Zur Deutung der Barockoper: *Il trionfo dell'amicizia e dell'amore* (Wien, 1711)', in *Musik und Geschichte. Leo Schrade zum sechzigsten Geburtstag* (Cologne, 1963), 96-145; Stefan Kunze, 'Die Entstehung eines Buffo-Librettos. Don-Quijote-Bearbeitungen', *Deutsches Jahrbuch der Musikwissenschaft* 12 (1967): 75-95.

6 Hermine Weigel Williams, 'Francesco Bartolomeo Conti: His Life and Operas' (diss., Columbia University, 1964); *idem*, 'Francesco Bartolomeo Conti: Nine Sinfonie', in Barry Brook, ed., *The Symphony 1720-1840*, Series B, vol. II: *Italians in Vienna.* (New York, 1983), xiii-xxxvi, 1-96; *idem*, 'The Sacred Music of Francesco Bartolomeo Conti: Its Cultural and Religious Significance', in Edmund Strainchamps and Maria Rika Maniates, eds, *Music and Civilization: Essays in Honor of Paul Henry Lang* (New York, 1984), 326-34.

7 A preliminary thematic catalogue was published in *The Symphony 1820-1840*, Series B, vol. II, xxxi-vi.

Part I

CHAPTER ONE

From the Medici to the Habsburgs

Francesco Bartolomeo Conti was born in Florence, Italy, on 20 January 1681/1682.[1] Little is known about his formative years except that before the age of seventeen he had become a highly esteemed theorbist in the service of the Medici family. Some measure of the young musician's talent and activities is revealed in correspondence dating from 1699 to 1701. In a letter of 11 March 1699 Don Diego Felipez de Guzman, Governor of Milan, had Secretary Sesto thank Cardinal Francesco Maria de' Medici for allowing Conti to participate in performances of the Carnival opera that season. Apparently the orchestra in Milan lacked a theorbist for the opera production and Cardinal de' Medici was asked to help fill the position with a theorbist in his employ. So delighted was the Milan audience with Conti's theorbo playing, Sesto asked if he might be engaged for the next Carnival season.[2]

A similar request for a theorbist came to Prince Ferdinando de' Medici in 1700. This time it was from Cardinal Fulvio Astali, asking if Conti could participate in the festival of the Accademia della Morte in Ferrara.[3] These letters, together with other correspondence between Cardinal Francesco and his nephew Prince Ferdinando, confirm that Conti played the theorbo for both sacred and secular performances, not only in his native city but also in other Italian cities as well.

In March of 1701 Conti travelled to Vienna, perhaps at the invitation of the Kapellmeister Antonio Pancotti. A letter written on 26 March 1701 by Marco Martelli, the Tuscan envoy in Vienna, to Cardinal Francesco Maria de' Medici in Florence seems to be the only extant document to mention this visit.[4] Martelli's letter describes the honour paid by Emperor Leopold I and other members of the Habsburg court to the young theorbo virtuoso since his arrival there at the beginning of the month. The letter also sets forth Conti's request to remain under the protection of the Medici family during what he described as his limited stay in the imperial city. On the basis of this request it appears that Conti had every intention of returning to Florence. What caused him to change his mind a few days after Martelli's letter was written and to accept a position as court theorbist remains a mystery.

At the time of Conti's appointment, the Hofkapelle included one lutenist, Andre Boor (Pohr), and two theorbists.[5] Orazio Clementi was the principal theorbist, earning a monthly stipend of 100 florins. He had served the court as the sole theorbist from 1680 until 1697 when, because of his age, he required an assistant to help him shoulder the burden of the musical performances. Georg Reutter was appointed theorbist for this express purpose in 1697 with a monthly stipend of 25 florins.[6]

If Clementi had any hopes that Reutter might some day be his successor, he was soon to be disappointed. Reutter was far more interested in playing the organ than the theorbo and in August of 1700 he assumed an additional position as one of the court organists.[7] This meant the Kapellmeister had to find a musician who could eventually replace Clementi. Conti surely would have been a prime candidate, given his reputation in Florence and perhaps that is why he happened to be in Vienna during the month of March. Obviously the emperor and the Kapellmeister were favourably impressed with his talent, for he was offered a position with the same stipend as Clementi.

By the beginning of the eighteenth century the Habsburg court was well served by Italian composers, instrumentalists, and singers. Therefore the addition of another Italian to the list of court musicians was not particularly newsworthy. The office of the Obersthofmeister recorded the appointment of Conti as court theorbist in the *Hofprotokollbuch* on 12 July 1701. This brief entry was followed by a recommendation from the Kapellmeister that a monthly stipend of 100 gülden be paid to the theorbist retroactively from 1 April 1701.[8] Confirmation by the emperor that he agreed with this contractual arrangement appears in the *Hofprotokollbuch* on 23 August of that same year.[9]

Conti must have led a busy and interesting life during the final years of Leopold's reign. As a theorbist, he would have been expected to participate in large-scale secular and sacred works as well as in more intimate chamber works. The theorbo was used either as a solo or as a *basso continuo* instrument, often supplanting the organ or harpsichord. It could also share the continuo part with other instruments such as bassoon, violoncello, and harpsichord.

Unfortunately, extant materials offer few clues about Conti's musical activities in Vienna from 1701 to 1705. Only an occasional reference in the court's financial records serves as a reminder that he continued to perform his requisite duties. For example, an entry in the *Hofrechnungsbuch:1702* credits 'Franciscus

Bartolomaeus Conti' with 1800 florins. A notation beside this amount explains that Conti's annual stipend is supposed to be 1200 florins, but since he had not been paid for his services at the court from the beginning of April 1701 until the end of September 1702, he was now entitled to eighteen months' pay.[10]

That Conti received no payment for his services until October of 1702 should not surprise anyone acquainted with the financial problems which plagued the imperial realm. Often the court was so delinquent in the payment of wages that soldiers were forced to serve for four months or longer without pay. Musicians did not fare any better. They had grown accustomed to waiting long periods of time for the payment of their promised stipends. The situation was deplorable in 1701 and it did not improve with time. Throughout Conti's entire tenure at the court, this same problem persisted. The passage cited from the *Hofrechnungsbuch* is only the first of many such notices regarding delinquencies in payment of his stipend.

One of the most difficult problems facing the Habsburgs for more than a century involved the procurement of funds for the imperial treasury. The manner in which this could be effected varied considerably. Leopold was dependent upon subsidies and upon the Peter's pence which he received from the pope and for which he had to pay with his good conduct. He was dependent upon the reigning princes of the empire, or perhaps even more upon their business instinct, which extracted profits from every service rendered for as much as could be extorted by taxation.[11]

Musicians did not always wait complacently until court officials paid their stipends. Conti resorted to written petitions; others found more expedient methods to gain the emperor's attention. One author relates the following about the musicians serving Leopold I before 1690: 'And if as might sometimes happen, their salaries were not regularly paid, they would strike'.[12]

The financial plight of the court musicians contrasts sharply with the opulence of the nobility. Many of the nobles amassed considerable wealth from spoils of war as well as from unscrupulous dealings at court. Display of this wealth fostered an architectural renaissance in Vienna, the fervour of which was not lessened by the War of Spanish Succession. The narrow alleys which still bore the scars of the siege of 1683 were slowly transformed into elegant streets lined with buildings built in the Baroque style. The Pestsäule (1682-86) on the Graben and the Lobkowitz palace (1685-87) present isolated, but none the less excellent, examples of this style as it manifested itself prior to 1700.

Changes were also taking place outside the medieval walls of Vienna. Fields and villages, burnt and devastated during the Turkish siege, once again breathed with new life. Revitalized vineyards covered the slopes of Klosterneuberg; *heuriger* taverns flourished in Grinzing. The countryside, however, was not simply restored to its former self; the nobles were bent on transforming the landscape here just as they had done in the city. They built palaces with extensive and costly gardens, using them as summer residences. Moreover, this penchant for 'town and country' living, already in vogue with the Habsburgs, was to persist among the wealthy classes for many generations. As the seventeenth century drew to a close, Vienna began to look more and more like the capital of an empire. Strangely enough this transformation took place during the reign of an emperor who was intent upon preserving the *status quo*.

When Leopold I ascended the throne in 1658, the Habsburg realm showed only faint signs of its future brilliance. Leopold gave no indication of strength as a ruler. Contemporary accounts describe him as a thin, sickly, and melancholy figure of pale complexion, hollow cheeks, and a gross underlip, a peculiar characteristic of the Habsburg family. He deplored change. He wished that nothing concerning his private affairs or those of the realm should be altered.

As to his interests, there seems to be general agreement among contemporary accounts. Abbé Pacichelli, an Italian tourist visiting Vienna between 1670 and 1680, described them in this way: 'Next to the passion for hunting, with the concomitant sport of angling, Leopold's second great hobby was music and the theatre'.[13] The Duke of Gramont observed that 'he is fond of music, and understands it so far, that he composes very correctly most doleful melodies'.[14] The Habsburg family was indeed gifted with musical ability. Leopold composed and performed music for the court; his second wife, Claudia of Tyrol, played several instruments. In each of Leopold's four residences – Hofburg, Laxenburg, Favorita, Ebersdorf – musical entertainments were regularly held, especially to celebrate birthdays and name-days.

Musicians in the employ of Leopold I had opportunities to participate in musical activities outside the imperial capital, sometimes even outside the Habsburg realm. When, in 1702, the initial phase of the War of Spanish Succession caused a cessation of musical entertainment in Vienna, Giovanni Bononcini decided to find another venue where he and his colleagues could perform. The place he chose was Berlin, residence of Elector Friedrich III of Brandenburg and his wife Sophie Charlotte. There, in the summer of that same year, Bononcini composed and presented his one-act opera *Polifemo*. Georg

Philipp Telemann happened to be in Berlin when *Polifemo* was staged and his eyewitness account of the event, later printed by Johann Mattheson, mentions the names of some of the musicians playing in the opera orchestra. They include, among others, the composer and his brother, Antonio Maria Bononcini, playing cello, Francesco Conti playing theorbo, and Sophie Charlotte playing cembalo.[15]

The death of Leopold I's daughter, Maria Josefa, on 14 April 1703 was followed by a requisite year-long period of mourning, thereby causing the ban on festive entertainments to be prolonged. A limited number of performances of secular and sacred dramatic works, however, were permitted at the court, albeit in more modest garb and this meant that once the turmoil over the war subsided some, if not all, of the musicians would have resumed their performance duties as needed.

How soon Conti actually resumed his court obligations remains known, but he was probably on hand to play the theorbo for the 1704 production of Attilio Ariosti's opera *I gloriosi presagi*. It was not unusual for operas composed expressly for the Habsburgs to include an aria featuring the theorbo as a solo instrument. What is noteworthy about this particular opera is that in the aria 'Bella mia, lascio ch'io vada', scored for alto, theorbo, and *basso continuo*, there appears one of the most virtuoso parts ever written for a theorbist. Did Ariosti compose this aria with Conti in mind? That possibility certainly exists since, as librettist for *Polifemo*, Ariosti was involved with musical events in Berlin in 1702 at the same time as Conti was performing there.

That Conti possessed talents beyond that of being a virtuoso instrumentalist was first brought to light with *Il trionfi di Giosuè*. This pasticcio oratorio was created with music by fourteen composers and given its initial performance in Florence in 1703. The score no longer survives, but the printed libretto by Giovanni Pietro Berzini does, and it is here that the composers are listed, each according to his place of origin. Among those so named are Francesco Conti ('fiorentino'), Giovanni Bononcini ('di Bologna'), Alessandro Scarlatti ('siciliano') and Tomaso Albinoni ('veneziano'). This same oratorio appears to have been sung again in Florence, only this time, with its title changed to *Giosuè in Gabaon*, it was dedicated to Princess Eleonora and performed (*c.* 1710) under the sponsorship of the Compagnia di San Sebastiano.[16]

In his role as a court theorbist, Conti was closely associated with some of the best composers in Europe and perhaps he availed himself of an opportunity to study composition with one or more of them. Men such as Marc'Antonio Ziani,

Giovanni Bononcini and Carlo Badia were at the peak of their careers.[17] Their dramatic works were in demand for every 'Day of Gala' at the Habsburg court.

Another musician who undoubtedly influenced Conti in the formative stages of his career was Johann Joseph Fux. Since 1698, Fux had been serving the court as a composer. Along with this position, he served as organist at the Schottenkirche on the Freyung and from 1705 to 1711 as Kapellmeister of St Stephen's Cathedral (Stephansdom), ultimately becoming the Hofkapellmeister during the reign of Emperor Charles VI. Fux occupied a commanding position in Vienna's musical life and was highly regarded as a teacher of composition.

Simon Molitor, noted for his pioneering research into documents pertaining to the musical life of the Habsburg court, was among the first to find evidence for an opera by Conti dating from the year 1704. According to Molitor's unpublished notes, Leopold I had a collection of operas composed at his command and staged for his enjoyment. In a document listing the contents of the emperor's opera collection, Conti is named as both court composer and theorbist. He is credited with an opera commissioned in 1704, which was dedicated to the emperor and performed for a court festival that same year. Unfortunately the opera's title is not mentioned.[18]

Since no opera by Conti with a date of 1704 has survived and no record of a 1704 performance of one of his operas for a court festival has been found, the notion that this music ever existed must await further evidence. Molitor thought he had found that evidence when he became aware of a catalogue of printed opera librettos available at the Biblioteca musicale 'G. B. Martini' in Bologna. Listed in connection with Conti's name were several librettos which the compilers of the catalogue believed he had set to music. Two had the same title, *Alba Cornelia*, but were by different librettists. One was associated with a 1704 production in Milan, and the other with a 1714 production in Vienna. Only the second one named the composer.[19]

Conti, of course, did have some contact with Milan when he was in the service of the Medici family and therefore it would not have been outside the realms of possibility to find him occasionally returning there to take part in musical events. Even the cathedral archives in Milan seem to corroborate this idea. A catalogue of the cathedral's music prepared by Claudio Sartori in 1957 cites works by a Francesco B. Conti (Florence, 1682-Vienna, 1732) and a Francesco Conti (Florence, 1760-Vigevano, 1822).[20] To the former are attributed four settings of the Magnificat, but an investigation into the musical compositions preserved in the cathedral's archives shows Sartori's catalogue to be in error. The settings of the Magnificat attributed to the Conti of Vienna are in fact by 'Doc. F. Conti' of Vigevano.

Further proof that Conti was not involved with the music of the Milan cathedral comes from a register of its musicians. The *Annali* lists only two musicians with the surname of Conti: Francesco Conti, the 'maestro di Duomo Novara' who died in 1730, and Francesco Conti of Vigevano, cited above.[21] There is no mention of a Francesco Conti with the middle name of Bartolomeo nor of one connected with the court in Vienna.[22]

On 5 May 1705 Emperor Leopold I died, bringing to a close an important period of Habsburg history. Joseph I succeeded his father and his ascent to the imperial throne was greeted with considerable optimism by his subjects. Joseph was particularly fond of Italians and encouraged their presence in Vienna. He also continued his father's interest in music, both by his patronage and by actual participation in the composing and performing of music for the court. The number of new works heard in Vienna increased considerably during Joseph's brief reign as did the number of musicans employed by the court.

Out of deference to the deceased emperor, the court observed a year-long period of mourning which caused festive musical events to be curtailed or eliminated altogether. Musicians who had served under Leopold I did not automatically retain their respective positions under the new regime. Their reappointments were dependent upon the recommendation of the Obersthofmeister and were subject to the approval of the emperor.

Whether or not Conti served as a theorbist under Joseph I is a matter of some disagreement among writers of his biographical profile. Köchel, for one, claims that Conti was not employed by the court from 30 September 1705 to 1 January 1708, but he offers not a shred of evidence to support his statement.[23] Carlo Schmidl contends that Conti's name is absent from the court register of musicians beginning on 30 September 1703 and continuing until 1711 when Charles VI was declared the new emperor.[24] Robert Eitner also believes Conti was absent from the court for eight years, but the dates he gives are for a period extending from 30 September 1705 to 1 January 1713.[25]

Enough evidence exists in various court records to contradict the information presented by these three authors. For example, the Obersthofmeister compiled a list of musicians who were to serve Joseph I and a copy of this list was entered into the *Hofprotokollbuch* on 4 January 1706.[26] Under the heading of 'theorbist', two names appear: Orazio Clementi and Francesco Conti, both with yearly stipends of 1200 florins. Financial statements in the *Hofrechnungsbücher* provide additional evidence that Conti was in the employ of the Habsburgs without interruption from 1 April 1701 to 30 September 1706. Although his stipend was paid on an irregular basis, he nevertheless did receive the full amount of 6600 florins owed to him.

Sources other than court records also corroborate evidence that Conti was still in Vienna in the latter part of 1705, serving as a 'theorbist und Hof-Cammer-Musicus'. One is the *Kirchenbuch von St Stephan: 1704-1707*; another is the issue of the *Wienerisches Diarium* covering the period from 30 September to 2 October 1705. Both report that the marriage of Francesco Conti and Theresia Kuglerin of Edelfeld, the daughter of court violinist Ignaz Leopold Kugler, took place in Vienna on 1 October 1705.[27] There is no question that Francesco considered Theresia to be his first wife. He himself makes that very clear in several official documents, not the least of them his last will and testament dated 19 July 1732. In that same document, Francesco also refers more than once to his son, Ignazio, and to his sister, Cattarina Angela Conti.[28]

In the absence of birth or baptismal records, it has been difficult to determine the year or place of Ignazio's birth. At the time of his death on 28 March 1759, the obituary published in the *Wienerisches Diarium* stated he was 60 years old. On the basis of that information, the year of Ignazio's birth was figured to be 1699 and, since Conti did not move to Vienna until 1701, the place of birth was thought to be Florence.

Molitor drafted two handwritten versions of a biographical sketch of Francesco Conti. Both versions underscore the fact that Molitor was not aware of the theorbist's marriage to Theresia in 1705 nor had he found any pertinent marriage or baptismal documents in Florence. He was therefore left with the problem of finding a plausible explanation for the birth of Conti's first and only child, apart from suggesting that Ignazio might have been born out of wedlock. He reasoned that a talented musician, such as Francesco, would have been in great demand in his native city and therefore could have received sufficient funds to justify marriage at an early age. Then, without giving any sources to support his story, he relates that Francesco arrived in the imperial city with his infant son but without the baby's mother. Molitor suggests that the mother may have died in childbirth and this was the reason why Francesco took his sister, Cattarina Angela, to Vienna so that she could care for his child. Molitor also contends that the baby was initially named Francesco, then Francesco Ignazio and finally just Ignazio.[29]

In the testament cited above, Francesco mentions that Ignazio reached the 'age of majority' on 16 July 1729. If this date pertains to a birthday, as it presumably did, then at least the day and month, if not the year, of Ignazio's birth can be determined. Is it possible that Ignazio was born in Vienna on 16 July 1706, a date that would have been nine and a half months after Francesco's marriage? Is it possible that Ignazio was named for Theresia's father, Ignaz Leopold Kugler?

In the course of research undertaken to write a biographical profile of Conti, Josef Schneider came to the conclusion that the *Wienerisches Diarium* incorrectly stated how old Ignazio was at the time of his death, causing a projected birth date of 1699 also to be in error. Schneider figured Ignazio's birth date to be 16 July 1705 based upon the 'age of majority' phrase in the 1732 testament.[30] His calculation may be correct, but if it is, then Ignazio's birth took place prior to the marriage of Francesco and Theresia in October of 1705. Schneider did not know the date or place of this marriage nor did he and Molitor realize that the Conti-Kugler union was the first of three marriages for Francesco.

Notes

1   Ludwig Ritter von Köchel was one of the first to indicate the exact date of Conti's birth; he based his information on a baptismal register in Florence. Köchel, in *Johann Josef Fux* (Vienna, 1872), 94n2, contends that the year of birth should be 1682, not 1681, because the Florentine calendar of that era calculated the beginning of a new year from the 25 March, not from the 1 January. Other scholars have reckoned the year of birth to be 1681 based upon information published at the time of Conti's death, namely that he was then fifty-one years old. Wulf Arlt's article 'Zur Deutung der Barockoper', in *Musik und Geschichte* (Cologne, 1963), 98n5, sets forth the idea that Köchel may have misinterpreted the date supplied to him by not realizing an adjustment for the Florentine calendar had already been factored in. There may be other explanations for the discrepancy between Köchel's date of 1682 and Conti's stated age at death. For example, when asked for the year of his birth, Conti might well have responded that it was 1681, never bothering to adjust the year to conform to the calendar system in use in Vienna. It could also be argued that Conti was considered to be in the fifty-first year of his life when he died, since he had already celebrated his fiftieth birthday on 20 January 1732.

2   Letter (11 March 1699) from Secretary Sesto of Milan to Cardinal de' Medici in Archivio di Stato di Firenze, Collazione Mediceo, filza 5655.

3   Letters (6, 13 May 1700) from Cardinal Astali to Cardinal de' Medici in Archivio di Stato di Firenze, Collazione Mediceo, filza 5599.

4   Letter (27 April 1700) from Pier Antonio Gerini, Secretary for Ferdinando de' Medici, to Cardinal de' Medici in Archivio di Stato di Firenze, Collazione Mediceo, filza 5781.

5   Andre Pohr served the court from 1697 until his death in 1728. See Ludwig Ritter von Köchel, *Die Kaiserliche Hof-Musikkapelle* (Vienna, 1869), 71, 78.

6   Ibid., 70.

7   Ibid., 66. By 1703 Reutter is no longer listed as a court theorbist.

8   The terms gülden and florin are used interchangeably throughout the court records. There is, however, a difference between a thaler and a gülden. Figured on a 2:3 ratio, 40 thaler equal 60 gülden.

9   Vienna, Staatsarchiv, *Hofprotokollbuch: 1700-1709*, fol. 201v. For the original wording of these three entries, see appendix.

10   Vienna, Finanz- und Hofkammerarchiv, *Hofrechnungsbuch: 1702*, fols 193v-210v. For a complete tabulation of the amounts and the dates of payment of Conti's stipend from 1 April 1701 to 30 September 1706, see this author's *Francesco Bartolomeo Conti: His Life and Operas* (diss., Columbia University, 1964), 22.

11   Paul Frischauer, *Prince Eugene* (New York, 1934), 130.

12   E. Vehse, *Memoirs of the Court: Aristocracy and Diplomacy of Austria* (London, 1856), II, 69.

13   Ibid., II, 8.

14   Ibid., I, 474.

15   Johann Mattheson, *Grundlage einer Ehren-Pforte* (Hamburg, 1740), 359.

16   The month when *Il trionfi di Giosuè* was first performed under the sponsorship of the Compagnia di San Marco has yet to be discovered. Since the libretto, printed in Florence by V. Vangelisti, has a publication date of 1703, it may be safe to assume that, under the Florentine calendar system, both the printing of the libretto and the premiere performance took place after 25 March. See Renzo Lustig, 'Saggio bibliografico degli oratorii stampati a Firenze dal 1690 al 1725', *Note d'archivio* (1937): 112, 249; Mario Fabbri, *Alessandro Scarlatti e il principe Ferdinando de' Medici* (Florence, 1961), 52-3.

17   Although the men named were most likely among the principal role models for Conti's career as a composer, one should not overlook the possibility that the women who were active as composers in Vienna during Leopold's reign could have influenced his work as well.

18   Simon von Molitor, 'Materialien zur Musikgeschichte', vol. A-D, fasc. viii, fol. 51. Since 'Hofkomponist' is used in connection with Conti's name, the inventory of Leopold I's operas probably was undertaken sometime after 1713.

19   Bologna, Biblioteca, *Catalogo del Regio Conservatorio di Musica 'G. B. Martini'* (Florence, 1942), V, 133.

20   Milan, La Cappella musicale del Suomo di Milano, *Catalogo della musiche dell'Archivo* (Milan, 1957), 146.

21   Milan, *Annali della fabbrica del Duomo* (Milan, 1885), II, appendix, 158.

22   A number of musicians living in the eighteenth century were named Francesco Conti and hence the confusion with the Conti that is the subject of this book. Further confusion has resulted from the spelling of his first name as 'Francisco' in the court records and from the occasional use of the diminutive spelling of his last name as 'Contini', the latter usually reserved to designate his son. Sometimes both the Conti and Contini version of Francesco's surname are in the same document. For example, a libretto for the *Intermedi* (1717)

published in Dresden indicates the third intermezzo is the composition of 'Signore Francesco Conti o Contino, Maestro di Capella di Sua Maesta Cearea'.

When 'Francisco' (surname omitted) has appeared in connection with a musical event in London, there have been attempts to link that name with Francesco Bartolomeo Conti. For example, several theatrical notices, reprinted in Part 2: 1700-1717, vol. I of *The London Stage 1660-1800,* mention a 'Signior Francisco', either as a performer or as one for whom a benefit concert was being presented. Two of these entries, paraphrased from the *Daily Courant,* are related to events that took place on 5 March 1702/3 and 18 May 1703 and the index for the volume in which they appear credits Francesco B. Conti with both of them. The second of these two events also mentions that 'there will be perform'd an Extraordinary Entertainment by an Eminent Master on the Arch-Lute, who never perform'd there before, accompanied by Mr Dean and others'. On the basis of the given (first) name and the mention of the archlute, editors of *The London Stage* reasoned (incorrectly) that the 'Francisco' and the archlute player were one and the same musician and then jumped to the conclusion that this 'Francesco' must refer to the Francesco Conti of Vienna. The most likely candidate for the 'Francisco' mentioned in this announcement is the singer identified as the 'Emperor's Crooked Eunuch', listed in an entry for 25 December 1699 in *The London Stage 1660-1800,* Part 1: 1660-1700, 521, a conclusion reached in the general index covering all volumes of *The London Stage.* See the *Index to The London Stage 1660-1800,* Ben Ross Schneider, ed. (Carbondale, IL, 1979).

In the February 1705 issue of *The Monthly Mask of Vocal Music,* John Walsh published 'A song set by Mr. Francisco, sung at the new Theatre'. This song begins with the words 'Of Chloe's charms' and may have been composed by the singer 'Francisco' cited above, for whom another benefit concert was given in London on 14 June 1710 in the Great Room of Peter's Court. See *The London Stage 1660-1800* Part 2, vol. 1, 224.

The identity of the 'Eminent Master of the Arch-Lute' remains a mystery. One of the first times the lute was advertised in the *Daily Courant* as an accompanying instrument occurred on 19 March 1703. At a concert on 18 April 1707, which occurred just a few weeks after the Union celebration concert in which Conti participated, an archlute accompanied the singer Francis Hughes. Admittedly the theorbo was called *arcileuto* in Italian and the equation of these instruments with one and the same person is not unreasonable. Nigel North, however, in his *Continuo Playing on the Lute, Archlute and Theorbo* (Bloomington, ID, 1987), 7, makes a distinction between archlute and theorbo when he writes: 'the great Francesco Conti was employed at the Viennese court and was well known as an archlute player, whereas [Leopold] Weiss, whilst visiting Italy, probably always played a D-minor tuned theorbo'.

There were other skilled players of the archlute who might have been on hand to entertain the London audiences. One known for his archlute performances in that city at the beginning of the eighteenth century was Thomas Dean, Jr, son of the violinist Thomas Dean, though he may not have been the 'eminent master' in the announcement quoted above. If 'the eminent master' were indeed Conti, that would add an interesting perspective on why he might have written obbligato parts for the lute in some of his early cantatas. The author thanks Olive Baldwin and Thelma Wilson for calling her attention to the 17 May 1703 announcement in the *Daily Courant.*

23 Köchel, *Johann Josef Fux*, 94.

24 Carlo Schmidl, ed., *Dizionario universale dei musicisti*, I, 365, s.v. 'Conti'. Eleanor Selfridge-Field relied on secondary sources for information about the court musicians for her article on 'The Viennese Court Orchestra' in Brian Pritchard, ed., *Antonio Caldara* (London, 1987), 115-51 and therefore perpetuates inaccurate data found in Köchel, Schmidl, et al. In particular, she lists Conti as a theorbist from 1701-03 and 1711-32, and mistakenly believes no theorbist served the court after 1732 (see pp. 147 and 128).

25 Robert Eitner, *Biographisch-bibliographisches Quellenlexicon* (Leipzig, 1898-1904), III, 36, s.v. 'Conti'. An engraving owned by the Österreichische Nationalbibliothek captures the scene of a banquet in the Knights' chamber (Vienna). Of interest are the musicians shown in a gallery overlooking the banquet hall, for one of them, looking very youthful, is holding a theorbo. Could this be Francesco Conti? This engraving is illustrated in several books on Baroque music, but there appears to be some disagreement about the date of the scene depicted. For example, George Buelow, in *The Late Baroque Era* (Englewood Cliffs, NJ, 1994), 325, plate 49, dates the scene as 8 November 1705. Friedrich W. Riedel, in *Kirchenmusik am Hofe Karls VI (1711-1740)* (Munich-Salzburg, 1977), 312, gives 8 November 1712 as the date. See chapter three for more details about these engravings.

26 Vienna, Staatsarchiv, *Hofprotokollbuch: 1700-1709*, fol. 595.

27 Vienna, Stadtarchiv, *Kirchenbuch von St. Stephan: 1704-1707*, XXXVI, 361; *Wienerisches Diarium*, Nr. 226 (30 September-2 October 1705).

28 Vienna, Stadtarchiv, 'Testament / Francesco Conti', Nr. 6881/1732. Francesco spells his sister's name as Cattarina Angela Conti, but her name also appears in the court records as Catarin' Angiola Conti. For another document in which Conti names Theresia as his wife and also indicates her maiden name, see his petition of 1723, cited in chapter five.

29 Molitor, fasc. viii, fol. 4v.

30 Ibid.

32 Josef Schneider, 'Francesco Conti als dramatischer Componist' (diss., University of Vienna, 1902), 2 (original pagination).

CHAPTER TWO

The years 1706-1711

Joseph I was crowned emperor of the Habsburg realm on 19 March 1706. The change in imperial leadership was especially welcomed by Pope Clement XI whose prior relationship with the Habsburgs had been anything but cordial. Leopold I had remained faithful to the doctrines of the Roman Catholic Church throughout his reign, but this did not prevent him from exerting undue political pressure upon the papacy. When the King of France challenged the hereditary claims of the Habsburgs to Spain and to the kingdom of Naples, Clement XI was asked by both claimants to decide these territorial issues. He attempted to settle the disputes through diplomacy, but his efforts proved to be futile. Prince Eugene's army continued to advance towards Rome, exacting exorbitant amounts of tribute from residents along the way. Just when the pope had given up all hope of halting a Habsburg invasion of his realm, Leopold I died.

Clement expected the new emperor to be more receptive to his peace initiatives, but he soon discovered that Joseph I was a mean-spirited and arrogant young man who let nothing stand in the way of his power. He showed little respect for the pope and openly defied papal authority. One of Joseph's first acts as emperor was to order the papal nuncio, Davia, to leave Vienna. He also had the audacity to demand that Clement grant free passage for his imperial forces through the Papal States, all for the sole purpose of annexing the kingdom of Naples.[1]

Some measure of how great the tensions between the papacy and the Habsburgs had become during the initial year of Joseph's reign is revealed in a papal brief issued by Clement XI on 2 June 1706:

> The action of your Majesty's troops in throwing garrisons into the Pontifical States and unfurling their banners as in a conquered territory . . . is contrary to equity and reason, as well as to the regard due to the Holy See and the rights of the Church . . . Withdraw without delay your foot from where your soul would find certain damnation . . . take heed lest you stain the first-fruits of our

flourishing youth by scandalizing the whole Christian people and begin your reign by offending the Church.[2]

The pope's words angered the emperor, causing him to launch a verbal attack of his own. On 26 June 1706 he published a manifesto, considered by some historians to be one of the harshest statements ever directed by the Habsburgs against the papacy. In this manifesto Joseph declared the pope's words to be null and void. He further decreed that, as emperor, he had a rightful claim to all of Italy. As if to prove his point, he levied taxes against Italian territories considered by him to be imperial fiefs.[3]

Conti's career does not appear to have been adversely affected by all of this political turmoil between Vienna and Rome. During his first year serving the new emperor, he presented the court with two major works – one secular, the other sacred. The secular work was *Clotilde*, a *dramma per musica* which may have been one of the 'kleinen Opern' performed in the private chambers of the Hofburg between 7 and 16 February 1706.[4] The reason operas were not being staged in the court theatre during this particular Carnival season, as would have been customary, was that the court was still observing a period of mourning for Leopold I.[5] Neither a score of Conti's *Clotilde* nor any contemporary descriptions of a 1706 performance are known to exist. Therefore it is not possible to know how his setting of Giambattista Neri's libretto compares with one composed by Giovanni Maria Ruggieri in 1696, the year the libretto was published.[6]

The tradition of commissioning a work specifically for the Carnival season seems to have been instituted at the Habsburg court at the turn of the century. Before 1700 the months of January and February afforded occasions for celebrations because the 6 January and the 21 February were, respectively, the birthday and name-day of the Empress Eleonora, third wife of Leopold I. Both occasions gave ample opportunity for opera performances. After 1700 an opera for Carnival time was given in addition to those staged to honour Eleonora. Eventually her birthday and name-day celebrations disappear from the list of 'gala' events, leaving only the Carnival opera as the main attraction for the first two months of the year.

It was considered a privilege to compose the Carnival operas; commissions for this important season of entertainment were usually reserved for composers of the first rank. Marc' Antonio Ziani and Giovanni Bononcini, for example, wrote most of the Carnival operas between 1703 and 1709. If Conti had been trying his hand at composing operas for the court, as Molitor has suggested, he quickly rose to a position of prominence with his works. The appearance of *Clotilde* during the Carnival season of 1706 (if indeed it did appear as Köchel claims) places Conti on a level with the established composers of the court, even though he lacked any official title or stipend acknowledging his contribution.

The sacred work was *Il Gioseffo*, an oratorio whose text was obviously chosen to pay homage to the new emperor. The libretto is based upon Genesis 39:1-23. In this particular biblical passage, Joseph is portrayed as an honest man whose success in life was made possible because 'the Lord was with him; and whatever he did, the Lord made it prosper'.[7] The exact date when *Il Gioseffo* was sung in the imperial chapel is not known. Only the year, 1706, appears on the title page of the manuscript. Since Joseph's coronation occurred in March of that year, it is entirely possible that Conti's oratorio was performed during that same month, a time that coincided with the Lenten season.[8]

Although only Part I of the full score for *Il Gioseffo* is extant, the manuscript offers important clues about Conti's role as both a composer and a performer.[9] Of primary interest is Noafa's aria 'Bramo un core', scored for violins in unison, viola, and mandolino, with the latter tuned a whole tone lower than its usual tuning. The mandolino part involves very elaborate figuration and seems designed to show off the talents of the performer, but who was the mandolino player?[10] The answer may be found in a most unlikely source – a London newspaper.

The *Daily Courant* for 1 April 1707 printed this notice:

> To Morrow being Wednesday the 2d of April, Signior Fr. Conti will cause to be perform'd, at Mr. Hickford's Dancing-Room in James street in the Hay-Market over-against the Tennis Court, the Consort of Musick compos'd by him for her Majesty, and which he had the Honour to have perform'd at Court the Day the Act for the Union pass'd. Signiora Margarita, the Baroness, and Signior Valentino will sing in it, accompanied with several Instruments, and the said Signior Conti will play upon his great Theorbo, and on the Mandoline an Instrument not known yet. The Consort will begin at 8 a Clock at Night. Tickets to be had only at White's Chocolate-House, and at the Smyrna Coffee-House, at a Guinea a Ticket.[11]

On the day of Conti's concert, the following announcement appeared in another source:

> Wednesday 2 Concert.
>   Music. By direction of Sig. Francisco Conti, the Consort of Musick compos'd by him for her Majesty, and which he had the Honour to perform at Court upon

the Union-day. La Signiora Margaretta, the Baroness, and Il Signior Valentino are to Sing therein, and there is to be several Instruments, and the said Signior Conti is to play upon his Great Theorbo, and La Mandelitta, an Instrument hitherto unkown.

Comment. At Hickford's Dancing Room in James's-street in the Hay-Market, over against the Tennis Court. At 7 p.m. Tickets 21s.[12]

Both notices confirm that Conti was in London at least as early as 6 March 1707, for that was the day the Act of Union was passed.[13] They also provide information about a hitherto unknown composition by Conti. He not only composed a 'Consort of Musick' for a very special occasion at the court, but he was also invited to participate in the performance before Her Majesty the Queen. A month later, the general public was to have an opportunity to hear this same 'Consort' in a performance directed by the composer.

Conti's reputation as a player of his 'great Theorbo' was enough to attract London audiences to his concerts, but what was especially newsworthy on this occasion was his playing of an instrument that hitherto had not made its way into that city. This is not surprising, given the fact that the introduction of the mandolin as an obbligato instrument appears to have been a fairly recent development on the Continent. In the 1670s the first printed music specifically composed for this instrument became available and similarly the first mandolins Stradivari made also date from this decade.[14] Early examples of arias with an obbligato mandolin part can be found in one of Alessandro Scarlatti's cantatas of 1699, Francesco Mancini's *Alessandro il Grande in Sidone* (1706), and Conti's *Il Gioseffo* (1706). Additional examples can be found in compositions spanning the next several decades, including several more works by Conti. Other composers who wrote arias with an obbligato part for mandolin include Ariosti, Fux, Gasparini, Lotti, and Vivaldi.[15]

Conti also seems to have been in the forefront of contributing to the solo repertoire for the mandolin. His 'Sonata al mandolino solo e basso' is considered a milestone in the history of that genre.[16] The sonata appears in a collection of works for solo mandolin along with two anonymous partitias and four compositions by Fillipo Sauli. Conti's sonata is unusual in that the mandolin part is accompanied by a 'Basso' part supplied in a separate manuscript.[17] Not one of the compositions in this collection is dated, but there is reason to believe some, if not all, of the music was created before 1711.

There was only one nine-month period when Conti was not paid his usual monthly stipend by the Habsburg court. That period extended from 1 October 1706 to 30 June 1707 and coincided with Conti's trip to London. At the beginning of July 1707 Conti petitioned the court to be reinstated as a theorbist. His petition was granted by an official decree from Joseph I and this decree was forwarded to the Hof-Controlor for his enactment.[18] During Conti's absence, Filippo Sauli had been appointed assistant theorbist with a monthly stipend of 25 florins and he continued to hold this position throughout most, if not all, of Joseph I's reign.

Few facts about Sauli's career have come to light. His name is entered in the *Hofprotokollbuch* where he is listed under the title 'Musicus Instrumentista'. A later hand has crossed out this title and inserted 'Tiorbista' above his name in the main text as well as in the index to that volume.[19] In addition to playing the theorbo, there is evidence that he may have had to play the mandolin at least once while Conti was in London. The 19 March 1707 production of Attilio Ariosti's *Marte placato* required a mandolin player for the obbligato part in the aria 'Se tu m'amassi'. Sauli was probably the person chosen to execute the part, for his works for mandolin discussed earlier indicate he had intimate knowledge of the instrument.

How long Sauli served the court is not known. On the basis of financial records, it appears that he was in the employ of the court at least until 1709. The death of Orazio Clementi in August of 1708 was certainly one factor that might have convinced the court to retain Sauli for an indefinite period of time. One other event suggests Sauli might have been active as a performer for the court as late as 1711. The Carnival opera that year was Conti's *Il trionfo dell'amicizia e dell'amore* and it includes an aria scored for two mandolins. Since this is the singular example of this instrumental combination in Conti's music, the particular scoring may have been created so that Conti and Sauli could perform together.

Sauli was not named on the list of musicians drawn up to serve Charles VI, but he continued to express an interest in performing at the imperial court. In July 1722 he filed a petition requesting that he be reinstated as a theorbist, citing Conti's busy schedule as a composer and Ignazio Conti's mediocre abilities as a theorbist as reasons why his talents could be put to good use. The court did not agree with his premise and the petition was rejected.[20]

Although Conti resumed his duties as court theorbist in the summer of 1707, he did not deny himself the opportunity to engage in other musical activities at home and abroad. His name appears among the twenty-four composers who contributed to a pasticcio oratorio performed in Florence in 1708. The score is lost, but three librettos survive. One (D/*Hs*) has the title *L'onestà combattuta di Sara*; the other two (I/*Fn;* I/ *Fm)* have *Sara in Egitto.* All three list the composers and, in addition to 'Francesco Conti fior', they include Alessandro Scarlatti, Francesco Gasparini, Antonio Caldara, Giuseppe Orlandini, Francesco Veracini, Carlo Cesarini, and Lorenzo Conti.[21] The last named was a Florentine composer of sacred music whose numerous oratorios were performed in his native city throughout the first three decades of the eighteenth century. It is tempting to speculate that he and Francesco were related, but no documents have been discovered to support this idea.

It was also in 1708 that Conti was elected a member of the Accademia Filarmonica in Bologna. Founded in 1666 this academy was comprised of composers, singers, and instrumentalists. Its primary function was to offer member musicians a forum for discussing theoretical works and for performing their new compositions.[22] Whether or not Conti ever travelled to Bologna to take advantage of his membership is not known.

Contemporary assessments of Conti's theorbo playing are few in number, but each attests to his superior talents. One worth noting is a comment made in the English language edition of François Raguenet's *Parallèle des Italiens et des Français en ce qui regarde la musique et les opéras* published in London in 1709. The anonymous translator (who obviously was a resident of London) supplied his edition with lengthy and informative footnotes on every page. In one of these notes which concerns the quality and quantity of first-rate Italian musicians, he writes: 'For the Theorbo, the first of all was the late *Tedeschino* of *Florence*; but *Contini*, who was two Years since here in *London*, has out-stripp'd him'.[23]

Earlier in the same year that the English edition of Raguenet's essay was published, Conti's music once again entertained London audiences. This time it was in the form of a pasticcio version of his 1706 *Clotilde,* arranged for the Queen's Theatre in the Haymarket by that theatre's business manager, John Jacob Heidegger. The initial performance took place on 2 March 1709 and several more performances were given throughout that month.[24] Aside from the overture which is credited solely to Conti, the other forty or more numbers consisting of arias, duets and a chorus appear in published editions without the names of their composers.

One of the few sources with eyewitness information about *Clotilda* is the 1709 edition of Raguenet's essay cited above, most notably in *A Critical Discourse on Opera's and Musick in England* which the anonymous translator appended to his edition of the French text. In a footnote to the main essay, the English writer discusses the aria 'Del' fallo sul camin' from *Clotilda* and credits Gasparini with its composition.[25] The appended *Discourse* contains a review of the recent run of Italian operas on the London stage and it is here that the writer comments on *Clotilda*. He describes 'the novelty of Spanish habits' and mentions that 'there are . . . several good Airs compos'd by Bononcini, Scarlatti and Contini, but . . . many others . . . had no effect upon the Stage'.[26]

Charles Burney offered his own assessment of the staging of *Clotilda* during the month of March 1709:

> And this revived opera (*Camilla*) and *Pyrrhus and Demetrius* were alternately performed till the 2d of March, when a new opera called *Clotilda* was brought out, for the performance of which the boxes on the stage were again advanced to fifteen shillings. After two representations of this new drama, *Pyrrhus and Demetrius* was exhibited once, which was followed by two performances more of *Clotilda*, when it gave way to *Camilla*, and *Pyrrhus and Demetrius*. After this it was performed three times, and then wholly laid aside. This opera was composed by Conti and printed by Walsh, half in English and half in Italian as it was performed. The composition was not contemptible; and yet it seems to have come into the world and gone out of it so quietly as scarcely to have left any memorials of its existence.[27]

The performances of these three Italian operas engendered varying responses from those who attended them. Typical was the response of Charles Dering. In a letter written to his friend John Percival on 17 March 1708/9 on the occasion of a benefit concert for Nicolini, he confesses that he did not particularly 'relish' the first opera he attended, but after the third such production, that being *Clotilda*, he found himself 'growing in love very fast with operas'.[28]

Burney's statement that *Clotilda* was 'wholly laid aside' after the March productions is not quite accurate. It is true that at that time no further productions of *Clotilda* were planned. At least that is the impression given by an advertisement for a performance of Alessandro Scarlatti's *Pyrrhus and Demetrius* on 2 April 1709, which was to feature an entirely new stage set fashioned out of one previously used for *Clotilda*.[29] Two years later, however, *Clotilda* was staged once again at the Queen's Theatre on 16, 19, and 22 May 1711 'at the desire of several Ladies of Quality . . . And by reason of the Hot Weather, the Waterfall will play the best part of the Opera'.[30]

Given the popularity of Walsh's editions of the 'songs' from *Clotilda*, there is every reason to believe that individual selections from this score could have been included in some of the concert programmes listed in the calendar of entertainments for London. The singers who participated in the 1709 production of *Clotilda* were frequently the very same who were featured in these concerts and they might have been inclined to repeat a repertoire which brought them fame on the stage.[31] Prior to 1710 the advertisements for these concerts gave a general idea of the programmes to be performed such as the type of music (instrumental solos, Italian airs) and the names of performers, but they omitted details about the music that would be heard. After 1710, advertisements tended to be more specific. One printed on 25 April 1713 indicated a performance at the Queen's Theatre of the songs in the pasticcio *Dorinda* would conclude with the chorus from *Clotilda*.[32]

Performances of these pasticcio operas on the London stage were subject to the whims of the singers. According to the anonymous translator and editor of the Raguenet essay cited above, singers would frequently omit portions of the songs they were to sing, thereby distorting the beauty of the composer's original work. Such was the case with the Gasparini aria 'Del' fallo sul camin' which this translator says was truncated by the singer who 'omitted the most beautiful part of that song'. This same singer wanted to eliminate the song entirely, 'alledging it to be a composition not proper for the theatre'. The song, however, met with the audience's approval and therefore the translator recommends that before judging one of these Italian operas, one should 'consult the original, and not the copy printed here in London, where, as we observ'd before, the most beautiful of all the musick was wanting in the second part'.[33]

John Walsh wasted no time in printing music from these Italian productions for the benefit of the general public. An announcement in the *Daily Courant* concerning a publication with music from *Clotilda* appeared on 31 March 1709. Conti's name is noticeably absent from the advertisement and from the edition itself which included music by Corelli along with items from *Pyrrhus and Demetrius*, *Love's Triumph*, and *Clotilda*, all arranged for two flutes. On the occasion of another Walsh edition issued a few weeks later and devoted solely to a vocal score of *Clotilda*, the announcement for it in the *Daily Courant* acknowledged both the librettist (Neri) and the composer (Conti).[34] Walsh also published other editions of the *Clotilda* music in 1709 such as *The Symphonys or Instrumental Parts in the Opera Call'd Clotilda*. That same year William Babell made arrangements for harpsichord of arias and duets from *Pyrrhus* and *Clotilda* and printed them in *The 3rd Book of the Ladys Entertainment or Banquet of*

Musick.[35] His 1709 edition was followed with another published some six years later. So popular were these publications that some began to appear in pirated editions. The November 1709 issues of *The Post Man* and *The Tatler* carried a notice in which Walsh accused a former apprentice, Luke Pippard, of having 'lately coppied [sic] on me the Opera of *Clotilda*'.[36]

Conti's involvement with musical events outside Vienna did not jeopardize his relationship with the imperial court. On the contrary, he seems to have been rewarded financially for adding a bit of international lustre to his reputation. The imperial director of music, Joseph von Paar, recommended to the emperor that an increase of 10 florins be made in the theorbist's monthly stipend beginning 1 July 1709; his recommendation received approval.[37] Conti may have found intellectual satisfaction in the actions taken on his behalf by Joseph von Paar, but he would have to wait a considerable period of time before he saw any monetary boost in his stipend. Funds in the imperial treasury had been depleted by the extravagant lifestyle of the Habsburgs and the court simply had to postpone payment to those in its employ. To restore solvency to the treasury, Joseph I ordered taxes be levied against the clerics in the territories conquered by Prince Eugene. He further demanded great sums of money from the papacy.

This was not the first time a financial yoke had been placed upon the Roman Catholic Church nor would it be the last. The libretto Conti set for his second oratorio is a reminder that history can repeat itself. *Il martirio di San Lorenzo*, performed first in 1710 and again in 1724, represents the only extant example of an oratorio by Conti based upon the life of a saint.[38] During the first half of the third century, St Laurence, a deacon of the church in Rome, was served notice to surrender the treasures of the church to the prefect of Rome. According to accounts recorded in fourth-century martyrologies, St Laurence took the treasures and distributed them to the poor of the city. He then brought these people before the prefect, presenting them with the following words: 'These are the treasures of the Church'.[39] His defiance of Roman authority caused him to be martyred in the year 258.

Apart from regularly scheduled musical events in which Conti was expected to participate, little else can been discerned about his activities in 1710. That he was dividing his time between performing and composing seems a foregone conclusion, given the fact that in January of the following year his *Il trionfo dell'amicizia e dell'amore* was presented as the opera for Carnival season.[40] Who provided the libretto for this *dramma pastorale* is open to debate, for the title pages of both the libretto and the extant scores do not reveal the author's identity.

Credit for the libretto usually has been assigned to Francesco Ballerini because it is his signature that appears on the dedication page.

What little biographical information has been uncovered about Ballerini (Ballarini), an alto castrato, is documented in Wulf Arlt's study of *Il trionfo dell'amicizia e dell'amor*; yet, his research has gone virtually unnoticed by some of the more recently published profiles of this singer.[41] In the absence of birth and death records, Arlt relied upon a combination of contemporary documents and secondary sources to piece together some of the more salient facts regarding this singer's activities. For example, he reasoned that Ballerini had to have been born around 1670 or earlier because a remark in a letter written 13 May 1688 by Ranuccio II of Farnese to the Duke of Mantua implies the singer was, by that date, well established in his career.[42]

Apparently Ballerini had sung in a number of Italian cities (Venice, Mantua, Florence, among others) before he made his appearance in Vienna in Antonio Draghi's *Musica di camera,* performed there on 26 July 1695. Whether or not this was his first encounter with the imperial city is a matter of conjecture, but from this point forward, he seems to have maintained a close association with the Habsburg court. In fact, sometime between the end of 1695 and the end of 1696, Ballerini was appointed a 'Cammer Musicus' to serve the Empress Eleonore Magdalena. In this position he was engaged to participate in performances of dramatic music but was not expected to undertake other singing assignments related to the Hofkapelle. Consequently, even though his name is among the cast of singers for the dramatic works in which he sang a role, it is not included in the regular list of court singers.

That Ballerini was something of a celebrity before the turn of the century is revealed in two letters dated 28 March and 21 April 1697 which were sent from the Elector Johann Wilhelm to the Empress Eleonora. This correspondence mentions that he was involved in a production of an opera 'written expressly for him' which was staged twice in Düsseldorf in 1697 – once during the Carnival season and again in connection with the festivities associated with the marriage of Gian Gastones de' Medici and Anna Maria Franzisca of Saxony-Lauenburg.[43] By 1699 Ballerini was back in Vienna to sing in at least one of the two operas by Bononcini which were staged for the court that year.

Under what circumstances Ballerini left the sphere of musicians who were engaged for the benefit of the empress is not known, but by 1700 the singer was aligned with other musicians who were associated first with Leopold I, and then with Joseph I. What is more, Ballerini remained in the employ of the court until

1711. At that point in time, a mandatory reduction in the court staff (instituted by the empress-regent) caused him to be removed from the 'active' list of musicians. He continued to receive his regular stipend until the actual reduction in staffing was put into effect in December of 1712, after which date he was pensioned, receiving 800 florins until 1729 (possibly the year of his death).[44]

While Joseph I was still alive, Ballerini petitioned the court for permission to build a public opera house in Vienna, perhaps intending to replicate the system of public theatre which he had experienced in Venice. Although the petition is undated, the contents and subsequent response to it suggest a date of 1708. Ballerini did indeed obtain the 'privilege' to build the theatre.[45] What he did not obtain were the necessary funds to initiate the project, nor did that situation change when the next emperor came to power. Charles VI was not at all in favour of relinquishing the court's monopoly on this grand form of entertainment, and so Ballerini's dream never became a reality.

With the poets Pietro Antonio Bernardoni and Silvio Stampiglia holding appointments at the court during the reign of Joseph I, it is perhaps fair to ask how it happened that Conti and Ballerini made contact with each other and created a very delightful piece for the theatre. If Ballerini is indeed the librettist of *Il trionfo dell'amicizia e dell'amore*, then this collaboration between librettist and composer was repeated at least once more in 1717 when Conti set Ballerini's text for the last of three intermezzos created for performance with the opera *Giove in Argo* in Dresden that year. Stampiglia provided the text for the first and second intermezzos with music by Alessandro Scarlatti.

Conti may also have collaborated with Stampiglia during this period, for one of his cantatas sets a text by this poet. Unfortunately, the cantata is not dated, but since a number of his other cantatas, especially those featuring the flute as an obbligato instrument, may also date from this same period, it is conceivable that the Stampiglia work does too. Joseph I played the flute (as well as the cembalo) and Conti may have designed these works with the express purpose of providing opportunities for the emperor to perform.[46]

If Conti expected his compositions to attract this particular emperor's attention and ultimately win for him an increase in pay or an appointment as court composer, he was soon to be disappointed. Joseph I died 17 April 1711, causing festivities in Vienna to be curtailed for the traditional period of mourning.[47] As had happened during a similar period of mourning for Leopold I, some musicians left Vienna in order to stage their works in other cities. Conti did not leave. While others mourned the death of an emperor, he remained to mourn the death of a family member. His wife Theresia died on 15 April 1711.[48]

Notes

1   Ludwig, Freiherr von Pastor, *The History of the Popes* (London, 1941), XXX, 38-9.

2   Ibid., 49-50.

3   Ibid., 52.

4   Köchel lists *Clotilde* as a *dramma per musica* by Giambattista Neri and Francesco Conti performed during Carneval in Februrary 1706. See Ludwig Ritter von Köchel, *Johann Josef Fux* (Vienna, 1872), 524. Franz Hadamowsky does not include *Clotilde* in his list of works performed in 1706, but he quotes the following from fol. 455v of the 1706 *Protokolle des Obersthofzeremonieamtes* with respect to events occurring between 7 and 16 February: 'Private Cammerfestinen und Recreationen mit Musik, Balletten, Verkleidungen und kleinen Opern', indicating there were opportunities when *Clotilde* might have been performed. See his 'Barocktheater am Wiener Kaiserhof', in *Jahrbuch der Gesellschaft für Wiener Theaterforschung 1951/52* (Vienna, 1955), 98.

5   The official period of mourning ended on 19 June 1706.

6   Giambattista Neri (d. 1726) was born in Bologna. In addition to writing poetry and librettos for seven operas and seven oratorios, he served as secretary to Prince Filippo Ercolani, who was both the state counsellor to the three emperors under whom Conti also served (Leopold I, Joseph I, and Charles VI) and the imperial ambassador to Venice. S.v. 'Neri' in *The New Grove Dictionary of Opera*, III, 571. Ruggieri's *Clotilde* was presented during Carnival in the Teatro S. Cassiano, Venice.

7   *The Holy Bible*, Revised Standard Version, 1952.

8   A number of works reportedly performed in 1706 are cited by Köchel without specific day and month indicated. It could be that these works were intended for more festive performances but because of the period of mourning they were restricted to private performances within the Hofburg, and therefore not covered by the *Wienerisches Diarium*.

9   A manuscript score for Part I is in A/*Wn*: Mus.Hs. 18148; no score for Part II is known. Parts for violins, viola, and violoncello are available in manuscript for both Parts I and II in A/*Wn*: Mus.Hs. 18149.

10   The mandolinist does not show up as a separate category in the court roster of instrumentalists and therefore the name of the person responsible for executing the mandolin parts is not listed.

11   This notice was repeated on 2 April 1707.

12   *The London Stage 1660-1800*, Part 2: 1700-1729, I, 144-5.

13   Conti may have brought some of his cantatas with him when he arrived in London, for at least one, *Il Rosignolo*, was copied by a Mr Cousser for a collection of cantatas he began preparing in 1706 (according to the date inscribed on the first folio). For more about this and other cantatas, see part II, chapter eight.

14   Of the two known 'mandolini' made by Stradivari, the Cutler-Challen Stradivari mandolin, signed on the inside of the central back rib 'Antonio Stradivari Cremona 1680', was recently

acquired by the Shrine to Music Museum, Vermillion, South Dakota. See 'La Voce' (Fall, 1997): 2 (newsletter of Claire Givens Violins, Inc.).

15 For a listing of works by these composers which include the mandolin, see James Tyler and Paul Sparks, *The Early Mandolin* (Los Angeles, 1989), 27-8.

16 Tyler and Sparks, *The Early Mandolin*, 26. A person named Francesco Conti has been credited with writing a treatise related to mandolin performance practice entitled 'L'accordo della Mandola è l'stesso della Chitarra alla francesco Schola del leutino, osia Mandolino alla Genovese'. This treatise, dated *c.* 1770-80 and located in GB/*Ge*, is presumably by a Francesco Conti who lived in the latter half of the eighteenth century. Contrary to what has been written by James Tyler (op. cit., 140), this Conti is not known to be related to Francesco Bartolomeo Conti.

17 This manuscript is located in the archives of the University of Prague (CS/*CSSR*: Pu II. KK 36). The composer of the sonata is indicated as 'Sigr. Francesco Contini'.

18 The three stages of this transaction – petition, imperial decree, enactment of the decree – were not recorded by the Obersthofmeister until 21 January 1710. See Vienna, Staatsarchiv, *Hofprotokollbuch: 1710-1713*, fol. 23. Entries in the *Hofrechnungsbuch* for 1710, fol. 205; 1711, fols 169, 290; and 1712, fol. 160 confirm that Conti was credited with a regular stipend from the time of his 1707 petition to 1 October 1711.

19 Vienna, Staatsarchiv, *Hofprotokollbuch: 1700-1709*, fol. 697.

20 The full petition recorded in the *Hofprotokollbuch* on 3 July 1722 is quoted in Köchel, *Johann Josef Fux*, 394, no. 75.

21 The title page of this oratorio's libretto reads: 'Oratorio a quattro voci da cantarsi nella Congregazione ed Ospizio di Giesù Maria e Giuseppe e della SS. Trinità posta nella Compagnia di San Marco'. See Renzo Lustig, 'Saggio bibliografico degli oratorii stampati a Firenze dal 1690 al 1725', *Note d'archivio per la storia musicale* (1937):116, and Ursula Kirkendale, *Antonio Caldara* (Graz, 1966), 142.

22 S.v. 'Bologna', in *The New Grove Dictionary of Music and Musicians* (1980): III, 5.

23 *A Comparison between the French and Italian Musick and Opera's*, Anonymous, trans. (London, 1709), 51n35.

24 Additional performances are recorded for 5, 12, 15, 19, 24, and 26 March 1709. See *The London Stage 1660-1800*, Part 2: 1700-1729, vol. I: 1700-1717, Emmett L. Avery, ed. (Carbondale, IL, 1960), 186-8.

25 *A Comparison between the French and Italian Musick and Opera's*, 14-15, 15n12.

26 Ibid., 81. Note that the title of the pasticcio is spelled *Clotilda*, whereas the title of the opera for the imperial court is spelled *Clotilde.*

27 Charles Burney, *A General History of Music* (London, 1789), IV, 210.

28 Judith Milhous and Robert D. Hume, eds, *A Register of English Theatrical Documents 1660-1737* (Carbondale, IL, 1991), 437.

29 *The London Stage 1660-1800*, Part 2: 1700-1729, I, 189.

30 Ibid., 249-50.

31 The Walsh vocal edition listed the singers: Mrs [Katherine] Tofts, Mrs [Margarita] de l'Elpine, Mrs Lindsey, Valentino Urbani, Nicolino Grimaldi, Ramondon, and Lawrence.

32 *The London Stage 1660-1800*, Part 2: 1700-1729, I, 300. This same chorus, as well as the overture to *Clotilda,* were revived in London in 1730 as part of a pasticcio opera entitled

Ormisda which was prepared for the stage by Handel. For more on Handel's use of Conti's music, see chapters six and seven.

33   *A Comparison between the French and Italian Musick and Opera's*, 15n12.

34   William C. Smith, *A Bibliography of the Musical Works Published by John Walsh During the Years 1695-1720* (London, 1948), nos 295 and 296.

35   William C. Smith, *A Catalogue of Vocal and Instrumental Musick Published by John Walsh and His Successors 1706-90* (London, 1953), nos 29, 191, 208, 209.

36   Don J. Neville, ed. *Studies in Music: Opera I* (London [Canada], 1979), s.v. 'Conti', no. 50.

37   Vienna, Finanz- und Hofkammerarchiv, 'Report to Emperor Charles VI concerning payment of stipend to Francesco Bartolomeo Conti', (n.d., but *c.* 1713). Joseph von Paar was the first person appointed to the newly created office of *Musik-Oberdirector* in 1709. He served a brief time before being succeeded by the Marchese Scipione di S. Croce, who held that position from 1709 to 1710. Information contained in a document in the Vienna, Finanz- und Hofkammerarchiv contradicts Köchel's statement (*Johann Josef Fux*, 219) that the Marchese Scipione was the first to be appointed director of music.

38   In his revised biographical sketch of the composer, Molitor indicates that the oratorio was first heard in August of 1710 but offers no documentation to support his data. The performance of this same oratorio on 23 March 1724 occurred at a time when the resources of the imperial treasury were drained by the excessive expenditures of Charles VI.

39   *The Oxford Dictionary of the Christian Church* (Oxford and New York, 1997), 958.

40   There is some disagreement among sources about performance dates for *Il trionfo dell'amicizia e dell'amore*. The *Wienerisches Diarium* lists three dates: 21 January, 10 and 15 February of 1711. Other sources list two: 22 January and 11 February.

41   Wulf Arlt, 'Zur Deutung der Barockoper: *Il trionfo dell'amicizia e dell'amore* Wien 1711', in *Musik und Geschichte: Leo Schrade zum sechzigsten Geburtstag* (Cologne, 1963), 105-109. His article was apparently unknown to the person who prepared the biographical profile published in *The New Grove Dictionary of Opera* (1992): I, 293, s.v. 'Ballerini, Francesco'. Note, the surname is spelled variously as Ballarini or Ballerini.

42   Excerpt from the letter quoted in Arlt, 'Zur Deutung der Barockoper', 105. See also Antonino Bertolotti, *La musica in Mantova* (Milan, 1891), 115.

43   Letters quoted in Alfred Einstein, 'Italienische Musiker am Hofe der Neuburger Wittelsbacher', *Studien für Musikwissenschaft* 9 (1907-1908): 402.

44   In the latter part of 1702, Ballerini's brother, the cleric Dom Francesco Maria Ballarini, arrived in Vienna to begin his duties with the imperial family. The similarity of the two brothers' given (first) names undoubtedly caused, and probably will continue to cause, confusion about their respective identities. Arlt also mentions that there may have been yet another brother, Antonio, who eventually came to Vienna as well. See Arlt, 'Zur Deutung der Barockoper', 106n45.

45   Cited in Alexander von Weilen, *Geschichte des Wiener Theaterwesens von den ältesten Zeiten bis zu den Anfängen der Hof-Theater* (Wien, 1899), 124. The actual document is in the Harrach'schen Familienarchiv, Vienna. See also Arlt, 'Zur Deutung der Barockoper', 107, where a relevant excerpt is quoted.

46   See part II, chapter eight, for a discussion of Conti's use of the flute in his cantatas.

47   The cancellation of the production of *Giunio Bruto*, intended for 1711, was probably directly related to the emperor's death. The music was composed by Cesarini, Caldara, and A. Scarlatti and the scene designs were by Filippo Juvarra. An illustration of the watercolour

showing the scenery for Act III, Scene xvii (taken from a presentation copy of the score prepared for Joseph I) is in George Buelow, *The Late Baroque Era* (Englewood, NJ, 1994), 3.

48 The year of Theresia's death is given in several documents written by Francesco, including one concerning money owed him by the court. See Vienna, Finanz- und Hofkammerarchiv, *Österreichische Hoffinanz* rote, Nr. 860, 9 April 1723. This document is discussed in chapter five.

CHAPTER THREE

The years 1711-1713

In the intervening period between the death of Joseph I and the coronation of Charles VI, Dowager Empress Eleonora Magdalena served as regent. Her interests in the affairs of state were primarily financial; her objectives were stabilization of the court economy and restoration of the treasury's solvency. She had already experienced how an extravagant lifestyle could wreak havoc with a political entity, for such had been Duke Ranuccio's lifestyle, which had reduced the Duchy of Parma to political and cultural insignificance by the close of the seventeenth century. She also knew that Ranuccio's disregard for financial responsibility had been replicated on a much larger scale by her own husband (Leopold I) and her recently deceased son (Joseph I). If the affairs of the imperial court were to be spared a similar fate at the hands of a new emperor, some measure of reform would have to be introduced. Eleonora knew she could not expect restraint in matters of luxury from Prince Charles. Even Leopold I, who was particularly fond of Charles, harshly criticized his son's extravagances. For this reason Eleonora acted promptly to curb court spending.

Among the several decrees she issued was one entered in the court records on 3 September 1711. In essence this decree stated that only the most talented of the musicians currently serving the court should be retained and that the 'Capellmeister' would have sole responsibility for licensing them.[1] The decree eventually had its desired effect; it caused the number of active court musicians to be reduced substantially. It also insured that long overdue stipends and retroactive rises would be paid.[2] Enactment of the decree did not happen as quickly as Eleonora had hoped. In fact, Charles was crowned emperor in Frankfort on 22 December 1711 and had made his triumphal entry into Vienna on 26 January 1712 before any benefits of the decree could be realized.

As far back as 1486, when Maximilian I was crowned emperor, the coronation ceremonies of the imperial realm had been conducted in Frankfurt. Preparations for the 1711 event officially began in August of that year, with Gottfried von

Bessel, a Benedictine monk from the Stift Göttweig in Austria, assigned the task of organizing not only the intricate details of the coronation festivites but also the protocol events leading up to that festival day. By the beginning of October, delegations of envoys and ambassadors from Bohemia, Brandenburg, Hanover, and Saxony had arrived in the city for the purpose of convening the assembly that would formally choose the next emperor. Musicians from the various court chapels associated with these envoys gradually made their way to the coronation site. Some arrived in October to assist in the preliminary festive services of worship. Others, in particular those being sent from the Hofkapelle in Vienna, arrived in the last week of November. According to the records preserved in the Haus-, Hof-, und Staatsarchiv in Vienna, 'Francesco Contini' was among the imperial singers and instrumentalists who made that trip to participate in the actual coronation event. Detailed descriptions of this historic occasion are available in several sources, such as the Mainz *Diarium* and the *Direcktorium* (1727), a manuscript preserved in connection with the Hofkapelle in Vienna.[3]

The new emperor was as dedicated a musician as his Habsburg predecessors had been and he delighted in performing and composing. Nevertheless, he did not permit his intense interest in music to interfere with the full implementation of his mother's decree. A passage in the *Hofprotokollbuch: 1710-1713* explains the procedure by which a more financially responsible policy for the musical aspects of court life was finally achieved. The director of music, Ernest (Graf) Mollart, appointed a committee to evaluate the credentials of each member of the current staff of musicians. That committee consisted of Marc' Antonio Ziani (Kapellmeister), Johann Joseph Fux (Vizekapellmeister), and Kilian Reinhardt (Konzertmeister). Their responsibility was to review each musician and file their respective comments with Mollart. He, in turn, submitted the committee's findings to the Obersthofmeister.[4]

To facilitate tabulation of this information, the Obersthofmeister divided the requisite pages of the *Hofprotokollbuch* into two columns: the right one listed the name of the musician; the left one contained the committee's evaluation of the musician's qualifications. The left column also included the committee's inquiry into other matters such as the number of musicians needed to perform at court events. For example, Ziani decided three organists were sufficient to participate in the daily chapel services.[5] While this seemed to be the opinion of just one member, other comments represented a consensus of the committee as a whole. A case in point was the committee's statement that twenty-four singers, six to a part, constituted a sufficient number to perform the current repertoire of court music.[6]

Occasionally differences of opinion did arise among the three members concerning the qualifications of specific individuals. In comments pertaining to Johann Angermayr, Reinhardt considered him to be worthy of remaining in the service of the court, but Ziani and Fux did not.[7] When Conti was evaluated by this committee, he fared better than some of his colleagues. Not only did he receive the committee's unanimous endorsement of his qualifications but he also gained sole rights to the position of court theorbist. This privilege came about as a result of a comment made by Ziani in which he declared that one theorbist was sufficient and no more need be employed.[8]

By the method described above, the first phase of the Empress-Regent Eleonora's decree was accomplished. Further action on her decree did not happen until the end of 1712, at which time the actual reduction of the staff took place (see table 3.1) and the stipend of each musician who continued on the roster was entered into the *Hofprotokollbuch*. Under 'Tiorbista' only one name appears: Francesco Conti is listed with an annual stipend of 1440 florins. This represented a monthly increase of 10 florins to be paid retroactively from 1 October 1711.[9]

As detailed as the court records appear to be, they nevertheless distort the instrumental potential available to the composers for their compositions. Noticeably lacking from the court payroll are musicians credited with playing the chalumeau, flute (traversière), baryton, harp, and mandolin; yet, Conti's compositions require these instruments, either in solo or accompanying roles. Actually all five of these instruments are called for in his opera *Il trionfo dell'amicizia e dell'amore*, first performed in 1711 and revived in 1723.[10] Interestingly, this opera was not affected by the decree requiring the staff of musicians to be reduced, for the premiere took place prior to the issuance of the decree and the revival occurred in 1723 at a time when the number of instrumentalists employed by the court was exceptionally large.

Although extra musicians were engaged from time to time for special occasions, there is evidence that some of the regular court musicians were adept at playing more than one instrument.[11] For example, Maximilian Hellmann is listed as the tympanist in the 1712 roster, but a court document of 1729 refers to him as a 'cimbalist'.[12] Investigation of this musician's duties reveals that Hellmann did indeed serve the court in a dual capacity, thereby lending credence to the notion that the variety of instrumentation could exceed the number of instrumentalists listed in the court's financial records.

Table 3.1

Number of musicians assigned to the Hofkapelle

Instrument	April 1712*	December 1712**	April 1721***
Violin and Viola	18	18	23
Violoncello	4	3	4
Violone	3	2	1
Gamba	3	2	1
Theorbo	1	1	1
Lute	1	1	1
Organ	4	3	6
Cornett	2	2	2
Corno da caccia	0	2	1
Oboe	9	4	5
Bassoon	4	3	4
Trumpet	6	8	16
Trombone	5	4	4
Tympanum	1	0	2
	61	53	73

*   *Hof-protokollbuch: 1700-1713*, fols 215-26 (date of re-evaluation)
**   *Hof-protokollbuch: 1700-1713*, fols 401-5v (date of reduction)
*** Köchel, *Johann Josef Fux*, 225.

Conti never ceased to have trouble with the Finance Ministry. Months often passed before he could collect even a small portion of the money owed to him. As if this were not bad enough, he suffered further insult by not being credited with the correct amount of his stipend. His financial dilemma had become so critical and complex by 1713 that an interested colleague wrote a 'Report to Charles VI' in support of Conti's monetary claims.[13] The anonymous writer of this report lodged several complaints with the comptroller. He complained the amount of the stipend being paid was incorrect because the comptroller had failed to credit the monthly increase granted to Conti by Joseph von Paar in 1709. He also complained about the housing subsidy. He reported that Conti had never been given any housing allowance, as was the custom during this period of Habsburg rule. Since accommodation at the court was very limited, soldiers, musicians, and other court personnel were housed with residents of Vienna. They were expected to pay for their housing with the special subsidies provided for that purpose. This arrangement, in practice, had a serious flaw: the Finance Ministry was reluctant to furnish a housing allowance to the staff and consequently the staff felt no obligation to pay the rent owed to their landlords. According to the writer of the 'Report', the sum of 100 florins per year would constitute an amount commensurate with that granted to other musicians for their housing. This meant Conti was entitled to 1200 florins to cover his expenses since his arrival in Vienna. Where Conti resided during these twelve years is not known.[14]

A number of engravings related to court activities were made by Johann Adam Pfeffel (1674-1748) and Christian Engelbrecht (1672-1735). Among them are two depicting scenes that took place on 8 November 1712. One shows the interior of the Hofkapelle on the occasion of a performance of a Te Deum. The other is a view of a festive meal being served in the Ritterstube, the ceremonial room of the Hofburg. On the balcony overlooking this room is positioned a group of musicians, and in the upper left hand corner are two theorbists, one more distinctly pictured than the other. Friedrich Riedel has suggested that the theorbists depicted here are Francesco Conti and Georg Reutter. If this is indeed the case, this engraving would take on added significance, for no other engravings of Francesco or of other members of his family have come to light, although by this date, Reutter's duties were primarily confined to that of court organist.[15]

Few of Conti's cantatas and liturgical works are dated, making it almost impossible to know the extent of his contribution to the chamber and church music performed at the court during the interregnum. Three of his cantatas for soprano and *basso continuo* may have been composed between 1711 and 1713. They appear in a manuscript collection with nine other cantatas by Giovanni Bononcini, Antonio Caldara, Emanuele d'Astorga, and Andrea Fiorè.[16] Except for the two cantatas by Caldara, which are dated March 1712, the remaining works in the collection provide no information as to when they were composed. Nevertheless, it is possible that all twelve cantatas were written no later than 1713, since the composers represented therein were, or could have been, in Vienna during the interregnum. For example, Bononcini was at the court until the early part of 1713, and therefore his three cantatas could have been completed before his departure. Astorga came to Vienna for a limited time from early 1712 until 1714 and Fiorè may have been present when several of his dramatic works were performed there between 1710 and 1713. Although not one of Conti's works carries a date of 1712, there is no question that he, too, was actively participating in musical events associated with the court that year. With the curtailment of festive events during the period of mourning for Joseph I, it is a foregone conclusion that the composers would use another medium such as the cantata to express their creativity.

Notes

1 Ludwig Ritter von Köchel, *Johann Josef Fux* (Hildesheim, 1974), 312.
2 Ibid., 221.
3 For an exceptionally detailed description of the coronation proceedings, see Friedrich W. Riedel, 'Die Kaiserkrönung Karls VI (1711) als musikgeschichtliches Ereignis', *Mainzer Zeitschrift, Jahrgang 1960/61* (1966): 34-40.
4 Vienna. Staatsarchiv, *Hofprotokollbuch: 1710-1713*, folios 215-25.
5 Ibid., folio 218.
6 Ibid., folio 215v.
7 Ibid., folio 217.
8 Ibid., folio 219. On this same folio, Ziani and Reinhardt agreed with Fux's contention that the court needed no more than twelve violinists and four violists. They were asked to evaluate seventeen violinists and violists. Of these, two were praised for their virtuoso playing.
9 Ibid., fols 402 and 420. Mollart made provision for all increases in musicians' stipends to be figured retroactively from October 1711, the month immediately following the issuance of Eleonora's decree.
10 In her chapter 'The Viennese Court Orchestra' in Brian W. Pritchard, ed., *Antonio Caldara* (London, 1987), 129, Eleanor Selfridge-Field mentions that 'the sole baryton player was an Italian'. She presumably based her statement upon Köchel's listing of musicians in *Johann Josef Fux* (Hildesheim, 1974), 368, where only one name appears under the category 'Baritonist', that of Marc. Ant. Berti, whose service to the court extended from 1721 to 1740. Conti's *Il martirio di S. Lorenzo* and *Il trionfo dell'amicizia e dell'amore*, however, include parts for two baryton players, and since these works had performances in 1710 and 1711 and revivals in 1723 and 1724, there had to have been other musicians at the court who played this instrument.
11 One such special occasion occurred in May 1724, when Johann Adam (Graf) Questenberg travelled from Jaroměřice to Vienna to participate as a theorbist in the performance of Caldara's *Euristeo*. This particular production was presented by the nobility and members of the imperial family, with Charles VI conducting from the harpsichord.
12 *Nieder-österreichische Herrschaftsakten* W/Wien, 61/A.32, Nr. 817-29, February, 1729.
13 Vienna, Finanz- und Hofkammerarchiv, ('Report to Emperor Charles VI concerning payment of stipends to Francesco Bartolomeo Conti'). On the final page of this document are the words 'Carl placet', meaning that Charles VI approved the requests made in the report.

14 Not every musician serving the court had to find lodging with local residents of Vienna. For an extended period of time Fux lived in the Schottenstift on the Freyung. He was eligible for this desirable residence because he was organist at the Schottenkirche.

15 See Friedrich W. Riedel, *Kirchenmusik am Hofe Karls VI (1711-1740)* (Munich-Salzburg, 1977), 38, 312. Riedel claims that this engraving depicts a scene dating from 8 November 1712. By this date Conti was the only full-time theorbist serving the court, but it is possible that Reutter could have assisted in this event, for although his primary duty at the Hofkapelle in 1712 was as organist, he probably continued to perform as a theorbist.

George J. Buelow includes this same engraving in *The Late Baroque Era* (Englewood Cliffs, NJ, 1994), 325, but he labels the scene as taking place at a banquet in the 'Knights' chamber (Vienna), following the Ceremony of Oaths of Allegiance sworn to Charles, Archduke of Austria, on 8 November 1705'. If the year given in Buelow's caption is correct, it would lend credence to Riedel's claim that the two theorbists are Conti and Reutter, for both are listed in the 1705 court records as theorbists.

The Ritterstube was used for many different kinds of ceremonial and religious events. The only occasions when the emperor dined in this room were for the festive meals served there at Christmas and Easter, and on St Andrew's Day (30 November), and for the high feast of the Order of the Golden Fleece. Other events held there include the baptism of Maria Theresa (13 May 1717) and musical performances, such as that of Fux's Te Deum (K. 271).

16 Lawrence E. Bennett, 'The Italian Cantata in Vienna, 1700-1711: An Overview of Stylistic Traits', in Pritchard, ed., *Antonio Caldara*, 208.

CHAPTER FOUR

The years 1713-1722

The death of Kapellmeister Antonio Pancotti precipitated several changes in the roster of musicians who were to serve Emperor Charles VI. Marc' Antonio Ziani became the new Kapellmeister and into his former position of Vizekapellmeister was placed Johann Josef Fux. The promotion of Fux left only one person, Carlo Augusto Badia, holding the title of Hofcompositor. He had served in this capacity from 1696 and was to continue in this same position until his death in 1738.

Badia was soon joined by Francesco Conti, but the precise date when Conti became an official court composer is difficult to determine. The first reference to him as 'Tiorbista und Hof-Compositor' occurs in a March 1714 entry in the *Hofprotokollbuch*.[1] There the appointment is treated as an accomplished fact. The purpose of the entry was to confirm that his annual stipend of 1440 florins was to be paid retroactively from 1 January 1713. This newly authorized stipend was to run concurrently with the one Conti had been earning as a theorbist. This meant that his annual income of 2880 florins exceeded the stipend of the Kapellmeister, which at the time was only 2500 florins. That Conti received his new appointment at the very beginning of 1713 cannot be ascertained solely from the *Hofprotokollbuch*; yet, that is precisely the conclusion Köchel has drawn.[2] He disregards the fact that there was really no vacancy until 25 January 1713, the date when Fux advanced from the position of court composer to Vizekapellmeister.

Ceremonial aspects of life at the Hofburg did not undergo radical changes with the arrival of the new emperor. The conduct of the imperial realm under Charles VI resembled that of his immediate predecessors. Preserving the *status quo* seemed to be the guiding principle behind every decree. Even court festivities continued to follow a well-worn pattern as if in obedience to an invisible law of the Habsburg dynasty.

Though the Habsburg family was extremely fond of music, occasions when secular dramatic works could be offered were relatively few: Carnival season, the birthday and name-day of Elisabeth Christina, the birthday and name-day of

Charles VI, birthdays and name-days of other members of the immediate family, weddings, and coronations. Thus the operatic events at the court in Vienna differed markedly from those in the cities of Hamburg, Venice, and London where few limitations were placed on the number of operas that could be presented to the public. Venice, for example, boasted several public opera houses where composers were encouraged to produce their works. Here the number of performances a single opera could have was limited primarily by the public's response.

This was not the case with operatic works presented in Vienna. With the exception of the opera for Carnival, which usually enjoyed several performances during a single season, other works composed for one of the specific occasions cited above, the so-called 'Days of Gala', usually had but a single performance.[3] That these were regal affairs is obvious from the following description penned by a contemporary of Charles VI:

> On the Days of Gala the Court is extremely gay and nothing is to be seen but Gold and Diamonds. The Days of this kind that are celebrated with most splendor are those of St. Charles and St. Elizabeth, the Name-Days of the Emperor and Empress.[4]

One of the first opportunities Conti had as an official composer of the court to offer a dramatic work for one of the Days of Gala came on 28 August 1713. This was the birthday of Empress Elisabeth Christina and he was commissioned by Emperor Charles VI to compose an operatic work to celebrate the occasion. The resulting composition was *Circe fatta saggia*.[5] Making his debut at the court on this same occasion was the scene designer, Ferdinando Galli-Bibiena. This, however, was not Ferdinando's first encounter with the new emperor. In August of 1708 he was called to Barcelona to prepare the scene designs for *Il più bel nome*, a *componimento da camera per musica* with text by Pietro Pariati and music by Antonio Caldara. This work was presented as part of the festivities associated with the marriage of Charles, then King of Spain, to Princess Elisabeth Christina of Braunschweig-Wolfenbüttel. For his efforts, Ferdinando was given the title 'maestro maggiore e pittore di Camera e feste di Teatro'.[6] When Charles became emperor, Ferdinando and a number of other artists, poets, and musicians who at one time had been associated with the court in Spain, received appointments at the imperial court as they were needed. Between 1714 and 1716 Ferdinando collaborated with Conti on six additional operatic productions.[7]

Thereafter the responsibility for creating the scene designs for many of Conti's later operas fell to another member of this illustrious family, Giuseppe Galli-Bibiena.

Conti must have greatly pleased the empress with his music for, with few exceptions, every year thereafter she commissioned him to provide a dramatic composition in celebration of either her name-day or birthday for as long as he was court composer. She also commissioned him to compose two works and revise another to honour her husband's birthday in 1721 and again in 1723, and his name-day in 1724.[8] Conti therefore gained control over the music performed for some of the Days of Gala. This was no small feat. Competition was keen to secure these coveted occasions when a new work or a repeat performance of a previously composed work could be presented. Not only was there competition among those officially associated with the Hofkapelle. There was also competition from composers whose sphere of activity was primarily centred in Italy and from composers who resided in Vienna but did not hold court positions. Among those in this latter category was Maria Margherita Grimani, one of several women whose works were heard in the imperial theatre and chapel between 1705 and 1715. Grimani's *Pallade e Marte*, a *componimento dramatico* presented on 4 November 1713 for the name-day of the emperor, earned for her the distinction of being the first woman to have an operatic work performed for the entertainment of the Habsburgs.[9]

With the production of his *Alba Cornelia* as the 1714 Carnival opera, Conti secured for himself another one of the coveted court events. The Carnival opera was, musically speaking, an ambitious enterprise because a full-length opera was required for entertainment in this festive season in contrast to the more modest dimensions of most works created for the Days of Gala. This placed the composer of such a work in the enviable position of contributing one of the few, sometimes the only, major opera heard in Vienna in any given year. Conti contributed no less than twelve Carnival operas between 1714 and 1732.

Collaborating with the staging of *Alba Cornelia* were two of the best known choreographers and dancing masters of the period, Alessandro Phillebois and Simon Pietro Levassori della Motta, whose dances were wed to the music of Nicola Matteis, the younger. These same three persons continued to maintain a working relationship with Conti whenever dances were to be incorporated into his dramatic productions. Matteis provided the *ballo* music for twelve more of Conti's operas, with *Issipile*, the Carnival opera for 1732, marking their final collaboration. Although Matteis's contributions to *Alba Cornelia* and *I Satiri in*

Arcadia no longer survive, some of the other *ballo* music he created for Conti's operas has been preserved.[10]

The singers Conti had available for his operatic productions were limited primarily to those in the employ of the court. The roles in his operas and oratorios were rarely filled by internationally recognized stars imported for that purpose, although several made guest appearances at the court and sang in his productions. This meant Conti was spared the harrowing experience of having to deal on a daily basis with the personalities of celebrated singers such as Faustina, Senesino, Farinelli, and Cuzzoni.[11] Although contemporary writers made disparaging remarks about the imperial singers, any evidence to the contrary remains a matter of conjecture, for although contemporary Viennese accounts comment on composers, librettists, ballet masters, and scene designers, they are peculiarly silent on the subject of singers.[12] What cannot be disputed is that the singers who participated in Conti's secular and sacred dramatic works must have been well-trained musicians, for the roles they sang were often very demanding. In the early 1720s , a few singers who already had well-established careers in Italy accepted appointments at the court and Conti benefited from their talent and experience. One was the soprano Anna d'Ambreville; another was the tenor Gaetano Borghi. Coincidentally, both of these singers had appeared in Alessandro Scarlatti's *Tigranes*: Borghi sang the role of Doraspe in the Naples première in 1715 and Ambreville sang the role of Meroe in the Livorno production of 1716.

Some of the singers who started to work with Conti during the early stages of their careers eventually became well known beyond the confines of the imperial realm. Perhaps the most famous of them was Francesco Borosini (*c.* 1699-1754), who had a dual career in Vienna – first as a singer and then as an impresario. He is listed as a member of the Hofkapelle in January of 1713 with a stipend of 1080 florins. After petitioning the court twice, once in July 1716 and again in April 1719, he was successful in having his stipend increased to 1800 florins, thereby making him one of the highest-paid tenors in the employ of the court. His appearance in the title role of *David* in 1724 seems to have marked the last time he worked with Conti in Vienna, for shortly thereafter he accepted an offer from Handel to go to London for the 1724-25 season. His arrival there was announced in the *Weekly Journal* (17 October 1724), but the wording of that announcement was anything but complimentary: 'We hear that . . . Signior Borseni [sic], newly arrived from Italy, is to sing the Part of the Tyrant Bajazet. *N.B.* It is commonly reported this Gentleman was never *cut out for a Singer*'. Borosini returned to Vienna at the conclusion of that one theatrical season, and before long he became the co-director of the Kärntnertor-Theater, a position he held from 1728 until 1746. He then returned to London where he again was involved with the theatre, reportedly as 'Manager of the Opera' at the King's Theatre in the Haymarket for at least the 1746 to 1747 season. He may also have sung some minor roles, though this is difficult to document. During this second sojourn in London, Borosini's collection of a portion of Caldara's vocal canons was published under the title of *One Hundred Cantici*.[13] Here indeed was a versatile and gifted musician who was capable of assuming a great variety of tasks.

The cast of *Alba Cornelia* consisted of eight singers, including Francesco Borosini and his father Antonio. Both men are listed in court records as tenors and therefore it is a bit of a surprise to find Antonio playing the part of the comic servant, a role scored in the bass clef. In Köchel's listing of musicians who served the court under Leopold I, Joseph I, and Charles VI, he includes Antonio with the tenors but also indicates that this singer terminated his duties in 1711.[14] Court records, however, contradict Köchel's data. According to an April 1712 entry in the *Hofprotokollbuch*, a committee consisting of Ziani, Fux, and Reinhardt, who were charged with reviewing the status of musicians currently in the employ of the court, recommended that Antonio Borosini and his son be retained as tenors. In his comments supporting this decision, Ziani reveals that Antonio had 'quit' his position during the reign of Leopold I but later rejoined the court staff, together with his son, shortly before the death of Joseph I.[15]

Unlike his father, whose appearance in *Alba Cornelia* came when he was close to retirement and was the only role he ever sang for Conti, Francesco Borosini (*c.*1690-1754) was at the threshold of his career. His performance in *Alba Cornelia* marked the beginning of a long and productive association with the composer. He is known to have sung in at least fifteen operas and four oratorios by Conti, all of them performed prior to his appearance on the London stage in the 1724-25 opera season (see table 4.1).[16] Some of the other singers who had roles in *Alba Cornelia* also continued to appear as performers in subsequent works which Conti composed for the court. They include the soprano Regina Schoonjans and the alto castrato Gaetano Orsini. The stability of the roster from which Conti could draw his singers allowed him to compose with specific voices in mind, and indeed some of his singers are cast in predictable roles from one opera or oratorio to the next.

The annual stipend of a court singer was considerably higher than that paid to instrumentalists. Some singers earned 1080 to 1800 florins per year, the latter sum

Table 4.1

Works by Francesco Conti which list Francesco Borosini as a performer

Date	Opera/Oratorio	Role
1714	*Alba Cornelia*	Lentulo
1714	*I Satiri in Arcadia*	Damone
1715	*Teseo in Creta*	Tauride
1715	*Ciro*	Sibari
1716	*Il finto Policare*	Turbone
1717	*Sesostri, rè di Egitto*	Amassi Tiranno
1718	*Astarto*	Agenore
1718	*La colpa originale*	Dio
1719	*Don Chisciotte in Sierra Morena*	Don Chisciotte
1719	*Galatea*	Ulisse
1721	*Alessandro in Sidone*	Crate
1721	*Naaman*	Gesi
1721	*La via del saggio*	Ercole
1722	*Archelao*	Archelao
1722	*Pallade trionfante*	Marte
1723	*Creso*	Esopo
1723	*Il David perseguitato da Saul*	Valore
1724	*Penelope*	Ulisse
1724	*David*	Saul

exceeding the stipend of the Vizekapellmeister. There was, however, a notable exception to the aforementioned stipends. The prima donna received annually 4000 florins.

The singer who held the position of prima donna from 1713 until 1722 was Maria Landini.[17] Although her official debut at the court did not occur until she appeared in the title role of Conti's *Alba Cornelia*, Landini had already made her presence known there on 1 October 1710 when she sang in one of Fux's operas, *La decima fatica d'Ercole*. This particular opera, performed in the Favorita, featured the theorbo with an obbligato or concertizing part in two of the arias. Presumably Conti was the theorbist and therefore may well have had an opportunity to be introduced to Landini three years before she participated in one of his creations.

Prior to her appointment at the imperial court, Landini had sung operatic roles in several Italian cities. For example, she is listed among the singers for two of Caldara's operas. One was *Gli equivoci nel sembiante*, produced in 1703 for Ferdinando Carlo, Duke of Mantua, in the Teatro nuovo at Casale. The other was *L'inimico generoso*, produced 11 May 1709 in the Teatro Malvezzi at Bologna.[18]

On 28 August 1714 Landini played the lead in Conti's *I Satiri in Arcadia*, a three-act opera with a *licenza*.[19] That she agreed to be cast in two of Conti's works within the same year perhaps should be viewed as a tribute to the composer's talent and personality, for the success of a composer often depended on his or her ability to please the prima donna. Landini's apparent enthusiasm for Conti's music was matched by the composer's high regard for her talents. One wonders, however, what other powers of attraction fostered such an intimate friendship between these two musicians. Was Landini charmed by Conti's appearance and personality? Molitor has hinted that even Empress Elisabeth Christina was exceptionally fond of Conti for more than musical reasons.[20] Was Conti so impressed with Landini's beauty, or even her financial worth, that he asked her to be his second wife? For whatever reason, these two musicians decided to marry sometime between September 1714 and the forthcoming Carnival season. *Ciro*, the Carnival opera for 1715, lists 'La Contini' as the person playing the leading soprano role.[21]

Marriage did not interfere with Landini's career. She maintained her coveted position of prima donna, being cast in the leading role for every one of Conti's operas until 1721 and every one of Fux's operas from 1714 to 1720. These appearances were in addition to all of the other musical events to which she lent her talents during the course of this same period. The stipend of 4000 florins paid to Landini, when added to that earned by Conti, netted this couple an annual income of 6880 florins a year – a considerable sum in those days.

Wealth must have come as somewhat of a surprise to Conti, for he seems to have been accustomed to more humble circumstances. Landini, however, had come to expect luxurious living. Her first husband, Mallo di Castelnovo, had been a man of means, steeped in the pleasures of aristocratic life. At his death, he left Landini with three children (Ferdinando, Francesca, and Caterina) and a considerable estate which included a residence in the city of Vienna and another in Hieteldorf, a suburb of Vienna.[22] Hieteldorf was a favourite haunt of the nobility. Even Charles VI found it a desirable area in which to stage a chase. One of the features of the Hieteldorf residence was its extensive garden adorned with exotic treasures from the Orient. The garden must have been exceptionally beautiful because according to a contemporary assessment it was valued far in excess of the house itself.[23] Landini was able to share this inheritance with Conti, ensuring both of them and members of their respective families a life of ease and elegance.

Despite intense competition from other composers, Conti's musical endeavours earned for him an outstanding reputation among his peers. In large measure his success can be attributed to the ideal working relationship he had with Pietro Pariati, the court poet who was appointed to that position in July of 1714 upon a recommendation from Apostolo Zeno. Previous to his arrival in Vienna, the position of *poeta cesareo* had been filled successively by Pietro Antonio Bernardoni (1672-1714) and Silvio Stampiglia (*c.* 1690-1725). Bernardoni held that position from 1701 until 1705 during the reign of Leopold I. He then remained at the court, writing librettos for Ariosti, the Bononcini brothers, Fux, and Ziani, among others, until his death in January 1714.

Silvio Stampiglia succeeded Bernardoni as *poeta cesareo* in 1706. He had previously worked in Naples, Rome, and Florence, achieving notable success with a number of composers, not the least of them being Alessandro Scarlatti. Word of Stampiglia's poetic talent spread far beyond his native land. Some of his works were even put before the imperial court as early as 1697 when his *Il trionfo di Camilla regina dei Volsci* was presented there a year after its premiere in Naples. Ever eager to attract the finest poets Italy had to offer, Joseph I presented Stampiglia with an offer that he readily accepted. His initial stipend was only 1440 florins, but the amount of his annual stipend was soon increased to 4000 florins, a sum earned by only one other court poet between 1706 and 1740 – Apostolo Zeno.

Between 1706 and 1711 Stampiglia wrote the librettos for three oratorios and five operas for presentation at the court and during this same period he may also have written some cantata texts, including the undated one set by Conti. There is no telling how many more major dramatic works Stampiglia might have produced for the court had not his enthusiastic patron died. When the new emperor came to the throne, Stampiglia remained in the employ of the court, but clearly Charles VI showed little interest in him or his work. Instead, the emperor gave his commissions to the newly appointed poet, Pietro Pariati, whose work he had come to know in Spain. Charles wanted nothing better than to be entertained in a similar fashion now that he was in Vienna.[24]

It did not take Stampiglia long to realize that his talents were not going to be put to good use by the imperial family. As early as 1714 he started to petition the court to allow him to return to Italy. His request, however, was not granted until 1718, the year when Zeno was appointed to the senior position as court poet. Between the time of his first petition and the subsequent granting of his request, Stampiglia's health deteriorated. He suffered from a respiratory illness that seriously curtailed his activities. A move to his native city, Rome, was expected to improve his condition and for a time he did resume writing works dedicated to various members of the Habsburg family.[25] Unfortunately, the climate in Rome did little to improve his physical condition, and so once again he moved, this time to Naples. There his condition continued to deteriorate, aggravated by other physical mishaps from which he never recovered. He died on 26 January 1725.

Stampiglia left his mark on Vienna with his distinctive style of *dramma per musica*. That same style characterizes *Alba Cornelia*, an anonymous libretto set by Conti for the 1714 Carnival season. As far back as 1733, Allacci credited Stampiglia with this libretto, but more recently there have been attempts to attribute the work to Pariati.[26] Even before his appointment was made official, several of Pariati's works had been presented in Vienna. His *Ercole in cielo*, a *serenata*, was performed on 1 October 1710 and again on 1 October 1713 to honour the birthday of Charles, first as King of Spain and then as emperor. Pariati also wrote the libretto for *Il voto crudele*, an oratorio performed in the imperial chapel in 1712.

During his twelve years serving the imperial court, Pariati provided the composers of Vienna with numerous sacred and secular librettos. Fux set several of these, including *Angelica vincitrice d'Alcina* and *Costanza e fortezza*, the two works most discussed in contemporary Viennese accounts of the court's operatic entertainment. It was to Francesco Conti, however, that Pariati offered the majority of his librettos and the first time their collaboration can be confirmed on the basis of the surviving materials was in August 1714. Instead of celebrating the empress's birthday with the usual *serenata* or *festa teatrale*, consisting of a single act plus *licenza*, Conti and Pariati presented the court with a three-act *favola pastorale* entitled *I Satiri in Arcadia*.

An interesting facet of Pariati's poetic genius lay in his flair for the comic. One of the first times Pariati may have had an opportunity to test Conti's adeptness at setting music to his comic episodes was in the 'Tuberone e Dorimena' intermezzos presented with the three-act pasticcio *L'Atenaide*, to which Ziani, Negri, and Caldara each contributed one act.[27] *L'Atenaide* was presented in celebration of the empress's name-day on 19 November 1714 and apparently was so well received that it had several additional performances later that same year. Zeno is listed as librettist for the opera, but since he usually delegated the writing of comic episodes to Pariati, there is every reason to believe this same situation prevailed here. This particular set of intermezzos proved to be of historical importance, for it was the first time in Vienna comic scenes were created independent of the host opera with which they were staged.

The staging of Antonio Lotti's *Giove in Argo* in Dresden in 1717 represents one of the first recorded events when Conti's ability as a composer of comic intermezzos was experienced by audiences outside the Habsburg realm. Between the acts of this *opera seria* was inserted the comedy 'Vespetta e Milo', itself a miniature pasticcio. Not only did two librettists contribute to these intermezzos (Silvio Stampiglia and Francesco Ballerini), but so also did two composers (Alessandro Scarlatti and Conti). The interpolation of intermezzos into an otherwise serious production was a phenomenon virtually unknown to the Dresden stage before this particular production took place.

In 1718, Pariati and Conti collaborated on *Amore in Tessaglia*, commissioned for the empress's birthday that year. Although the subtitle *componimento da camera per musica* suggests this is a chamber work, in reality it is a substantial one-act opera requiring seven singers and a chorus. It is even conceivable that the premiere might have mirrored the description John George Keÿssler (1689-1743) gives in his travel diary of imperial name-day and birthday celebrations:

> On the 4th of November and also on the empress's birthday, operas are exhibited, each of which costs the emperor about sixty thousand guldens; for the magnificence of the theater, the splendor of the decorations, the richness of the habits, and the performance in the orchestra, surpass any thing of the kind in Europe.[28]

Between 1714 and 1718, Pariati's librettos were more frequently used for court entertainment than those of any other poet. Evidently his works were popular with the composers and well received by the Habsburgs. This favourable reception, however, did not alter the poet's official status at the court, for Pariati never advanced from his position as 'kaiserlicher Kammerdichter'. When Stampiglia was granted permission to leave the court in 1718, Charles VI did not promote Pariati to the vacated post. Instead, he offered it to Apostolo Zeno and his appointment, which became effective in March 1718, carried an annual stipend of 4000 florins, a sum that exceeded that earned by Pariati by 1600 florins. The emperor's choice of Zeno for the coveted post was applauded by the adversaries of Pariati, who were displeased by his presence at the court and hoped to see him removed.[29] This appointment also caused Zeno some embarrassment. A statement entered in the *Hofprotokollbuch* in April 1719 declared his title to be 'primo Poeta' and 'Historico'. Since Zeno did not want to offend Pariati, he requested the word 'primo' be omitted from his title and the request was granted.

Zeno's published correspondence concerning his appointment reveals the sincere regard he held for Pariati. For example, in a letter to Andrea Cornaro in Venice dated 1 October 1718, Zeno explains that he wanted his title changed to 'Poeta e di Istorico Cesareo' so as not to destroy his long-standing relationship with Pariati, for whom he had the highest opinion and in whom he had a very good friend.[30] With Zeno in residence at the court, the partnership of the two poets was activated once again, but with one important difference. Pariati no longer served as a silent partner. Zeno acknowledged, especially in his correspondence, the assistance given him in their collaborative works. In a letter to Pietro (Pier) Caterino Zeno written 7 November 1718, two days after the initial performance of *Ifigenia*, Zeno tells his brother that he received considerable assistance from Pariati in the writing of the libretto and it was in large measure that assistance which was responsible for the success the work enjoyed at its premiere.[31]

Several excellent librettos were created for Conti as a result of this renewed partnership, most especially *Don Chisciotte in Sierra Morena*, the *tragicommedia* which was staged during the Carnival season of 1719. Although the use of *scene buffe* and intermezzos had long been in vogue, the comic opera *per se* was as yet little known, especially in Vienna.[32] It was, therefore, with particular interest that the Habsburg court viewed this five-act operatic production. In addition to delighting the Viennese audiences with its multiple performances during the 1719 Carnival season, *Don Chisciotte* also provided comic entertainment for other European cities as well and rocketed his reputation as a composer to new heights.

This year of 1719 was an extremely busy one for Conti. Following the successful production of *Don Chisciotte*, he turned his attention to composing the oratorio *Dio sul Sinai* for the Lenten season. No sooner was that work completed than he became involved with opera productions for Hamburg where *Cloris und Thyrsis* and *Tigranes,* both containing his music, were brought to the stage. In August of this same year, Conti shared in the festivities celebrating the wedding of Maria Josefa and Friedrich August II. Although he did not have a *dramma per musica* or *festa teatrale* presented on this auspicious occasion, as did Zeno and Caldara with *Sirita* and Pariati and Fux with *Elisa*, he did have the opportunity to contribute *L'Istro*, a festive cantata set to a text by Zeno and composed expressly to honour the bride and groom.[33] There is also the possibility that one or more of Conti's undated sacred compositions might have been presented in connection with the wedding, for several of these manuscripts are found only in the archives in Dresden, the city where the married couple settled.

On 19 November 1719, the empress's name-day, Conti offered *Galatea vendicata*, a *festa teatrale* with text by Pariati. Since Conti often fêted the empress on her name-day, this performance would not normally be cause for special attention. The reason it is singled out here, however, is that the final aria, 'Cor costante, ed umil', and the preceding 'Introduzione' are scored for obbligato mandolin and theorbo parts. Conti, of course, was a skilled performer on these instruments, but only once before had he included both of them in the same work. It occurred in *Il trionfo dell'amicizia e dell'amore*, with the mandolin appearing in an aria in Scene ix of Act II, and the theorbo in an aria in Scene xiii of this same act. Never before had he combined the instruments within the same number. The uniqueness of this aria from *Galatea vendicata* raises the question of why Conti decided to use the instruments in this way since he could play only one of them. He must have created this unusual scoring for some reason other than to display his own talent. The mandolin was not used very often by Conti in his own music after 1713, but in the year before *Galatea* was presented, this instrument is included as an obbligato instrument in Act III of *Astarto*, the Carnival opera for 1718.

Conti, of course, was not the only one to take an interest in the mandolin. Other composers also incorporated the instrument into their works for the court. For example, Fux calls for a 'Citarina o Mandolino' in his *Diana placata* (1717). If a mandolin instead of a 'citarina' was used when the opera was initially staged, it seems reasonable to assume that Conti would have been the musician chosen to execute the part, given his intense involvement with the instrument a decade earlier.

By the same token, Conti could have played the mandolin part he wrote for *Galatea*, but who then played the theorbo? The date of *Galatea* may hold the answer to that question. It was presented just five days before Ignazio Conti, Francesco's son, began his duties as a paid apprentice theorbist under the tutelage of his father. Apparently Francesco decided to score the final numbers in *Galatea* for both the mandolin and theorbo as a way of introducing his son to the imperial family. Perhaps Ignazio needed this occasion to demonstrate his ability as a theorbist in order to receive an appointment to the court. Whatever the reasons might have been for creating an opportunity for what appears to have been a father-and-son performance, the results were at least positive. On 24 November 1719 Ignazio was officially appointed a Hof-Scholar with an annual stipend of 360 florins, the standard amount granted to all who held this sort of apprentice-type position.[34]

The reputation Conti held as a performer and composer was not to become a family tradition, as was the case with the Leopold Christian and Franz Glätzl families: four members of the Christian family played trombone and three of the Glätzl family played the oboe.[35] Although Ignazio studied the theorbo with his father, he gained only enough proficiency to make himself eligible for a minor appointment on the court staff. Obviously his talent as a performer was too modest to withstand the competition offered by other musicians. It is for this reason that, despite his father's prestige and influence, Ignazio was to remain a Hof-Scholar throughout his entire career in Vienna. That he possessed other musical talents beyond that of performer was revealed during the final phase of his father's career.

In the first month of 1720, Eleonora Magdalena, widow of Leopold I, died. Out of respect for a deceased member of the imperial family, the court required a year-long period of mourning. This meant that most of the regularly scheduled theatrical events had to be cancelled, a situation with which Conti was by this time all too familiar, having experienced several other periods of mourning since his arrival at the court in 1701. During the twelve months when operas and similar festive works could not be offered, the court composers either sought commissions from other patrons living outside the imperial city or they turned their attention to writing chamber music and works of a religious nature. Conti composed an oratorio, *Mosè preservato,* and a cantata, *Cantata allegorica,* the latter commissioned to honour the name-day of Maria Teresa on 15 October 1720. It is possible that some of his liturgical works which are no longer extant, such as his setting of the *Stabat mater* text, may also have been written during this period.

Since the majority of Conti's secular and sacred dramatic works can be dated, they have served as convenient reference points for developing a biographical profile of the composer. There are other works, however, that are equally important for rounding out details about his life; yet, they are often overlooked simply because they lack information relating to place and date of performance. Some are secular (the cantatas); others are sacred (the masses and liturgical works). For example, the double chorus Te Deum with full orchestral accompaniment is definitely a festival work and presumably it would have been used to commemorate an important event, possibly one celebrated in the cathedral of St Stephen's.[36] Two of his masses seemed to have been composed around 1720 and 1721 and they were most likely intended for services of worship that took place at the Schottenkirche in Vienna. The scoring suggests that one of these masses was written for a festival service that was dictated either by the liturgical calendar or by some imperial event. The other one may have been composed as a commemorative mass. There is even the possibility it could have been performed in memory of a person related to his own family. A remark made by Maria Landini Conti, in her testament of 1721, reveals that her first husband, Mallo di Castelnovo, was buried in the Schottenkirche. This information comes by way of her request to be buried next to her deceased husband in the Schottenkirche, if her death should occur in Vienna. Given the number of commemorative masses both she and Francesco requested in their testaments to be said after their deaths, it is reasonable to assume Castelnovo would have wanted similar acts of remembrance and devotion from his family.

Not many years after his second marriage, Conti once again found himself a widower. The leading role in his opera for the 1721 Carnival season, *Alessandro in Sidone*, marked Maria Landini's final appearance on the stage. Soon after this performance she became very ill. In May of the following year she travelled, or at least had made plans to travel, with Conti to Padua. The reason for their trip invites speculation: was Landini returning to her place of birth? did she have relatives there? was she seeking help for her illness? The only known reference to this trip is in a letter of 9 May 1722 from Apostolo Zeno to Antonio Vallesnieri in Padua, in which Zeno asks Vallesnieri to assist in any way possible his esteemed friends, Maria Landini and Francesco Conti.[37] If the trip to Padua was sought to restore Maria's health, it did not have the desired effect. She died in July 1722. This must have been an especially devastating experience for a composer whose major works, both secular and sacred, revolved around her presence in the leading soprano roles. How many of his other works requiring a soprano soloist she performed may never be known, since the vocal parts in the chamber and liturgical works are not assigned in the scores to specific singers.

Landini's testament, dated 30 May 1721, not only gives a glimpse of the material possessions which were to be included in her estate, but more importantly it provides information about various members of the Landini, Castelnovo, and Conti families. In her distribution of items of value, she seems to have wielded an even hand. She provided amply for everyone, beginning with her devoted servant Francesca Autelli and continuing on to members of the immediate family. They included a daughter Francesca who was married to Signor Pilastrina, a son Ferdinand who was Captain of the Grenadiers in Mantua, another daughter Caterina, Ignazio whom she calls her son ('*mio figlio*'), her sister-in-law ('*mio cognata*') Caterin (Cattarina) Angela, and finally her husband Francesco Conti. She also leaves a portion of her estate to her sister, Christine Landini, who was living in Rome. Included in the inheritance were valuable furnishings, elegant dresses, a pair of diamond earrings, a gold watch inherited by Ignazio, and a considerable amount of money. From her remarks to Francesco concerning how she wanted her wishes carried out after her death, it is evident that she was very much in love with him. Moreover, she recommends as strongly as possible that he take care of her daughter Caterina, who has expressed a desire to remain in Vienna rather than returning to Italy.[38]

Notes

1   Vienna, Staatsarchiv, *Hofprotokollbuch: 1713-1717*, fols 131v-32.
2   Ludwig Ritter von Köchel, *Johann Josef Fux* (Hildesheim, 1974), 363.
3   This does not mean that an opera designed for one imperial event could not be repeated for another. Sometimes an opera or *serenata* was repeated exactly as originally written; other times a work had to undergo revisions in order to honour a different member of the imperial household. Upon rare occasions a birthday or name-day work could have several performances within the same year. See, for example, *L'Atenaide* (1714).
4   Karl Ludwig Pöllnitz, *The Memoirs of Charles Lewis* (Dublin, 1737-38), I, 238-9.
5   The name of the librettist for *Circe fatta saggia* is not known. That this *serenata* may not have been the first of Conti's works for the court in 1713 is suggested by Alexander von Weilen. He lists Conti's *L'ammalato immaginario* as possibly having been performed during the Carnival season on 26 February 1713, but he does not offer any documentation to support his information. No score of this work is extant. See his *Zur Wiener Theatergeschichte* (Vienna, 1901), 74. Köchel, in *Johann Josef Fux*, 530, also includes in a list of works presented at the court in 1713 a *serenata* by Conti entitled *Ammalato immaginario,* which he indicates was performed in February during Carnival. For a different interpretation of this work, see chapter ten.
6   Joseph Rafel Carreras y Bulbena, *Carlos d'Austria y Elisabeth de Brunswich Wolfenbüttel a Barcelona y Girona* (Barcelona, 1902), 124. Various spellings of Elisabeth's name are given in the eighteenth-century sources consulted. The title pages of works by Conti performed in her honour usually have her name spelt as Elisabetta Cristina and only occasionally as Elisabeth Cristina, whereas the *Wienerisches Diarium* has Elisabeth Christina (see, for example, the entry for 19 November 1726), the version adopted for this book.
7   Franz Hadamowsky, 'Barocktheater am Wiener Kaiserhof. Mit einem Spielplan (1625-1740)', in *Jahrbuch der Gesellschaft für Wiener Theaterforschung 1951/52* (Vienna, 1955), 46. Ferdinando was the elder brother of Francesco Galli-Bibiena.
8   The works, as indicated by the title pages of the scores, are *La via del saggio* (1 October 1721), *Il trionfo della fama* (4 November 1723), and *Galatea vendicata* (1 October 1724). For example, the title page for the revised version of *Galatea* reads: Galatea Vendicata / Serenata nell' Imperial Favorita / Per il Felicissimo Giorno Natalizio / della / Sacra Cas:a e

Catt:a Real Maestà / di / Carlo VI / Imperadore de' Romani Sempre Augusto / per comando / della Sac: Ces:a e Catt:a Real Maestà / di / Elisabetta Cristina Imperadrice Regnante / L'Anno 1724 / La Poesia è di Pariati/ Poeta di Sac. Maestà. Ces:a e Catt:a / La Musica è di Franco Conti, Tiorbista e Comp: di Sac. M. Ces:a e Catt:a. (A/*Wn*: Mus.Hs. 18137).

9   Maria Grimani may have been a relative of the Grimani family of Venice, owners of several theatres in that city, and/or the ambassador Pietro Grimani who in 1713 was instrumental in securing an alliance between Venice and the Habsburgs against their common enemy the Turks. Other women composers active in Vienna during this period were Camilla de Rossi and Caterina Benedicta Grazianini. See Julie Anne Sadie and Rhian Samuel, eds, *The Norton / Grove Dictionary of Women Composers*, 196, 198 and 395.

10   For a discussion of the *ballo* music, see chapter seven.

11   Conti had but one occasion to work with Faustina when she made a brief guest appearance at the court in 1717. At that time she sang the role of Grilletta in the intermezzos performed with Conti's *Sesostri*. Seven years later, Faustina accepted the imperial court's offer to return to the Vienna stage and sing various roles during the 1724-25 season. Although she was paid the exceptionally generous stipend of 15,000 florins, this was not enough to secure her permanently for the court; in 1726 she accepted Handel's offer to sing in London. S.v. 'Bordoni' in *The New Grove Dictionary of Opera*, I, 546.

12   In an oft-quoted letter of 4 November 1730, John George Keÿssler offered the following remark on the singers he heard during his brief sojourn in Vienna: 'It is a saying among the Italians, that Vienna is the hospital of the *virtuosi* singers and that they never go thither till they are worn out; at least here are no Farinelli's, Senesino's, or Caristini's'. See his *Travels through Germany, Bohemia, Hungary, Switzerland, Italy, and Lorrain*, (London, 1760), IV, 189, [Letter LXXXII].

13   For a study of Francesco Borosini's involvement with Caldara and his collection of canons, see Glennys Ward, 'Caldara, Borosini and the One Hundred Cantici, or some Viennese canons abroad', in Brian W. Pritchard, ed., *Antonio Caldara* (London, 1987), 302-42.

14   Ludwig Ritter von Köchel, *Die Kaiserliche Hof-Musikkapelle in Wien von 1543-1867* (Vienna, 1869), 67, 71.

15   *Hofprotokollbuch: 1710-1713,* (April 1712), fol. 217, where the marginal comments read: 'beÿ dem Borosini erinnert der Ziani dass beÿ Kaÿser Leopold er in diensten gewesten seÿ und dieselbe Quittirt habe, und ist er nicht lang vor absterben Kaÿsers Josephi mit seinen Sohn wider aufgenohmen worden'. Francesco, the given (first) name of Antonio's son, is not mentioned here. Although Ziani and Reinhardt concurred in their recommendations concerning Antonio Borosini and his son, Fux questioned whether or not Heinrich Holzhauser should be retained instead of the two Borosini tenors. Reinhardt assured Fux that this was not an option.

16   Several of the manuscripts of Conti's dramatic works fail to list the names of the singers. It is therefore possible, even probable, that Borosini participated in some of these in addition to those listed in table 4.1. For instance, the oratorio *Dio sul Sinai* (1719) lacks the names of the performers, but Borosini probably sang the tenor role of Mosè. Borosini also sang roles in operas (4) and oratorios (2) by Fux between 1715 and 1719 and in a number of operas and oratorios by Caldara between 1717 and 1729.

17   Landini's appointment at the court presumably became official on 1 January 1713. For a brief summary of the singers serving the imperial court, see Franz Hadamowsky, 'Barocktheater

am Wiener Kaiserhof ', 63. His information is based primarily on the *Parteienprotokoll des Obersthofmeisteramts*.

18 Ursula Kirkendale, *Antonio Caldara* (Graz, 1966), 32, 51. For the Bologna production, Kirkendale suggests that the singers were procured from the Teatro San Giovanni Grisostomo in Rome.

19 On the title page of the manuscript (A/*Wn*: Mus.Hs. 17210), the opera's title is spelt *I Sattiri in Arcadia*.

20 Simon von Molitor, 'Materialien zur Musikgeschichte', folio 9.

21 Prior to her marriage to Francesco Conti, Maria Landini was known professionally by her maiden name and therefore was listed in opera and oratorio scores as 'La Landini'. After her marriage to Conti, she was listed variously as 'La Contini', 'La Conti' or 'La Sig. Conti' in the scores or as 'Maria Landini Contini' in the court records. Even after 1715 she occasionally was referred to as 'Maria Landini' by those who knew her before her second marriage. Never was she referred to as 'Maria Contini-Landini'; yet, this is the way her name appears in John Henry van der Meer's *Johann Joseph Fux als Opernkomponist* (Bilthoven, 1961) and in subsequent sources dependent upon Van der Meer's work. In Giovanna Gronda's *La carriera di un librettista* (Bologna, 1990), 287, she lists the singers who participated in works based upon librettos by Pietro Pariati. There is an entry for 'Landini Conti Maria' and one for 'Lorenzani Contini A. M.'. To the last named Gronda credits three works – *Orfeo ed Euridice* (1715), *L'oracolo del fato* (1719), and *Teseo in Creta* (1715) – because the name of the person who sang the leading soprano role in each was given as 'Contini'. Gronda assumed, incorrectly, that this was Conti's third wife. The dates of the works in question leave no doubt that the 'Contini' performing them was none other than Maria Landini.

22 Vienna, Stadtarchiv, 'Testament / Maria Landini Conti', Nr. 21693/1722. Her testament was recorded in the *Totenprotokoll* on 3 July. Also in the Stadtarchiv are the *Kameral-Zahlamts-Bücher*. The volumes for 1722 (Nr. 782, p. 110) and 1723 (Nr. 764, p. 160) have entries concerning Maria Landini Conti and her son who is referred to here with the French form of his surname, Ferdinand de Chateauneuff.

23 Vienna, Stadtarchiv, 'Testament / Francesco Bartolomeo Conti', Nr. 6881/1732.

24 For an overview of Pariati's life and works, including his involvement with the Habsburgs before 1714, see chapter nine.

25 That Stampiglia was still considered part of the imperial staff is made evident in various ways. For example, in the preface to the printed libretto for his intermezzos performed with Lotti's *Giove in Argo* in Dresden (1719), he is referred to as a poet in the service of the Emperor Charles VI.

26 Lione Allacci, *Drammaturgia* (Venice, 1755), col. 19; Giovanna Gronda, 'Repertorio', in her *La carriera di un librettista*, 187-8. For more about this libretto, see chapter nine below.

27 Obviously this statement would have to be modified if it can be proven that Pariati did indeed write the libretto for *Alba Cornelia*, for it includes a number of *scene buffe*.

28 John George Keÿssler, *Travels through Germany*, IV, 189 [Letter LXXXII cited above].

29 These adversaries were primarily members of the court in Modena and included Count Carlo Antonio Giannini, who was in Vienna at the time of Pariati's arrival in 1714, and Duke Rinaldo of Modena. For a fuller discussion of why there was considerable animosity between the duke and Pariati, see chapter nine.

30 'Del Sig. Pariati abbiate migliore opinione; e so di avere in lui un buon amico'. Quoted from Apostolo Zeno, *Lettere* (Venice, 1785), II, 436-7.

31 'L'assistenza del nostro Sig. Pariati è stata molta, e sommamente biovevole per la buona riuscita del Dramma . . .' Quoted from Apostolo Zeno, *Lettere*, II, 445.

32 Alessandro Scarlatti's *Il trionfo dell'onore* was produced in Naples in 1718, the first comic opera composed for that city. For a modern edition commissioned by San Francisco Opera for performances in 1982, see Hermine Williams, ed., *The Triumph of Honor* (St Louis, MO, 1982).

33 Maria Landini Conti sang the role of Venere in *Elisa* for the 1719 production, but that same role was sung by a castrato for the revival in 1722.

34 Information can be found in: the *Hofprotokollbuch: 1718-1723*, fols 187, 193; the *Österreichische Hoffinanz* rote Nr. 830, 4 January 1720; and the *Kameral-Zahlamts-Buch*, Nr. 7 (1720), fol. 124v. The last two documents are located in the Finanz- und Hofkammerarchiv, Vienna. *Galatea vendicata* was revived in 1724 at which time the 'Introduzione' was omitted and the mandolin and theorbo were eliminated from the instrumental accompaniment of the final aria. For more on this particular aria, see chapter nine.

35 Information provided by the *Hofprotokollbuch: 1710-1713*, fols 220v-222r.

36 An engraving by J. C. Hackhofer entitled *Das Te Deum Laudamus in der Hoff Capellen* (1705) is in A/*Wn*: Bildarchiv, 36 N 1, V, S. 80. This engraving is reproduced as an ،illustration in a number of articles and books that concern the performance of sacred music in Vienna. See, for example, Maria Teresa Muraro, *L'opera italiana a Vienna prima di Metastasio* (Florence, 1990), 225.

37 Zeno, *Lettere*, III, 332.

38 Maria Landini Conti gives this information in her testament dated 30 May 1721. See Vienna, Staatsarchiv, 'Testament / Maria Landini Conti', Nr. 21693/1722

CHAPTER FIVE

The years 1722-1732

The pace at which Conti's works were being performed between 1722 and 1724 offer no hint that his career as a composer would soon be coming to an end. Some of his most important secular and sacred dramatic works date from this period: *Archelao, Pallade trionfante, Creso, Il David perseguitato da Saul, Il tronfo della fama, Penelope, David,* and *Meleagro.* Not only was he composing new works, but he was also overseeing the revivals of several others, such as *Il trionfo dell'amicizia e dell'amore, Galatea vendicata,* and *Il martirio di San Lorenzo.* In addition he continued to fulfil his duties as a theorbist, performing the continuo and virtuoso obbligato parts in his own and other composers' works as well. All of this was happening at a time when a number of his operas and intermezzos were being staged in Hamburg, Braunschweig-Wolfenbüttel (Brunswick), Breslau, and Jaroměřice.

Conti did not let his composing and performing career interfere with personal affairs that he considered to be important, especially when they were related to financial matters. Court documents show that on 9 April 1723 Conti petitioned the imperial treasurer for payment of 283 florins. This was the amount he was entitled to receive as the rightful heir to first wife's pension that was still outstanding from a period extending from 1 August 1710 to 15 April 1711, the date of her death. In other words, Conti laid claim to that part of Theresia's annual pension of 400 florins which the court had failed to give her. In his petition, Conti explains that the pension, granted by Emperor Joseph I, had not been paid in a timely fashion by Baron Pilati, the paymaster for the treasury, and hence his request for the unpaid portion. Several abbreviated versions of the petition were filed at the same time as the main one, and together they initiated a favourable response from the court.[1]

This petition is significant for several reasons. First, it provides a source in which Conti states, in his own words, that Theresia Kuglerin was his first wife and that her death occurred on 15 April 1711. Second, it is the only document which mentions that Theresia received a pension, although it offers no information as to why she might have been entitled to one. Third, it underscores the ongoing problem Conti had in collecting money he was rightfully owed by the court. Lastly, it raises the question of what prompted Conti to file his petition at this date. Could it be that the loss of income after the death of his second wife had caused him some financial problems?

On 4 June 1723, according to a report printed in the *Wienerisches Diarium* that day, a number of the Hofkapelle musicians left Vienna for Prague. They were being sent there to help celebrate the coronation of Charles VI as King of Bohemia. One of the events scheduled in connection with the coronation was the première of *Costanza e fortezza*, an opera with libetto by Pariati and music by Fux. When it came time for the actual performance, however, it was discovered that the number of imperial musicians present was not sufficient to meet the demands of the score and of the venue where it was being held. Thus it happened that several musicians from the Dresden court, who had come to witness the festivities in Prague, were invited to augment the orchestral forces. Among those who accepted the invitation was Johann Joachim Quantz. He was so impressed with the occasion that he later wrote down his impressions.[2] Quantz begins by mentioning that only about twenty musicians from Vienna were on hand to play the orchestral parts for Fux's opera. Since that proved to be an insufficient number, extra musicians were drawn from whoever was at hand. They included students, members of a nobleman's chapel, and even foreigners who happened to be in Prague at that time. Quantz acknowledges that he (playing oboe) and some of his colleagues from Dresden – Weiss (theorbo), Graun (cello) – were among the foreigners who played in the *ripieno* group of the orchestra.

Of interest are his comments about Conti. He describes him as a highly inventive and zealous, if now and then an equally bizarre, composer of music for the church as well as for the serious and comic theatre. He also declares him to be one of the greatest theorbists of his day and makes a point of noting that Conti played the first theorbo part for Fux's opera performance, whereas the equally renowned theorbist from Dresden, Silvius Leopold Weiss, was assigned to the *ripieno* part. His remarks subsequently earned for Conti the title 'first theorbist of the world'.[3]

Some, if not all, of the Hofkapelle musicians remained in Prague for a considerable time after the coronation. Confirmation of this comes from the list of singers who portrayed the roles in *Il trionfo della fama*, a *serenata* by Conti which was performed in that city on 4 November 1723, the name-day of Charles

VI. Four of the five singers – Ambreville, Gaetano, Borghi, and Praun – were the same who had sung in many of his previous productions. Only the soprano castrato, Giuseppe, may have been a recent addition to his usual cast. The scoring of this *serenata* is indicative of its celebratory nature; it calls for trombe, clarini, and timpani in the 'Sinfonia' and 'Licenza'.

After Conti returned from Prague, presumably in the latter part of November 1723, he had occasion to write to Benedetto Marcello (1868-1739). This letter, sent from Vienna and dated 25 December 1723, is the only example of his correspondence that has survived.[4] Conti's reason for writing a letter was prompted by the receipt of four psalms representing a sample of the cantata-like settings Marcello had made based upon G. A. Giutiniani's Italian paraphrases of the Vulgate version of the biblical psalms. In the letter, Conti thanks Marcello for giving him the privilege of being one of the first to see the fruits of his labour. He then adds his words of praise for what Marcello had accomplished and encourages him to go forward with his worthwhile project. From the tone of the letter, which of course is couched in the flowery language of the day, it seems that Conti and Marcello may have been acquainted with each other for a considerable period of time. They, of course, not only shared an interest in music for the church; they also had in common some of the same experiences. That their friendship might have extended over a fairly long period of time is suggested by an event that took place in 1712. In December of that year, Marcello was admitted as a member of the Accademia Filarmonica of Bologna, the very organization of which Conti became a member in 1708.

Marcello ultimately limited himself to setting the first fifty of the 150 psalms. The completed project numbered eight volumes, with several issued in 1724 and the remainder in 1726. Conti was far from being the only person who offered words of praise and encouragement to Marcello. Other composers, among them Bononcini, Mattheson, and Telemann, were similarly impressed with what he had done and they, too, were eager to communicate their support for his work. Their letters of endorsement, along with Conti's, appear in the prefatory sections of the published volumes.

Shortly after the first volume of his psalm settings was published, Marcello received an invitation to compose some musical entertainment for the imperial family. The resulting work, which carries the descriptive title of *Serenata da cantarsi ad uso di scena*, was performed at the imperial palace on 1 October 1725, the emperor's birthday.

The high regard for sacred music held by the musicians of the Hofkapelle was in part responsible for the founding of a new organization in Vienna in 1725 known as the Cäcilien-Bruderschaft. This was a highly structured society whose extensive list of officers involved some twenty musicians. One of the by-laws of the organization made it clear that there was to be equal representation from those who were German and those who were foreigners. This rule was obviously prompted by the great influx of Italian musicians to the court. Fux and Caldara shared the position of what would be comparable to a vice-president's position and Gaetano Orsini was the treasurer. Among the officers designated as the six advisors was Francesco Conti. His duties seemed to be less specific than those assigned to the other officers. For example, Francesco Borosini was in charge of the accounts and records and Christian Payer was one of two officers designated to visit the sick of their society.[5] It would appear that this Bruderschaft was similar to the societies founded in Italian cities, such as the one which sponsored Scarlatti and Pergolesi to compose settings of the *Stabat mater* for use in the Holy Week devotions attended by its members.

At the start of the 1724 opera season, Conti was still without a prima donna. Ever since the Carnival season of 1721, he had relied solely upon Regina Schoonjans to play the leading female role. This soprano was no stranger to the Vienna stage, nor to Conti. In fact, she had played the seconda donna in every one of Conti's operas since 1714. Fux was of the opinion that Schoonjans had been unfairly treated because her stipend was considerably less than that granted the prima donna, the implication being that her vocal technique equalled or even surpassed that of Maria Landini. For some unknown reason, neither ability nor years of service helped Schoonjans advance to the position vacated by the death of Conti's second wife. Instead, the court appointed Maria Anna Lorenzani as the new prima donna.[6] Information about her background is limited to one sentence provided by an eighteenth-century source in which she is said to have been a 'virtuoso' in the employ of the Prince of Darmstadt and considered by all to be an excellent singer.[7] Nothing else about her life or career prior to her arrival in Vienna has been uncovered.

Lorenzani's first engagement with Conti occurred in the October 1724 revival of *Galatea vendicata*. For this performance Conti composed a new aria, substituting it for the opening aria in the 1719 score. The reasons for this substitution may be several, not the least of them being that Lorenzani may have wanted to sing an aria that had been specifically written for her rather than for Maria Landini. That same year Lorenzani appeared in another of Conti's one-act operas, *Meleagro*. Evidently she was making a good impression with her performances, for in 1725 Conti engaged her to sing the leading role in his three-act Carnival opera, *Griselda*. The *Wienerisches Diarium* announced the first presentation of this opera on 6 February 1725 and indicated that it had met with praise from all who attended. On Saturday of that same week *Griselda* was again performed at the court. This was to have been the production attended by Elisabeth Christina and Charles VI, but those plans had to be postponed because the empress was ill. Three days later the empress had fully recovered and she, together with the emperor, was then able to attend the opera's final performance.

The reporting of musical events held at the court and in the principal churches played an important part in every issue of the *Wienerisches Diarium*. This bi-weekly journal, first issued on 8 August 1703, devoted itself to the coverage of both *Ausland* and *Inland* events. The domestic reporting mainly involved activities of the court, including descriptions of hunts, marriages, and festivals. Also featured were notice of baptisms and deaths, and a 'personal mention' section, in which important people entering or leaving Vienna were listed. In 1721, the character of this reporting changed considerably when the publication passed from its original owner, J. B. Schönwetter, to Johann Peter van Ghelen. Whereas earlier issues of the *Diarium* merely announced the events presented at the court, the later issues gave more extensive coverage of the works performed. They published the title of the work, the names of the composer, librettist, ballet master, and scene designer. They even occasionally included a synopsis of a libretto, as was done in the 13 February 1724 issue which carried a full synopsis of Conti's *Penelope*, and often commented about an audience's response to a performance. The *Diarium*, therefore, was and continues to be an invaluable source of information.

An exceptionally useful source for information about Conti's private life is his testament of 1732. Here he makes known that he was married for a third time on 8 April 1725 and that his bride was none other than the new prima donna, Maria Anna Lorenzani. This meant that their combined stipends netted them an income of 6800 florins per year, a sum Conti had grown accustomed to receiving with Maria Landini. Unfortunately, this third marriage did not last very long nor did it bring with it the professional rewards that had been anticipated. The reason was that soon after they were married, Conti suffered some sort of illness which curtailed his career. He was not able to fulfil his duties as a theorbist nor was he able to provide the new prima donna with the wealth of leading roles he had hoped to create. *Griselda* was the only new composition he is known to have composed in 1725 and the only full-length opera by him in which Maria Anna participated. She did, however, sing the leading role in several other major productions, including two operas by Fux: *La corona d'Arianna* (1726) and *Orfeo ed Euridice* (1728), the latter having been previously staged in 1715 with Maria Landini singing the same role. A similar situation occurred with the 1725 revival of Conti's *La colpa originale*, for Maria Anna was cast in the role of Eva, which Maria Landini had sung in 1718.

In 1726 Conti collaborated with the new court poet, Claudio Pasquini, to offer two works in celebration of the name-days of Maria Theresa (5 October) and Elisabeth Christina (19 November). The first one, *Il contrasto della bellezza e del tempo*, a *componimento per musica da camera*, was really a glorified cantata requiring only a soprano role, sung by Maria Anna Lorenzani Conti, and an alto role, sung by the castrato Gaetano Orsini. The second was *Issicratea*, a *festa teatrale,* which was scored for three sopranos, an alto, and a bass. The soprano roles were sung by one castrato and two females, one of whom was the soprano Anna Hülverding ('La Helferding'), making her first appearance in a work by Conti. Lorenzani was not listed as one of the participants.

No new compositions were offered by Conti for the entertainment of the court between 1727 and 1731; illness had indeed brought a halt to his creativity. Several documents found among extant court records speak of Conti's failing health. Of these, one mentions that his illness caused him to return to Italy: 'Fran^{co} Conti – impotens in Italia'.[8] Although no specific place in Italy is indicated, it is more than likely that he returned to his native city of Florence, where he owned a house on the Strada nel corso de' Barbari.[9] No doubt this place would have afforded him a comfortable place in which to recuperate.

Conti's temporary relinquishing of his duties precipitated several changes at the court. Musicians lost no time in applying for both of his positions and the Kapellmeister was equally anxious to receive applications. Ever since 1711 when the Empress-Regent Eleonora's decree caused a reduction in the number of musicians permitted to serve the court, Fux had spent much effort in rebuilding the Hofkapelle staff. By the mid 1720s, he had increased the number of musicians to a level he considered sufficient to handle all of the imperial events and therefore he was not about to have any position go unfilled for any length of time. Conti's illness, of course, created two temporary vacancies, causing Fux some anxious moments in trying to fill them. Finding someone for the position of theorbist apparently was a rather difficult task. Since no one within the immediate vicinity of Vienna seemed qualified for the position, the court decided to bring

Joachim Sarao from Naples. According to a most elaborate account in the *Hofprotokollbuch*, Sarao had been living in Vienna for more than eight months before the court finally granted him the official position in January of 1727.[10] Needless to say, Sarao was highly insulted by this casual reception. Moreover, he and his family were in desperate straits because of the court's neglect of his stipend and his housing expenses. As soon as he assumed his duties in 1727, Sarao demanded that the court compensate him for his past inconveniences. The demands he made prompted Fux to recount for Sarao's benefit what had been the experience of other theorbists who had served the court in the past, making it clear that Sarao had no reason to expect the same stipend which was presently being paid to Conti. The initial amount of Sarao's stipend was 1200 florins per year.[11]

While Fux was fortunate to find a worthy replacement for the position of theorbist, he was not so successful with that for the position of composer. He tried to hire a retired musician from Innsbruck, but his petition on behalf of this candidate, Bernard Aprile, was not forceful enough to convince the Obersthofmeister that a replacement was needed, and that Aprile was the person best qualified for the position. The Obersthofmeister argued that, even though Conti had gone to Italy and Fux himself was only serving the court on a half-time basis because of his own failing health, the court could be adequately supplied with compositions by the current staff, which included Caldara, Badia, and Porsile, among others. And indeed, such proved to be the case.[12]

Ignazio Conti did not accompany his father to Italy. He continued his court duties as Hof-Scholar and, in his father's absence, found opportunities to have several of his works performed. On 15 October 1727 he presented his *Dialogo tra l'aurora e il sole*, a chamber work set to a text by Claudio Pasquini for the name-day of Maria Theresa. While this may not be the first work Ignazio composed for the court, it is the first which can be dated. Presumably it met with favourable comments from the imperial family as well as from his peers, for after this date Ignazio began writing compositions of a more ambitious nature. Two such works were presented in 1728, the opera *Pieria* and the oratorio *La destruzione di Hai*.[13] By his contribution to court festivities, Ignazio was able to keep his family's name in the forefront of court activities, even though his own talents were obviously inferior to those of his father. Ordinarily Francesco would have been pleased by his son's modest efforts to maintain the family's tradition of providing entertainment for the court, but unfortunately Ignazio succeeded all too well in drawing attention to the family name.

One day, in the summer of 1730, Ignazio and a Sicilian cleric, Steffano Bertoni, engaged in an argument which became so intense that a battle of words gave way to a battle of fists, in the course of which Ignazio struck Bertoni. An offence of this kind committed against a member of the clergy was considered very serious and caused Ignazio to be brought before an ecclesiastical tribunal. Besides having to do penance for his actions, Ignazio was also sentenced by the provost to six months in the Spielberg prison. Since it was the custom in that period for the prisoner to pay for his own maintenance, Ignazio was charged 50 florins 48 kronen. Only upon receipt of this money would he gain his release.[14]

Contrary to what Mattheson wrote about penalties incurred with this incident, Ignazio avoided an extended time in jail and was not exiled from Austria.[15] At the end of January 1731, he resumed his duties as Hof-Scholar and it was in that same year that Francesco also resumed some, if not all, of his duties at the court. Obviously Ignazio's imprisonment did not disrupt the privileged relationship with the Habsburgs which the Conti family had enjoyed for so many years.

Francesco's return to Vienna marked a new phase in his career as a composer. Not the least of the changes that greeted him was the fact that the librettists with whom he had collaborated in the past were no longer active there. Before the end of the third decade of the eighteenth century, the careers of Pariati and Zeno, who together had dominated the Viennese stage for more than a decade, were already on the wane. Zeno had become ill and consequently resigned his position so that he could return to Venice in 1729. At about the same time, Pariati also ceased writing for the stage for reasons that are not clear, but he chose to remain a resident of Vienna until his death in 1733. The court was anxious to fill these positions and before long several new poets were chosen for that purpose. One of those poets was Claudio Pasquini, whose appointment had taken place in 1726 before Conti left Vienna.

Another poet who was invited to serve the court was Pietro Metastasio (1698-1782). His appointment had been prompted by several recommendations, not the least of them coming from Zeno.[16] In fact, Zeno made it known that he wanted to choose his successor and the poet he regarded the most highly for the position was Metastasio. The Musik-Oberdirektor, Prince Pio of Savoy, acted favourably upon the recommendation and in his letter to Metastasio of 29 August 1729 offered him the position, it having been 'so far approved by his imperial Majesty'. Metastasio's appointment as *poeta cesareo* earned him a stipend of 3000 florins plus moving expenses. Since he was not taking on the additional position of imperial historiographer, his stipend was 1000 florins less than that given to Zeno.[17]

Metastasio delayed his arrival at the imperial court until July 1730 because he was obligated to supply the managers of a theatre in Rome with two librettos before his departure. Some idea of his first impressions of Vienna is revealed in letters he wrote to 'La Romanina', a friend in Rome. For example, he was struck with the regularity of the court events and a bit dismayed with the bitterly cold winter weather that he had to endure. He mentions some of the commissions he received, such as one for the birthday of Empress Elisabeth Christina, and even describes how his work was received when presented in its musical garb. Fux and Caldara were among the first to set Metastasio's librettti for the court, with *Enea negli Elisi, overo il tempio dell'eternità* and *Il Demetrio* coming to the stage before the end of 1731. Thus, by the time Conti set Metastasio's *Issipile* for Carnival in 1732, the court was somewhat acquainted with this poet's works.

During the time the performances of *Issipile* were taking place at the court, Metastasio secured an extra copy of the score and sent it to his friend 'la Romanina' (Marianna Benti Bulgarelli), the prima donna and director of opera in Rome. Since he included instructions for designing the scenery, he obviously hoped the opera would be staged in Rome, and perhaps it was.[18] In a letter sent with this score, he offers his own assessment of how the opera was prepared for the stage in Vienna. Judging from his complaints about the lack of rehearsal time, it is clear that he was not entirely satisfied with the conditions under which he had to operate. He nevertheless seemed pleased with the end result.

The partnership between poet and composer that Pariati and Conti had developed over the years was not be replicated with Metastasio. Even their single collaborative event showed that Conti was somewhat overpowered by the Metastasian text and decidedly overshadowed by Metastasio's popularity. Nowhere is this more evident than in the letters Metastasio wrote to 'la Romanina' about *Issipile*, for they are devoid of any comment about either the music or the composer. In a letter dated 23 February 1732, he commented that a much larger crowd than expected was on hand for the final performance, at the conclusion of which the emperor 'descended from his box' and came up to him to congratulate him on 'his labours' and to tell him that 'the opera was very fine'.[19] Metastasio viewed this scene of the emperor making his remarks in the presence of everyone assembled as something quite extraordinary, given the fact that 'it is difficult to obtain any notice from our patron, who is so reserved in public'.[20]

On 18 March 1732, the oratorio *L'osservanza della divina legge nel martirio de' Maccabei* was performed in the court chapel. The *Diarium* reported that the occasion included the customary sermon delivered in Italian. This oratorio was the last work that Conti composed for the Habsburg court in 1732, the year of the composer's death. In neither *Issipile* nor *L'osservanza della divina legge* did Maria Anna Lorenzani participate. Suffering from ill health, she resigned her court position at the beginning of April of that same year.[21]

Maria Anna left Vienna after her resignation; nothing else is known about her life. It is possible that she recovered from her illness, perhaps outliving her husband by a decade or more. Although documents in Vienna offer no clues as to where she might have gone, there are at least two sources that suggest she may have gone to Italy. One is the libretto for *Ormisda*, a *dramma per musica* presented in Genoa at the Teatro del Falcone in the spring of 1732.[22] This libretto, published by Giovanni Franchelli of Genova, does not indicate the librettist (presumably Apostolo Zeno) or the composer, but it does list the singers and the roles they performed. Cast in the leading role of Artenice is one with the name of Maria Anna Laurenzani. Could this have been Conti's wife? Certainly she would have been well suited for the part, a role that had also been sung by Faustina Bordoni ten years earlier when Orlandini's setting of *Ormisda* was produced in Bologna. Intermezzos were included with the Genoa libretto and the performers were none other than the famous duo of Rosa Ungarelli and Antonio Ristorini.[23]

The other source is Charles Burney. In his *General History*, he mentions that a 'Contini' who had come from Florence sang one season on the London stage in 1743. One of the operas performed in London that year was Galuppi's *Enrico*. The libretto for this opera was originally written for a theatre in Florence where it was presented in 1732 under the direction of the librettist-manager, Vaneschi. This, of course, was the very year that Maria Anna left Vienna, and it is not unreasonable to suggest she might have gone to Florence, making it possible for her to have participated in the première performance. Eleven years later, in 1743, Vaneschi adapted his *Enrico* for the London stage, using for the minor roles three 'female performers' who were brought from Italy for the production: 'These were Frasi, Galli, and Contini. The two first after transplantation from Italy, took root in this country and remained here in great public favor for many years; the third seems to have remained in England but one season'.[24]

On 19 July 1732, Conti drew up a new testament which was to replace the ones he had written on 30 November 1726, on 10 June 1732, and on 15 June 1732.[25] After a prefatory statement concerning his funeral, the saying of commemorative masses, and his wish to be buried in the parish ('nella Parochia'), he proceeds in this lengthy document to distribute a portion of his estate to each member of his immediate household. To Maria Anna Lorenzani he left a large sum of money and an amulet of precious stones. Curiously, he gives no hint of where Maria Anna might be residing, though from other sections of this document it is apparent that she is not living in either his home in Hieteldorf or his house in Florence.

His sister, Cattarina, appeared to receive the largest portion of the estate, but her inheritance does not seem to have been sufficient to sustain her in the months following her brother's death.[26] In fact, upon two occasions Fux petitioned the court to secure additional income for her. Fux set forth the argument that even though Cattarina was not legally entitled to a pension such as a widow might normally receive from the government, she nevertheless should be entitled to an equivalent compensation. Fux contended that the resignation of Maria Anna and the death of Francesco saved the court almost 7000 florins per year. It would therefore cause no inconvenience to the imperial treasury to grant Cattarina an annual pension of 200 florins.

The first of these petitions was acknowledged by the Obersthofmeister on 17 January 1733.[27] The second, filed on 21 April 1733, finally achieved a favourable response from the emperor.[28] The writing of these petitions was not an isolated occurrence for Fux. He was always concerned about the well-being of the court musicians and their families.[29] No injustice was too small for his attention, as shown by the kind and number of petitions he wrote, many of which initiated positive outcomes.

Some hint of the leisure enjoyed by Francesco and the members of his family can be seen from the fifth and seventh items of the testament, which refer to servants of the household. The high praise as well as the tangible wealth which Conti gave to one servant in particular, Francesca Autelli, attest to her singular loyalty to his family. He mentions her long years of service in his house but offers no other information that would provide a clue about her past. It is conceivable that Francesca Autelli may have been brought into the service of Francesco's household when he married Maria Landini, for his second wife also took particular care in her testament to provide for the well-being of this person. For his other servants, Conti requests that they each receive one month's salary from the date of his actual death.

The last member to be mentioned is Conti's son, Ignazio. To him he gave all of the remaining personal belongings and real estate, with the stipulation that such could not be mortgaged, sold, or disposed of without due regard for his sister Cattarina. Conti also made available to Ignazio a sizeable sum of money which included a separate inheritance from Maria Landini that she had originally willed to Francesco in her testament.[30]

On 20 July 1732, the *Wienerisches Diarium* printed the following:

> Lista deren Verstorbenen zu Wien
> in und vor der Stadt
> Den 20 Julii
> Herr Conti, Kaiserl. Hof-Music-Compositor, in dem
> Kirchnersch. H. auf der hohen Brucken / alt 51 J.[31]

This simple announcement of Conti's death parallels his almost unobtrusive entry into the service of the imperial court as a theorbist in 1701. He entered the Habsburg world merely as a performer; he left the court serving only as a composer.

Notes

1   Vienna, Finanz- und Hofkammerarchiv, *Österreichische Hoffinanz* rote Nr. 860 (9 April 1723).

2   See Friedrich Wilhelm Marpurg, *Historisch-kritische Beiträge zur Aufnahme der Musik* (Berlin, 1755), I, 219.

3   Ludwig Ritter von Köchel, *Johann Josef Fux* (Hildesheim, 1974), 226.

4   The 'Lettera del Signor Francesco Conti all' Eccelentissimo Signor Benedetto Marcello' appears on p. 4 of vol. 2 in the 1724 printed edition of Marcello's Psalms, which has since been reissued as a facsimile edition. See Benedetto Marcello, *Estro poetico-armonico* (London, 1967).

5   For a more complete listing of the members of this Bruderschaft, see Köchel, *Johann Josef Fux*, 169-72.

6   Maria Anna's surname is spelt Lorenzani in Francesco Conti's testament (1732) and in most of the court documents. This spelling is also found in the cast lists for *Griselda* (1725) and *La colpa originale* (1725). Other spellings include Laurenzana in the cast list for *Galatea* (1724) and *Meleagro* (1724) and Lorenzoni in Köchel's list of singers who were appointed to the Hofkapelle. The Lorenzani spelling has been adopted for this text.

7   Francesco Saverio Quadrio, *Della storia e della ragione d'ogni poesia* (Bologna, 1739-52), V, libro iii, 538.

8   Vienna, Finanz- und Hofkammerarchiv, *Nieder-österreichische Herrschaftsakten* W/Wien, 61/A.32, nos 817-29, February 1729.

9   This information is in his 'Testament / Francesco Barolotmeo Conti', Nr. 6881/1732.

10   *Hofprotokollbuch: 1725-1727*, fol. 493v. In her compilation of instrumentalists associated with the Hofkapelle between 1680 and 1770 appended to 'The Viennese Court Orchestra', in Brian W. Pritchard, ed., *Antonio Caldara* (London, 1987), 149, Eleanor Selfridge-Field incorrectly lists the dates when Joachim Sarao served the court as a theorbist.

11   Ibid., fol. 497.

12   Ibid., see the entry for 15 November 1727.

13   Simon von Molitor, 'Materialien zur Musikgeschichte', Musiksammlung Nr. 19239, vol. A-D, fasc. xviii, fol. 11v.

14   Vienna. Finanz- und Hofkammerarchiv. *Österreichische Hoffinanz* rote Nr. 930 (22 December 1730; 22 January 1731).

15   For Mattheson's version of this incident, see chapter six.

16   One author has suggested that, in addition to Zeno et al., Countess d'Althan may have been influential in securing Metastasio for the position. See Joseph Kennard, *The Italian Theatre from the Close of the Seventeenth Century* (New York, 1932), 14.

17   Several authors claim Metastasio's stipend of 3000 florins was 1000 florins more than that earned by Pariati. This claim is based upon inaccurate information; Pariati's stipend was 2400 florins.

18   Charles Burney, *Memoirs of the Life and Writings of the Abate Metastasio, Including Translations of His Principal Letters* (London, 1796; New York, 1971), 79-81.

19   Ibid.

20   Pietro Metastasio, *Tutte le opere di Pietro Metastasio* (Florence, 1832), XIV, 30-31.

21   A report to that effect is in the *Hofprotokollbuch: 1731-1732*, fol. 339, and it contains the official order to terminate her stipend as of the last day of March, 1732.

22   Claudio Sartori, *I libretti italiani a stampa dalle origini al 1800* (Cuneo, 1990), 330.

23   Charles Troy does not include this set of intermezzos in his list of performances by Ungarelli and Ristorini between 1716 and 1732. See *The Comic Intermezzo* (Ann Arbor, MI, 1979), 51.

24   Charles Burney, *A General History of Music,* Frank Mercer, ed., (New York, 1957), II, 841.

25   Vienna, Stadtarchiv, 'Testament / Francesco Bartolomeo Conti', Nr. 6881/1732. For the full text of the testament, see this author's 'The Life and Operas of Francesco Bartolomeo Conti', (diss., Columbia University, 1964), 260-64.

26   Cattarina inherited jewellery, furniture, religious artifacts, and the use of the houses in Hieteldorf and Florence until her death, at which time the property would pass to Ignazio.

27   This petition was filed one month after Conti's death on 26 August 1732, but it was not recorded in the *Hofprotokollbuch: 1733-1734* until 17 January 1733. See Köchel, *Johann Josef Fux*, 437, where the first petition is quoted in full.

28   *Hofprotokollbuch: 1733-1734*, fol. 99.

29   For other examples of petitions that show Fux's concern for the court musicians, see Vienna, Finanz- und Hofkammerarchiv, *Nieder-österreichische Herrschaftsakten*, W/Wien, 61/A.32, Nr. 164.

30   Vienna, Stadtarchiv, 'Testament / Maria Landini Conti', Nr. 21693/1722.

31   His death is also recorded in the *Totenprotokoll: 1732*, fol. 275.

CHAPTER SIX

The Conti legacy

On 23 February 1736, four years after Francesco Conti's death, the première of his oratorio *Gioseffo, che interpretata i sogni* took place in the court chapel. Although this work has some notable differences from his previous oratorio compositions, there is nothing to suggest that this work is not by Francesco. The score has one of the characteristic trademarks of this composer's oratorios – an aria with an obbligato part for the theorbo. What is uncharacteristic is that the theorbo is not given a virtuoso part nor even a true solo part. Did Francesco intentionally compose something less demanding for this instrument in consideration that someone other than he would be the performer?

During most of Conti's tenure at the court, the Lenten seasons were marked by performances of one or two, possibly three, different oratorios. In the 1730s, that number increased significantly. For instance, in 1735 the *Wienerisches Diarium* reported six different oratorios were heard during the Lenten season of that year. Some were newly composed, such as Caldara's *Gesù presentato nel tempio*; others were revivals, such as his son Ignazio's *La Debbora*. In 1736, the *Diarium* reported the performance of oratorios on 23 February and 1, 8, and 27 March, each by a different composer. Francesco's oratorio (cited above) was the first oratorio and Ignazio's *Il giusto afflitto nella persona di Giob* was the third.

Ignazio was quite active as a composer between 1733 and 1739. Five oratorios, four secular dramatic works related to the *serenata* or the *festa teatrale* genre, and one *a cappella* mass can be dated within this six-year period. Among his undated works, some of which may have originated in this same decade, are several cantatas, a sacred choral work, and a half dozen or more *a cappella* masses. For most of his secular works, Ignazio relied heavily on the librettos of Pariati's successor, Claudio Pasquini. His singular use of a work by Pariati came in 1739 when he composed *La colpa originale*, an oratorio based on the same text his father had set in 1718 and again in 1725. This would appear to be the last major work Ignazio had performed at the court and the reason for that may be linked to two events that happened in 1739.

On 16 December of that year, a petition was filed by Fux on behalf of Ignazio. It sought to have him named 'Compositore di Camera', noting that a number of his oratorios and 'Servizy di camera' had already been produced at the court. Fux was very candid in this petition, readily admitting that in the twenty years Ignazio had served as a Hof-Scholar he showed little inclination or talent as a therobist.[1] At the same time, Fux was rather emphatic in contending that his particular aspect of Ignazio's career should not prejudice an evaluation of his ability as a composer. Unfortunately, Fux's enthusiastic recommendation failed to secure the desired title and Ignazio was thus relegated to the position of Hof-Scholar until his death.

That same year Mattheson's *Der vollkommene Capellmeister* was published. Although the text contains some laudatory comments about Ignazio's father, it also seeks to destroy the family's reputation by retelling the episode that had landed Ignazio in jail. Mattheson quotes at length a letter from Regensburg dated 15 October 1730. The opening line of the letter contains the scandalous news that on September 10 in Vienna, the imperial 'Compositore di Musica', Francesco [!] Conti, was expelled from St Stephen's Cathedral'. Mattheson obviously believed his source and never doubted for one moment who had committed the crime. As a consequence, he succeeded in casting a dark cloud over Francesco's reputation and one that was not easily erased. To add insult to injury, Mattheson also included an epigram, in Latin, that is anything but complimentary to the composer, and it is inserted between the detailed description of the encounter with the cleric and a paragraph that praises Francesco's 'portrayal of gesture through musical notes'.[2] The account of the incident and the penalties levied against the perpetrator of the crime contained in the Regensburg letter are so far from the reality of what has been recorded in the court records, that one is left to wonder how such a deliberately damaging account could have been written. The letter indicates that after Conti was transferred from the ecclesiastical to the secular authorities, he would have to pay 1000 guilders to compensate the cleric whom he had beaten. It further states that Conti would have to remain in jail for four years and when released would be banned from Austria.

Why Mattheson felt compelled to destroy the reputation of one whose music he admired will forever remain a mystery. Several contemporary writers, aware that the subject of Mattheson's account should have been Ignazio and not Francesco, attempted to set the record straight, but their efforts initially met with limited success.

There is no way to know how Ignazio's life was affected by the Mattheson publication, although it does seem more than coincidental that he no longer composed music for the court after this date. From that time forward, his income was limited to his annual stipend as Hof-Scholar, a sum which did not adequately support his carefree pattern of living. By the time Ignazio died, he was left with nothing but a few personal items; he had spent all of the 14,000 florins he had inherited.

With Ignazio's career as a composer limited to a few works presented within a period of approximately ten years, it is understandable that he would not be the one to carry forth his father's reputation for creating effective dramatic works for theatrical entertainment, for writing majestic works for the church, or for introducing innovative elements into his compositional palette. For that aspect of the Conti legacy, one must look elsewhere.

The focus of this study of Francesco's life and music has been intentionally confined, in so far as is possible, to his association with the imperial court. Nevertheless, it is tempting to speculate, on the basis of the incomplete evidence at hand, about the possible influence which he may have had upon his contemporaries. Both during his lifetime and after his death – but especially during the 1720s when Conti was at the apex of his career – many of his works had revivals outside Vienna. It is important to note, however, that aside from his contribution to two pasticcio oratorios for Florence in the first decade of the eighteenth century, Perugia was probably the only other city in Italy where one of his works was performed. In fact, the majority of the non-Viennese performances of his music occurred in places located to the west and north of the imperial city: Breslau, Braunschweig-Wolfenbüttel, Brussels, Dresden, Hamburg, Jaroměřice, London, and Prague.

As early as 1718, Conti's operas began to make an appearance on the Hamburg stage. It did not take the Hamburg audiences long to appreciate Conti's *tragicommedia* type of opera. Not only did this type become extremely popular, but other types such as the *favola pastorale* (*Il trionfo dell'amicizia e dell'amore*; *Cloris und Thyrsis*) and an *opera seria* that lacked intermezzos (*Issipile*) also found favour. One of the composers for the Gänsemarkt-Oper who thought highly of Conti's dramatic works was Reinhard Keiser. In fact, it was Keiser's adaptation of *Il trionfo dell'amicizia e dell'amore* that first brought Conti's music to the Hamburg opera house. Johann Joachim Hoe prepared the Italian-German version of Ballerini's libretto and entitled it *Il trionfo dell'amore e della costanza / Die Triumph der Liebe und Beständigkeit*.[3] He retained approximately half of the

Italian arias, but altered the original scene divisions, eliminated the subtle humour of some of the recitatives (especially in Act III), and increased the use of the chorus (Act I, Scene i-iii). In the prefatory remarks to the libretto, Conti is said to be the composer, although it is doubtful if he can be credited for anything but the arias sung in Italian. Presumably the music for the remaining arias and the recitatives was composed by Keiser, although there is nothing in the extant manuscript to confirm this.

According to the libretto, the performance of this *favola pastorale* took place in January 1718 and marked Keiser's final opera production in Hamburg that season.[4] Shortly thereafter he was forced to leave the city because his extravagant expenditures had brought the Gänsemarkt-Oper, of which he was the impresario, to a state of bankruptcy. The opera house was closed for almost all of 1718, but when it reopened in November of that year, it began to feature a repertoire consisting entirely of imported works, many having had recent performances at the court in Braunschweig. This policy of staging works by non-resident composers continued for several years while Keiser was away, during which time several other operas by Conti became known to the Hamburg audience.

In January of 1719, a second pastorale involving music by Conti was staged. This time it was the pasticcio opera *Cloris und Thyrsis*, set to a libretto by D. Gazal, a Hamburg jurist. Following a successful debut, the opera enjoyed six additional performances.[5] The recitatives are in German and the arias, in Italian. Although *Cloris und Thyrsis* has the same plot as Pariati's *I Satiri in Arcadia*, it is textually and musically unrelated to Conti's opera of the same title staged in Vienna in 1714. On the initial page of the overture in one of the extant manuscripts of *Cloris und Thyrsis* (D/*MGs*: Mus 4074) is written the title of the opera, place and date of performance, and Conti's name as the composer Other sources also credit Conti with the opera, but if he did have a part in creating this work, his contribution may have been limited to the music for the Italian arias.

The pasticcio *Tigranes* which represents the collaborative efforts of Conti, Francesco Gasparini, Giuseppe Maria Orlandini, and Antonio Vivaldi, was brought to the Hamburg stage in 1719.[6] Gazal's libretto, fashioned from Antonio Marchi's *La costanza trionfante degl'amori e degl'odi* (Venice, 1716), is entitled *Die über Hass und Liebe siegende Beständigkeit oder Tigranes*. Unfortunately, the score has not survived, making it impossible to determine what each composer contributed. Performed with *Tigranes* was a set of intermezzos with Tuberone and Dorimena as the *dramatis personae*. It is more than likely that Conti had some responsibility for the intermezzos. He may have revived the 'Tuberone e

Dorimena' set which he composed in 1714 or he may have written new music for the same libretto.[7] Gustav Schmidt, in his discussion of the history of the intermezzos on the Hamburg stage, states that the performance of this opera marks the second time that intermezzos were produced at the opera house, the first having taken place in 1708.[8] There can be no doubt that *Tigranes* and its set of intermezzos delighted the Hamburg audiences, for there were no fewer than twenty-three productions between 15 May 1719 and 2 January 1722.[9]

Equally popular was the Italian-German version of Conti's *Don Chisciotte in Sierra Morena*. From 1722 until 1737 some twenty-seven performances were given, though not all used identical material.[10] In the year prior to its musical setting for Hamburg, the Zeno-Pariati libretto had been translated and adapted by Johann Samuel Müller for the opera house in Braunschweig. Since some of Hamburg's opera singers occasionally sought guest appearances in Braunschweig to augment their meagre salaries, it is conceivable that they had participated in one or more of the performances of this version of the opera, which was now entitled *Don Quixotte in dem Mohren-Gebürge* and may have initiated the idea of bringing it to the Gänsemarkt-Oper. When Mattheson prepared the score for the initial 1722 Hamburg production, he kept the Italian text for the principal arias but adapted Müller's German translation to the recitatives and folk arias. He considered the opera uncommonly beautiful and of clever invention, declaring it to be a model example of a satire.[11] After this and similar expressions of admiration, Mattheson's attempt to damage Conti's reputation through the use of maliciously false information appears strange, though perhaps not if one considers Mattheson's pronounced vanity and quarrelsome nature.

In the latter part of 1720 or the beginning of 1721, Georg Philipp Telemann arrived in Hamburg anxious to fill the void caused by Keiser's departure. His first opera was staged there on 28 January 1721 and from that point forward he began to take an active role as composer for the Gänsemarkt-Oper, securing for himself the position of director in 1722. His duties at the opera house were in addition to his regular duties as a teacher and supervisor of music in Hamburg's principal churches. During this same period he became interested in Conti's music, especially as it related to comic episodes. According to Mattheson, Telemann used music originally composed by Conti for his 'Il Capitano' to create his third part of the pasticcio *Der Beschluss des Carnevals*. Mattheson mentions that the première of this pasticcio took place on 11 February 1724 and supposedly the work was repeated three more times that month. Two years later, 'Il Capitano' was performed as a separate work.[12] Since 'Il Capitano' was reported to be entirely comic, it suggests that Telemann, who later became famous for his ability to set comic texts to music, was not only acquainted with Conti's comic style, but may also have been strongly influenced by it. Those who consider him to be 'a pioneer in the use of a bass voice in comic roles' use his version of *Pimpinone* (1725) to support their opinion; yet this very work shows that he was not only acquainted with Conti's score of this same text, but that he also patterned one of Pimpinone's (bass) arias on the corresponding aria in Conti's score, even going so far as to use the very same motive that dominates Conti's aria.[13] Telemann's esteem for Conti's operatic style, however, was not confined to the comic passages alone. Evidence of this can be found in his five-act *Aesopus beÿ Hofe* (1729), which is nothing more than a revision of Conti's 1723 score of *Creso*.[14]

When Keiser returned to Hamburg after extended sojourns in Ludwigsberg and Copenhagen, his new offerings for the opera house reveal a change in style – a change that relects the growing popularity of Italian opera in Germany. Although scholars are by no means agreed about the influences upon Keiser that might have fostered this new stylistic development, there are indications that Conti may have had some influence upon *Der lächerliche Printz Jodelet* and *Croesus*. Certainly the text and music of *Printz Jodelet* suggest that Keiser was familiar with the score of Conti's *Don Chisciotte in Sierra Morena*.

In *Printz Jodelet*, Keiser abandoned his usual manner of composing in order to imitate the new Italian style found in Conti's operas. Although he was not wholly successful, primarily because his uncontrolled repetition of certain elements in Act III turn into overworked clichés, his score nevertheless shows that he was becoming conversant with the *buffo* and *galant* styles.[15] The same cannot be said of Keiser's revision of his 1710 score of *Croesus* for a new production in 1730. If he was using 'Italian composers like Conti and Orlandini as his models', as has been suggested by Hellmut Wolff, there is little in the overall style of the 1730 score to corroborate this influence.[16]

By the end of the 1720s, a reformist influence was starting to pervade the Hamburg productions just as it was in Vienna, due in large measure to the advent of Metastasian drama. Mattheson wasted no time in championing the new style of opera libretto, characterized by a greater attention to the musical delineation of affections and by an economy of means applied to language. A prime example of this type of opera is Conti's *Issipile* which had performances in Hamburg in 1737 and 1738. Metastasio's libretto was translated into German by Christoph Gottlieb Wendt and given the title *Sieg der Kindlichen Lieber oder Issipile, Printzessin von*

Lemnos in einem Singspiele. Conti's score was adapted by Mattheson for the Gänsemarkt-Oper performances.

Conti's reputation as a composer of comedy was well respected at the Braunschweig-Wolfenbüttel court, as evidenced by the particular dramatic works chosen for revivals there in a twenty-year period extending from 1720 to 1740. They include two different types: the *tragicommedia* (*Don Chisciotte in Sierra Morena*; *Archelao*; *Alessandro in Sidone*) and the *opera seria* with interpolated intermezzos (*Sesostri, rè di Egitto*; *Astarto*). The *tragicommedia* appears to have been favoured, inasmuch as Conti's operas in this category were performed more than once. In fact, *Don Chisciotte* was so popular that it was staged four times between 1720 and 1738, with the earlier productions sung in Italian and the later ones in German.

Although somewhat less popular, the revivals of *Sesostri* and *Astarto* are perhaps more significant when viewed from a historical perspective. The intermezzo, so familiar to the imperial stage during Conti's entire career, was virtually unknown in Braunschweig (Brunswick). According to Gustav Schmidt, only five different sets of intermezzos were heard there between 1716 and 1730.[17] Of these, at least two were composed by Conti: 'Pimpinone e Grilletta' with *Sesostri*; and 'Farfalletta, Lirone, and Terrimoto' with *Astarto*. Interestingly, one of the singers for the *Astarto* production was Georg Caspar Schürmann (1672-1751), who was a composer of more than forty operas for the court in Braunschweig and whose own treatment of comedy was strongly influenced by these two sets of intermezzos.[18]

Conti may have contributed a third set of intermezzos for Braunschweig. When *Teodosio ed Eudossa* (with music by Fux, Gasparini, and Caldara) was performed there in 1716 and again in 1721, the production included two intermezzos (sung in German) with Tuberone and Dorimena as the *dramatis personae*. Any one of the three composers of *Teodosio* could have provided the music for the intermezzos, but Conti is probably the composer who can take credit for this aspect of the production. After all, he composed the music for the 'Tuberone e Dorimene' set of intermezzos (sung in Italian) for *L'Atenaide* (1714), an opera by Ziani, Negri, and Caldara which has the same plot as *Teodosio ed Eudossa* and a character, Eudossa, whose real name is Atenaide. The attribution of the 'Tuberone e Dorimena' intermezzos to Conti takes on added significance when considered in connection with yet another performance in Hamburg in 1719, as discussed above.

The 1732 première production of *Issipile* in Vienna generated considerable interest among other impresarios. The court theatre in Braunschweig staged a revival the following year in February and another in August 1736. *Issipile* also had a revival in Jaroměřice (Moravia) in October 1733 in a theatre built in 1722 by Johann Adam (Graf) Questenberg (1678-1752). In order to stage operas in a fashion similar to those put on by the Habsburgs, Questenberg utilized some of the finest talent in Vienna to augment his artists-in-residence, among them Giuseppe Galli-Bibiena who made several visits there in the 1730s. At the helm of Questenberg's musical activities was the composer František Václav Míča (1694-1744), whose career was certainly influenced by musicians associated with the Hofkapelle. Caldara, Conti, and his son Ignazio were among those whose secular and sacred works were performed not only in Jaroměřice but also in the other Moravian cities such as Brno. Unfortunately, information about specific compositions which enjoyed revivals in Jaroměřice is scarce and therefore it is not possible to reconstruct the repertoire that was of interest to both Questenberg and Míča.[19]

Three of Conti's operas appeared in Breslau within the same year, 1726: *Alba Cornelia* (during Carnival), *Il trionfo dell'amicizia e dell'amore*, and *Il finto Policare*. The libretto for the Breslau production of *Alba Cornelia* differed considerably from that staged in 1714, with scenes rearranged, new material added to Act III, and one of the comic characters eliminated. Perhaps the Breslau productions were staged by the same Italian troupe of Peruzzi and Brillandi that two years later, in 1728, presented Conti's *Alba Cornelia* and *Archelao* in Brussels.

Ever since Francesco's first contact with Dresden, which came with the performance of his intermezzo staged with the 1717 production of *Giove in Argo*, his reputation as a composer of the first rank became established there. In contrast to most of the other cities outside Vienna where interest was directed more toward Conti's secular dramatic works, here the emphasis was clearly upon his sacred music. Primary responsibility for this interest goes to Jan Dismas Zelenka, who spent considerable time in Vienna studying and listening to new works performed in the Hofkapelle and the churches of Vienna. He brought back to Dresden a number of sacred works by Caldara and Conti, among others, which he and Johann David Heinichen revised to suit the performance requirements of their court's chapel.[20]

Last, but certainly not least, Conti can lay claim to having influenced the two giants of Baroque composition – Bach and Handel. In 1716, when Bach was in

Weimar, he made a copy of Conti's *Offertorium de venerabilis* ('Languet anima mea'). How he came in contact with this music is not known, but the score obviously held a fascination for him for a number of years.[21] Sometime between 1717 and 1723, when he was living in Köthen, Bach and several of his copyists prepared orchestral parts of 'Languet anima mea' according to the slightly revised instrumentation desired by Bach. The part for the organist is notated a whole tone lower, suggesting that a performance of Conti's score may have taken place in Leipzig where the pitch of the organ necessitated this type of transposition to accommodate the other instruments.[22]

When Handel assembled the various components of *Ormisda* for a production at the King's Theatre in London on 4 April 1730, he took Conti's overture to *Clotilda* and used it to introduce his pasticcio.[23] From April until the end of June of that same year, *Ormisda* had thirteen additional performances, albeit with some notable changes. For the 21 April 1730 production, Handel substituted arias for twelve that were in his original score, and presumably it was this altered version that continued to be used for the remaining performances in the 1729-30 theatrical season as well as those in the following season, when another five performances were staged in November and December of 1730. Conti was in Italy during the time *Ormisda* was being produced in London. He was recuperating from his illness and may not have known that Handel had revived his music for this pasticcio.

One can only conjecture how Handel came to know Conti's music. It is entirely possible that he could have heard performances of Conti's music or even heard Conti himself perform as a theorbist on his visits to Dresden (1719) and Prague (1723). When he engaged Francesco Borosini for the 1725-26 opera season in London, he was put into direct contact with one of Conti's most prized singers who may have imparted first-hand knowledge about the composer's music. Handel may also have owned one of the various Walsh publications of *Clotilda* that contained the overture and final chorus and decided that the popularity of the music, gauged by the number of reprints it had, might translate into a theatrical success for himself.[24] Whatever the route of transmission, Handel can at least be credited with extending the theatrical usefulness of one of Conti's instrumental compositions.

There are several extant sources for *Ormisda*: a manuscript of the orchestral score in London (Add. Ms. 31551), a manuscript of the 'cembalo' score in Hamburg (M A/1036) which represents Handel's conducting score, and a Walsh edition of eleven favourite songs from *Ormisda*, published the same year as the performances described above.[25] At the top of the first page of the overture in both the London and Hamburg manuscripts is written 'del Sr. Conti', and from this ascription several of the original owners of these manuscripts believed, mistakenly, that Francesco Conti was the composer for the entire three-act opera, for no other names of composers are to be found in the extant materials. There were, of course, some other contemporary views expressed about who might have supplied the music for *Ormisda*. After attending a dress rehearsal of *Ormisda* at the King's Theatre on 2 April 1730, a member of the audience wrote a letter to a relative in which she explained that although there were several songs from the Italians, the major part of the opera was composed by Handel.[26] An announcement carried in the *Daily Courant* on 4 April 1730 held a different view and suggested that the music was 'probably by Bartholomeo Cordans and others'.[27]

The London manuscript of *Ormisda* represents a point in the performance schedule when the score underwent considerable revision. Judging from those revisions, wherein sections of the recitatives are crossed out and a majority (ten) of the substitute arias have been inserted on separate folios, the manuscript was probably put into this form shortly before 21 April 1730. Reinhard Strohm was able to identify the source of most of the arias and duets in *Ormisda*. There were some about which he either had no information or lacked sufficient proof for attribution. One was the overture. Another was the final number 'Tutte il ride'. Although the composer of this number is not known, the source can be identified as the concluding *coro* (SATB) of *Clotilda*. In the *Ormisda* manuscript, this number is scored simply as a single vocal line accompanied by continuo, whereas most of the other arias in *Ormisda* are scored for string ensemble. It should be recalled that this same *coro* was used to conclude *Dorinda*, another opera staged in London in 25 April 1713.

After 1732, Vienna continued to hear revivals of Conti's music, but almost all of the reported events involved works that were sacred. Exceptions were very few in number. For instance, according to the *Wienerisches Diarium*, *Penelope* was revived on 21 January 1739 and in that same year the Kärntnertor-Theater staged *Amor medico* which was based on excerpts from *Don Chisciotte in Sierra Morena* and in 1748 *L'ammalato immaginario* was produced at the Burgtheater. Almost a century later at least three of Conti's works were performed as part of the series of private house concerts organized by Raphael Kiesewetter, beginning in 1816 and extending until 1838.[28] The first of Conti's works performed there sometime between 1820 and 1822 was the cantata 'Clori nemica ed Irene' for two sopranos, *violini et hautbois unisoni*, viola, and continuo. In April 1826 and again in March

1827, the concert programs involved excerpts from his *Don Chisciotte in Sierra Morena* and in December 1834, the oratorio *David* was performed.

The mere tallying up of revivals, however, cannot measure the influence a composer's music may have had on future generations, nor can an investigation into the borrowing of one composer's music by others to create new works. For that, one has to engage in a comparative study involving compositions created by composers later in the century, a project reserved for another time and place.

Notes

1   Ludwig Ritter von Köchel, *Johann Josef Fux* (Hildesheim, 1974), 453. When, in 1722, Filippo Sauli petitioned the court to be reappointed as a theorbist, he also mentioned that Ignazio was not yet a very skilled player. See chapter two. See also Köchel, *Johann Josef Fux*, 394.

2   Johann Mattheson, *Der vollkommene Capellmeister* (Hamburg, 1739), §48, p. 41.

3   Mattheson contends Breymann translated and adapted Ballerini's libretto. See his *Der musikalische Patriot* (Hamburg, 1728), 189. Johann Joachim Hoe was active in Hamburg from 1711 to 1717.

4   Walter Schulze, in *Die Quellen der Hamburger Oper* (Hamburg, 1938), IV, 31, affirms that the date on the libretto is the correct one. Hans Joachim Marx and Dorothea Schröder, in *Die Hamburger Gänsemarkt-Oper* (Laaber, 1995), 371 and 476, give two dates for the first performance: 28 January 1718 (according to the *Hamburgischer Relations-Courier*) and 3 February 1718. Mattheson, in *Der musikalische Patriot* (Hamburg, 1728), 189, lists the performance in the year 1717.

5   The dates of performance given by Marx and Schröder, in *Die Hamburger Gänsemarkt-Oper*, 114, are: 23, 25, 26, 30 January 1719; 26 April, 3 May, and 26 June 1719. None of the January performances are listed in Paul Merbach, 'Das Repertoire der Hamburger Oper von 1718 bis 1750', *Archiv für Musikwissenschaft* VI (1924): 354-72.

6   See Mattheson, *Der musikalische Patriot*, 190. For the dates when *Tigranes* was performed, see Marx and Schröder, *Die Hamburger Gänsemarkt-Oper*, 378. Peter Ryom discovered that the arias contributed by Vivaldi come from his own setting of Marchi's libretto, *La costanza trionfante degl'amore*. See his *Verzeichnis der Werke Antonio Vivaldi* (Leipzig, 1974), 156.

7   A 'Tuberone e Dorimena' set of intermezzos was staged with the *Teodosio ed Eudossa* in Braunschweig in 1716 and 1721, and again the possibility exists that the intermezzo music was by Conti. For more on these performances, see below.

8   Gustav Friedrich Schmidt, in 'Zur Geschichte, Dramaturgie und Statistik der frühdeutschen Oper (1627-1750)', *Zeitschrift für Musikwissenschaft* VI (1923-24): 527.

9   Merbach, 'Das Repertoire der Hamburger Oper von 1718 bis 1750', 355-6.

10   In 1724 an episode occurred in Hamburg that mirrored the kind of tension that continually plagued the management of the opera house. On 21 September 1724, there appeared in the Hamburg journal *Der Patriot* an anonymous satire over the so-called 'opera war' being

waged between the impresarios of the Gänsemarkt-Oper. Three people associated with the theatre, including Telemann, were suspected of submitting the piece for publication. The satire was actually by Johann Philipp Praetorius and was intended to be inserted as an intermezzo, 'Il pregio del l'ignoranza oder die Bass-Geige', in Act III, Scene viii of Conti's *Don Chisciotte*, the scene that usually included marionettes, but the performance of that interpolated satire was forbidden by the Hamburg council.

11 Johann Mattheson, *Critica Musica* (Hamburg, 1722-25), I, 119.

12 Schmidt, in 'Zur Geschichte, Dramaturgie und Statistik der frühdeutschen Oper (1627-1750)', 523, considers *Der Beschluss des Carnevals* to be a set of intermezzos, and therefore viewed the 1724 production to be of historical importance, for it would have constituted the first set of intermezzos ever staged independently of an *opera seria* in Hamburg. Hans Marx and Dorothea Schröder treat *Der Beschluss* as a three-act opera and cast doubt on a 1726 performance of 'Il Capitano' apart from an attendant opera. See *Die Hamburger Gänsemarkt-Oper*, 82. The libretto of 'Il Capitano' (1726) is cited in Oscar G. T. Sonneck, ed., *Catalogue of Opera Librettos Printed before 1800* (Washington, DC, 1914), I, 255, Schatz no. 10270, which refers to this item as a one-act opera.

13 See chapter ten for a comparision of the Albinoni, Conti, and Telemann versions of *Pimpinone*.

14 For other influences stemming from *Creso*, see chapter nine.

15 Schulze, *Die Quellen der Hamburger Oper (1678-1738)*, IV, 52n44.

16 Hellmut Christian Wolff, 'The Neapolitan Tradition in Opera', *Report of the Eighth Congress of the International Musicological Society: New York 1961* (Kassel, 1962), II, 132.

17 Schmidt, 'Zur Geschichte, Dramaturgie und Statistik der frühdeutschen Oper (1627-1750)', 524.

18 Gustav Friedrich Schmidt, *Georg Caspar Schürmann* (Regensburg, 1933), I, 59.

19 Jiří Sehnal, 'Das mährische Musikleben in der Zeit Antonio Caldaras', in Brian W. Pritchard, *Antonio Caldara* (London, 1987), 254-5. Johann Adam Questenberg's early musical education took him to various parts of Europe, including Italy (1699), before he arrived in Vienna where he participated in opera productions as a theorbist. What kind of relationship he and Francesco Conti had, given their mutual dedication to the theorbo, is not known, but his desire to have performances of works by Francesco and Ignazio Conti in Moravia no doubt comes from his personal contact with both men.

20 See chapter twelve for a discussion of the influence Conti's music had upon Dresden's court chapel repertoire.

21 Johann Adam (Graf) Questenberg had contact with Bach upon a number of occasions and perhaps he was the conduit through which music by the court composers was made accessible to him. See Alois Pichta, 'Johann Sebastian Bach und Johann Adam Graf von Questenberg', *Bach-Jahrbuch* (1981): 23-8.

22 For more about the Bach versions of Conti's 'Languet anima mea', see chapter 12.

23 Charles Burney gives the date of the première as 31 March 1730 and then indicates (without citing specific dates) that there were thirteen more performances between 4 April and 14 May 1730. He also lists additional performances on 9 June; 24, 28 November; and 1, 5, 8 December 1730. See his *General History of Music*, Frank Mercer, ed. (New York, 1957), II, 766. In this edition, Mercer has added a note on page 767 that reads: 'the music to

Ormisda was by Francesco Conti. There is a copy in the British Museum [Library] Add. Ms. 31551'.

24   For more about these publications by Walsh and others, see chapter one. There is a minor error in the treble part of the Berlin 'cembalo' score (M A/1036) of Conti's overture which suggests that this score could not have been copied from the score that presently exists in the British Library.

25   In both London and Hamburg manuscript sources, the overture is scored only for violin and continuo.

26   Otto Erich Deutsch, *Handel: A Documentary Biography* (New York, 1979), 254.

27   *The London Stage*, Part 3, vol. I: 1729-1735, Arthur H. Scouten, ed. (Carbondale, IL, 1961), 47ff.

28   Herfrid Kier, *Raphael Georg Kiesewetter (1773-1850), Wegbereiter des musikalischen Historismus* (Regensburg, 1968), 62-3, 179.

Part II

CHAPTER SEVEN

The instrumental music

A chronological investigation of Conti's operas and oratorios reveals how difficult it is to generalize about his style of composition, for he tends to be a coordinator of styles. Through an assimilation of French, German, and Italian ideas and techniques, he creates his own musico-dramatic style, one that is as diverse as it is effective. This diversity is found most especially in the instrumental introductions to the secular and sacred dramatic works.[1]

Before the end of the seventeenth century, two clearly distinguishable types of overtures had emerged, the French and the Italian. The French overture is characterized by a strong rhythmic slow movement followed by an *allegro* fugue, after which there may be a return to a few bars of the initial slow movement. The Italian overture consists of three movements arranged in a fast-slow-fast pattern. The symmetry of this second type is emphasized further by the tonal relationship of the movements: tonic – related key (frequently the relative or parallel minor) – tonic. The final movement of the cycle is frequently a dance movement, a minuet or a gigue.

The regional preference which the terms 'French' and 'Italian' originally connoted was not continued in the eighteenth century. Both types were composed throughout the whole of Europe and England. Individual composers, of course, showed definite preferences in their use of the two models. Handel, for example, preferred the French type as an introduction for his operas; Antonio Lotti, who wrote primarily for Venice and Dresden, preferred the Italian type. Conti made use of both types in his opera and oratorios, sometimes even combining aspects of the two within a single overture.

The variety of textures and colours found in the instrumental accompaniments for Conti's vocal compositions is for the most part lacking in his overtures. The majority of them are scored for a four-part string ensemble, sometimes reinforced by woodwinds. Although the exact instrumentation is seldom designated at the beginning of an overture, an idea of the instruments required is frequently supplied either by performance directions within the context of the music or occasionally by extant part books. Deviation from the four-part scoring occurs most often in the slow movements, where Conti tends to omit the woodwinds and reduce the instruments assigned to the continuo line. Other examples include those of the string group being expanded with an obbligato part for violoncello or augmented by obbligato parts for oboes and bassoons or trumpets and timpani.

The particular attention to design and detail which Conti paid in the writing of the overtures to his secular cantatas and dramatic works was not wasted upon an inattentive or noisy audience, for the atmosphere in the court theatre differed markedly from the commotion and clamour in the public theatres of Venice and other Italian cities. A contemporary writer offered this description of the court's attitude toward music:

> The presence of a music-loving court and the rules of Spanish ceremonial naturally made any disturbance impossible, so that the overtures and symphonies of the Viennese operas could be of an intimate and subtle character, and need not, as in Italy, be a mere noisy signal for the rise of the curtain.[2]

The character of Conti's opera overtures might be more aptly described as vigorous and festive than 'intimate and subtle', owing to the greater emphasis he placed upon the *allegro* movements. In fact, many of the overtures of the Italian type consist of two fast movements separated by a mere four or five bars of chordal transition marked *adagio*. Some overtures do not even have a slow movement. One such example is the overture to *Galatea vendicata* (1719), which has three *allegro* movements of approximately equal length and importance.

Although Conti adopted specific models for the external design of his overtures, seldom did he adhere to any particular model with respect to the internal structure of individual movements. Even in the overtures for his oratorios, which in large measure are patterned after the French overture type, he experimented with ways to vary the internal design. Among the overtures that are fashioned internally on the French model described above (with its introductory slow movement, fugue, and a brief recapitulation to the opening bars of the introduction) are *Naaman*, *Il David perseguitato da Saul*, *David*, and *L'osservanza della divina legge*.

Several other overtures incorporate the French model within a more complex structure. In *Il Gioseffo* (1706), the title 'Entrée' suggests that the a French type of overture will unfold and indeed the opening nine-bar section, although lacking any tempo mark, does have the characteristics of a slow introductory movement.

There follows a *fugato* movement marked *presto presto*, at the conclusion of which is written the cue for a *da capo*. No *fermata* is at the end of the initial nine bars of the overture, only a double bar, but presumably the *da capo* pertained only to a repetition of those nine bars, thereby causing the overall structure to resemble the tripartite form of an Italian overture. The scoring also deviates from the norm, for it is in five rather than four parts with the division of the strings signalled by the clefs: violin (2), viola (2), and violoncello (continuo).

A few years after *Il Gioseffo* had its première in Vienna, the entire overture of this oratorio reappeared as the first of three movements for the overture to *Clotilda,* a pasticcio staged in London in 1709. This time the tempo for both the introduction and the fugue were specified as 'Largo' and 'Prestissimo' respectively. To the 1706 overture were added a brief 'Adagio' interlude and a 'Gigue', the whole resembling a combination of the French and Italian types of overtures. The popularity of the *Clotilda* overture is evident from the number and variety of editions published in London beginning in 1709 and from its inclusion as the overture to Handel's pasticcio *Ormisda*, which had its première on 4 April 1730 in London.[3]

Since the *Clotilde* score of 1706 no longer survives, there is no way to determine whether or not its overture was the same as the one which appeared with the London production of *Clotilda* in 1709. If, perchance, it was, then the overture to *Il Gioseffo* may be nothing more than a borrowing of the introduction and fugue from the 1706 opera overture. If, however, the overture to *Il Gioseffo* was newly composed for that oratorio, then the opening movement of the overture to *Clotilda* would represent a borrowing from that source for its opening movement. Admittedly, Conti's usual pattern for creating scores was seldom predicated upon borrowing material from his own or any other composer's works. One of the rare occasions when he did borrow music from one of his own scores can be found in the overture to *La via del saggio* (1721). The opening movement is the 'Minuetto Primo' from the overture to *Il trionfo dell'amicizia e dell'amore* (1711), and the second movement bears a close resemblance to the 'Largo' movement from the overture to *La colpa originale*, an oratorio he composed in 1718.

Of special interest are the opening movements of Conti's overtures structured on the Italian model. Here, more than in either the second or the third movements, Conti incorporates a considerable variety of forms and textures. By so doing, he avoids having any one form or idea completely dominate his musical material. This point is aptly illustrated by the opening movements of overtures written between 1724 and 1732 in which Conti utilized fugal procedure, symmetrical binary form, sonata forms, and through-composed organization. At first glance, his selection of these diverse designs seems random. A closer analysis, however, shows that the diversity resulted from Conti's continued attempts to develop certain musical ideas through experimentation. Thus, if one wants to understand how the overtures are related to each other, one must first examine how the separate musical ideas were developed.

One of these ideas – the use of binary form as a structural model – occupied Conti's attention in many of his opening movements. In them, he articulated the binary form by a combined tonal and thematic scheme. Since Conti was primarily interested in experimenting with thematic rather than tonal aspects of the design, he allowed one basic tonal concept to prevail in these movements: section one moves from a tonic to a dominant key; section two continues in the dominant, explores a related key, and concludes in the tonic key. Superimposed upon this simple tonal framework are two different concepts of thematic organization. One is based upon the principle that the themes exposed in the first section should be restated in the second in the order in which they originally appeared, with the initial theme coming at the outset of the second section. In the application of this principle of design, the thematic material cannot reappear in its original tonal context because section two begins in the dominant, continues with an elaboration of the initial theme in a related key, and concludes with a restatement of the second and closing theme coinciding with a return to the tonic key.

The tonal-thematic scheme described above can be observed most clearly in the opening movement of the 'Sinfonia' to *Ciro* (1715). In this case, section two is subdivided into three parts of equal length with both the first and third parts, in A major and D major respectively, devoted to a recapitulation of the entire exposition. The intervening second part develops the second theme in E major and concludes with cadenza-like figuration for the violins in A major. Therefore the tonal relationship between the first and second parts of this section gives the illusion of a tonic-dominant succession in the restatement of material, with the third part functioning more like a coda.

Another concept of thematic organization which Conti used in his binary movements centres around the principle that a return to the tonic key at the end of section two is to be accompanied by a restatement of the themes from the exposition. When Conti applied this idea to the binary form, he eventually succeeded in creating a structure that comes under the category of sonata forms.[4] The first evidence of this in Conti's works comes approximately at the mid-point of his career, that is, in the third decade of the eighteenth century at a time when other composers were also discovering this same principle of design. One of the overtures which paved the way for Conti's development of the sonata forms concept in his opening movements was the 'Introduzione' to *Circe fatta saggia* (1713). This particular overture is not in binary form; in fact, it constitutes a singularly different kind of overture. The difference lies not in the fact that this is a one-movement overture, but rather in the fact that it is constructed in three parts, the third part indicated by the words *da capo*. The treatment of the ternary design here bears only slight resemblance to the oratorio overtures composed according to a similar *ABA* design. For example, the 'Entrée' to the oratorio *Il Gioseffo* (1706) has the essential components of a French overture – introduction and fugue – but since the introduction is repeated after the *fugato* section, the overall structure can be diagramed as *ABA*. In the 'Sinfonia' to *Il martirio di S. Lorenzo* (1710), the *A* section is separated from its repetition by a mere five bars (adagio) that constitutes the *B* section.

A more complex situation obtains in the overture to *Circe fatta saggia*. Here the *B* section contrasts with the *A* section in length and tempo; it does not contrast tonally, because both *A* and *B* begin and end in the tonic key. More important than these features is the fact that both sections are related to each other thematically. Conti begins the overture with a four-bar theme and then devotes the remainder of the movement to an elaboration of that theme within a quasi-polyphonic framework, the whole becoming an exercise in thematic extension and development. The initial theme is developed in *A* by fragmentation, imitation, and inversion, with the original rhythmic and melodic contour of the theme fully preserved. The head motif of this same theme is developed in *B* through the process of transformation, with the identity of the original material considerably altered. While the procedure in *A* represents the same techniques Conti was to employ in all his works where there was a need for thematic elaboration and extension, the procedure found in *B* occurs in only one other overture, the opening movement to the *Alessandro in Sidone* overture. So striking is the similarity between the beginning of the *B* sections of both these overtures that there can be little doubt of the influence which the earlier work had on the later one

Another significant landmark in Conti's progression toward the creation of sonata forms in his instrumental music is the overture to *Don Chisciotte in Sierra Morena* (1719).[5] It constitutes the fourth in a series of opera overtures which Conti entitled with the French terms 'Entrée' or 'Ouverture' instead of the customary Italian terms 'Sinfonia' or 'Introduzione'. As the terminology suggests, all four of these overtures are dependent upon some aspects of the French overture. This dependence, however, is not to be found in the external design, for in each case Conti maintains the three-movement cycle of his Italian model. It appears instead in the design of the opening movements which have a modified version of a French overture with its traditional sequence of introduction and fugue.

In the earliest of the four examples, the 'Entrée' to *I Satiri in Arcadia* (1714) opens with a twenty-three bar introductory section that is repeated before the first movement continues with a fugue, the excellence of which reflects an influence from Fux. Then, in the manner of the Italian overture, are added a 'Largo' and a 'Gigue' as second and third movements respectively. This arrangement of a combined French and Italian type of overture is not unique to Conti. Handel, Lotti, and Fux, to mention but three of his contemporaries, composed overtures of a similar nature. What may be unique is Conti's peculiar application of the French model to his opening movements. On the one hand, he preserves in the introduction the dotted rhythmic character of the thematic material and the chordal texture – both distinctive features of the French overture – but he eliminates the characteristic slow-fast relationship between the introduction and fugue by marking the tempo *allegro* or *presto* for the introduction and calls for a repetition of that introduction before proceeding to the fugue.

In his 'Entrée' to *Il finto Policare* (1716), the second in this series of four opera overtures, Conti adopts a similar procedure, with one interesting variant. Here, in addition to the introduction being repeated before the beginning of the fugal section, the introductory material returns, in a slightly varied fashion, at the conclusion of the fugue (*AABA'*). In this position, it functions in a dual capacity: it not only unifies the opening movement but also serves as a transition to the final movement, which is composed in the manner of a minuet.

No new interpretation of the French model is presented in the opening movement of the 'Ouverture' to *Sesostri, rè di Egitto* (1717), the third overture in the series, because Conti patterned this overture after the one written for *I Satiri*. Similarly, the opening movement of the overture to *Don Chisciotte* bears a relationship to the overture to *Il finto Policare*, but this time Conti does more than merely imitate the 1716 model. In addition to eliminating the contrast in tempo between the introduction and fugue, and repeating the introduction before the start of the fugue, he explores other dimensions of structural design, such as thematically relating the theme of the introduction to the subject of the fugue and concluding with a return to the introductory material, albeit in a different tonal guise, giving the impression that this section is a transitional or middle movement. Superimposed upon the tripartite structure of the opening movement with tempo markings of 'Spiritoso' / 'Allegro' / 'Spiritoso' is an internal design that reflects Conti's concern for tonal and thematic unity.[6]

The significance of this particular overture is two-fold: it is the end product of a series of overtures in which Conti experimented with the combination of the French and Italian overtures and it forms one more stepping stone towards his realization of a design that exhibits the essential features of sonata forms. In fact, the type of tonal and thematic organization observable here is similar to that in the overtures to *Alessandro in Sidone* and *Pallade trionfante* where the most pronounced elements of sonata forms are to be found.

The opening movement of the overture to *Alessandro in Sidone* is organized as follows: exposition of main theme, elaboration of that theme forming an extensive bridge passage, exposition of second theme; development of main theme by fragmentation, inversion, and imitation; recapitulation of main theme, bridge passage, and second theme – all in the tonic key. The manner in which Conti has presented the musical material, however, is more suggestive of the thematic procedure found in a Baroque fugue than that found in sonata forms. For example, the main theme is expounded by violins 1 within a polyphonic texture. After a short bridge passage, the main theme is restated by violins 2 with the second presentation related to the first in the same way that a real answer is related to the subject of a fugue. At the corresponding place in the recapitulation, the main theme is introduced in *stretto*, the imitation occurring at the distance of one measure. Similarly, the influence of the fugue is felt in the extensive transition passage that links the first and second theme areas. This passage, comparable to a fugal episode, is comprised of a mosaic of motifs derived from the initial eight measures of the overture, and these motifs are imitated, one against the other, in all four instrumental parts.

The length of this transition passage delays the appearance of the second theme to the extent that the new thematic area actually concludes the exposition. The second theme, therefore, occupies the position of a closing theme, but in all other respects, the structural significance of the second theme area has been retained: the theme coincides with the dominant tonality; it contrasts with the first theme melodically and, most especially, texturally, since continuo-homophony has been substituted for imitative polyphony.

The contrapuntal texture returns at the outset of the development section where it becomes one of several devices used by the composer to effect a thematic metamorphosis of the initial material. Those devices include fragmentation of the main theme into separate motifs, inversion and alteration of the melodic contour of the original material, and imitation of the motifs. In this way, Conti transforms the main theme and thereby is able to make this development section distinctly different from a fugal episode. The recapitulation is approximately half the length of the exposition because here Conti has eliminated the extended bridge passage that had separated the main and second themes in the exposition. The combined length of the development and recapitulation equals the length of the exposition; thus, the entire movement is an example of symmetrical binary form.

The final movement of this overture also comes under the category of sonata forms. In contrast to the first movement, however, this one places the elements of sonata forms in a non-polyphonic texture. Perhaps it was this movement that prepared the way for Conti to compose two similar movements eighteen months later for the overture to *Pallade trionfante* (1722)

Unlike the overture to *Alessandro in Sidone*, in which the opening movement dominates the cycle, the overture to *Pallade trionfante* is balanced by two movements of approximately the same length separated by a slow transitional movement. In both outer movements, the contrapuntal texture has been discarded and thus the structure has become independent of the fugal procedure. Consequently, the style therein anticipates to a greater degree the character of the early Classical symphonic movements.

Although the departure from the fugal procedure strengthened the periodicity of the design, it also restricted the extent to which Conti was able to develop the thematic material. This resulted in the opening movement of this overture being only about one-third the length of that for the overture to *Alessandro in Sidone*. The concise presentation of material in this opening movement of the *Pallade* overture was replicated by Conti in several other overture movements in sonata forms, such as the third movement of the overture to *Pallade trionfante* and the first movement of the overtures to *Meleagro* (1724), *Issicratea* (1726), and *Il contrasto della bellezza e del tempo* (1726).

The overture to *Pallade trionfante* has been cited as proof that the Vienna opera overture had a direct influence upon the evolution of the Classical symphony. One of the first to make this claim was Hugo Botstiber:

> The development of symphonic form . . . must at least partially be regarded as the achievement of the Vienna opera composers of that period. The composer who is especially noteworthy in this respect is Francesco Conti, who has never yet

achieved the recognition he deserves. His *allegro* movements have very nearly the fully developed form of the later classical symphonies: the first section is repeated; after the repetition a development begins on the dominant; and the third section involves a return to the tonic. The appearance of a secondary theme, which recurs in corresponding tonality in the third part, is also to be noted. A classical example of this type is the introduction to *Pallade trionfante* (1722); another examples is the introduction to *Alessandro in Sidone* of which the development begins saucily with a reversal of the main theme.[7]

Others, such as Guido Adler, have also cited the overture to *Pallade trionfante* as a source for the type of instrumental music that predominated in the second half of the eighteenth century, but they fail to mention the overture to *Alessandro in Sidone*.[8] The reason why they do not may be attributed to Botstiber himself upon whose judgement they based their descriptions rather than consulting the sources anew. Although both overtures are mentioned by Botstiber, his comments are directed primarily toward *Pallade trionfante*, giving the impression that this opera's overture marks the earliest occurrence of sonata forms appearing in work by Conti. He also called attention to the *Pallade* overture simply by having all three movements printed in an appendix to his book.

Botstiber's emphasis on the *Pallade* overture succeeded in distorting another aspect of Conti's overtures. Although never stated, the implication of his comments is that once Conti stumbled upon this tonal-thematic design, which only long after the fact became known as sonata forms, he continued to utilize the design in subsequent overtures. This, however, did not happen. Throughout much of Conti's instrumental writing there is an unresolved tension between musical organization based upon contrapuntal procedures and that based upon continuo-homophony, but in the midst of this tension, elements continually emerge that show a close affinity with the sonata forms of the later eighteenth century. Seldom, however, are enough of these elements present in a single movement to create a structure that can, in retrospect, be embraced by the term 'sonata forms'. Those elements include: choice of the initial motif to underscore the tonality; presentation of motifs in small units reflecting the motivic style of the *buffo* arias; articulation of thematic materials so that the structure is audible by means of texture, orchestration, key, dynamics, and rhythm; transformation of motifs and extension of harmonic tension in the development area; and recapitulation of the exposition material in various ways without distortion of the underlying tonal framework.[9]

Although designs related to sonata forms are very much in evidence in Conti's overtures, especially in the opening movements, these most certainly were not the only designs utilized. Some have already been discussed; others deserve to be mentioned briefly. For example, the overture to *Penelope* begins with a *fugato* movement and the overtures to *Teseo in Creta* (1716) and *Issipile* (1732) open with through-composed movements. The 'Introduzione' to *La via del saggio* (1721) begins with a dance movement in triple metre. The second and third movements, as mentioned above, are based upon two earlier overtures by Conti.

In Conti's Italian type of overtures, the middle movements can vary considerably in style and length. At one extreme are the overtures to *Penelope* and *Meleagro,* both composed in 1724, in which the outer movements are separated by nothing more than two bars of music in a contrasting tempo and style. At the other extreme are a few overtures for which Conti composed a movement of considerable length. Among these is the overture to *Il trionfo dell'amicizia e dell'amore* (1711/1721). Here the middle movement, in binary form, is the most important of the three-movement cycle. It is the longest of the three and is scored for four instrumental parts instead of the three called for in the other two movements. What is even more interesting is that this middle movement, with the tempo marked *largo*, uses thematic material found in the opera itself, specifically in Act I, Scene x. This particular scene, consisting solely of an aria, contains the crux of the whole drama, for here Tirsi declares his love for Licori.

Alessandro in Sidone, *Pallade trionfante*, *Sesostri*, and *Issipile* are among the operas that also have overtures with middle movements that are of interest. The 'Adagio' movement of *Pallade trionfante*, for example, has a single motivic idea which is repeated over and over again by the upper strings against a descending chromatic line in the lower strings. The dynamic level in the last two bars is reduced to *pianissimo* as the movement comes to rest on a dominant chord of G minor. There is no resolution, simply a pause before the final movement begins in B-flat major, the key of the opening movement as well. This movement is so similar to the middle movement of the *Alessandro in Sidone* overture that the earlier work must have served as the model for the later one.

In *Sesostri*, one finds a four-movement cycle for the overture in which the second movement, the longest of the four, is fugal and the third movement is through-composed. In *Issipile*, the 'Largo' movement of the overture is in a minor key and has a very lyrical melodic part for the first violin, the nature of which suggests it was intended for a solo violin. The other three string parts accompany with pulsating chordal motion. Although the movement is only nine bars long, it gives the impression of being a substantial piece.

Twice Conti wrote overtures that added brass and timpani to the string ensemble. One was the 'Introduzione' to *L'Istro*, a cantata composed in celebration of a wedding at the court in 1719. The seven-part scoring calls for *tromba* 1 and 2, timpani, violins 1 and 2 doubled by oboes, viola, and *bassi*. In the first and final movements, Conti uses the trumpets and especially the timpani to articulate the design and make audible the musical structure.

The first of the three movements is in C major and consists of two distinct self-contained units – an introductory section that is of considerable length (forty-five bars) and a fugue. The full scoring is required for the entire introductory section, which itself is subdivided into three mini-sections, each centred on a single chord – tonic, dominant, and tonic – to accommodate the limitation of the timpani to tonic and dominant notes. The introduction opens with a fanfare-like theme in the two *tromba* parts, accompanied by the other parts playing a single tonic chord repeated once per each of the first six bars (ex. 7.1a). The interest thereafter shifts to the strings. They present a new theme and then alternate that with variants of the fanfare-like theme throughout the remainder of the introduction. Although the trumpets participate throughout, they are relegated to a subordinate role, either doubling the violins or reinforcing the tonic and dominant notes.

For the greater part of the fugue, the trumpets and timpani are silent. The fugue's subject and countersubject are presented and developed in a traditional fashion by each of the four string parts. In addition a third motif is introduced after two statements of the fugue subject and it is this motif that pervades, even dominates, the passages between and accompanying the various expositions of the fugual themes. Conti reserves the trumpets and timpani for the final three statements of the subject. In bar 99 the trumpets join the violins in presenting the thematic material while the timpani reinforces the bass, bringing the whole movement to a fitting climax (ex. 7.1b).

The middle movement is in A minor and is structured in repeated binary form. Here the scoring is limited to strings and woodwinds and Conti takes advantage of the versatility of these instruments and the *larghetto* tempo to introduce some chromaticism into the melodic and harmonic material. The final *allegro* movement is in binary form, its triple metre producing a dance-like character. The trumpets are scored as part of the tutti ensemble, with the first and second trumpets doubling their respective counterparts in the violins in the opening bars (ex. 7.1c). Thereafter Conti varies the texture and timbre by dividing up the strings, woodwinds, brass, and timpani into groups and using them in antiphonal or *concertato* fashion. For example, at the beginning of the second half of the movement, Conti alternates the woodwinds – solo oboes 1 and 2 and solo bassoons ('Haut. Soli; Fagotti soli') – with the tutti ensemble: four bars for woodwinds, four bars for tutti, twelve bars for woodwinds, six bars for tutti, and then there is a return to the scoring of the first part of the movement with the focus on the strings and brass (ex. 7.1d).

The other overture with this same seven-part scoring is the 'Sinfonia' to the opera *Il trionfo della fama* (1723). The similarity between the two overtures extends beyond the instrumentation and suggests the earlier work served as a model for the later one. A well-defined exposition opens the first of the three movements with the initial hammer stroke motif followed by a series of motifs that lend themselves to repetition and transformation. The style of the first forty-six bars is one that foreshadows the early Classical symphony, but the design does not mirror the same, for instead of the exposition concluding in the dominant, it ends in the tonic, thereby creating a closed form. Only a single crotchet rest separates that section from the following fugue that constitutes the middle section of the same movement. Here the scoring is reduced to the four-part ensemble. The interplay of subject and countersubject emphasizes the vertical rather than the horizontal flow of musical ideas and this results in a process that is more aptly equated with a development section than a fugal one. There is no noticeable division between the fugue and the concluding material, for one seems to be the logical outgrowth of the other. A return to the tutti scoring coincides with a restatement of a portion of the exposition. Once again, Conti has used the instrumentation to make audible the structure.

The middle movement is more elaborate than the brief interlude found in many overtures. It is in triple metre and typically has the scoring reduced to four-part strings (without oboes) The two basic motifs set forth by the violins in the first nine bars provide the thematic material for the remainder of the movement as the motifs are restated by bass and first violin. The tempo marked at the beginning is *tempo giusto* but the final two bars are to be played *adagio*.

The final movement balances the first in length and orchestral color, its triple (3/8) metre producing a sprightly dance-like character. Here the influence of the overture to *L'Istro* seems the strongest, especially in the variation of textures and in the *concertato* interplay of the strings and brass. The first twelve bars contain three distinct motifs which are restated in the dominant at bar 19 and then are concluded by a bridge motif. What follows is not a development section but rather

Example 7.1. *L'Istro*: 'Introduzione', (a) bars 1-6; (b) bars 97-103

(a)

(b)

Example 7.1 (continued). *L'Istro*: 'Introduzione', (c) bars 145-52; (d) bars 171-8

a spinning forth of the same three motifs, the whole comprising a through-composed finale. The strings rather than the trumpets are the dominating force in this very effective movement. Nevertheless, the trumpets and timpani actively participate throughout the entire movement, sometimes used alone either to set forth their own material (bars 61-4) or to accompany the violins (bars 87-91).

It was not uncommon in this period for court composers to take overtures from their operas and oratorios and recycle them as independent instrumental works with titles such as 'Sinfonia' or 'Sonata'. Caldara's overtures to his operas *Il trionfo della religione* and *Cajo Fabbricio* exist as independent pieces, the scoring altered to accommodate their use for other purposes. A number of opera overtures may have been used for liturgical or para-liturgical events. Such was the case with Conti's overture to *Pallade trionfante*. Under the title *Sinfonia à 4*, it became part of the Hofkapelle repertoire and was performed as an independent instrumental work throughout a period extending some thirty years from the date of its initial composition.[10]

In addition to the overtures that introduce the operas and overtures, Conti's dramatic works also contain a few independent instrumental pieces. In the oratorios, these take the form of self-contained numbers, sometimes entitled 'Preludio', which offer an opportunity for a soloist to display performance skills with an obbligato instrument such as the theorbo.[11] There is also a 'Preludio' in *Penelope* (Act II, Scene xi). It appears at the conclusion of a recitative involving the two comic characters in which Dorsilla tells Tersile that she is about to play some music that will touch his heart. There immediately follows the fourteen-bar 'Preludio' that serves to introduce Tersile's aria 'Bravo bene'. The obbligato part in the 'Preludio' consists of a series of arpeggiated chords in the treble register. This performance by Dorsilla becomes the subject of Tersile's aria. He exclaims over the manner in which she executes arpeggios, and challenges her to imitate his vocal line consisting of trills and other types of virtuoso passage. The nature of the musical material suggests that the accompaniment may have been intended for a harp or for a harpsichord, viola da gamba, and continuo, this latter combination having been used by Fux for a strikingly similar number, 'Sento nel core', in his *La decima fatica d'Ercole*.

Most of the independent pieces that occur in the operas are in the form of dances performed at the end of an act in place of an intermezzo. In fact, every one of Conti's full-length operas, with the exception of *Il trionfo dell'amicizia e dell'amore*, has at least one act which is to be concluded by a 'Balletto'. Music for these dances has not always been preserved in the opera manuscripts. For example, the three acts of *Alba Cornelia* (1714) should conclude with 'Balli', according to information supplied on the title page and stage directions that immediately follow the last musical number of each act, but no music for the dances is included in the score.

The term 'Balletto' is used to refer to a series of stylized dances in which no prescribed pattern of organization is operative. For example, the 'Balletto Primo' that concludes Act I of *Il finto Policare* consists of the following: Marche, Aria, Bourée, and Rétirade. Here, as in so many other 'Balletti', the music is in *particello* with only the two outermost instrumental parts supplied. This type of layout obscures the variety in texture and scoring that prevailed during the actual performance. That such variety is characteristic of the dances in Conti's operas can be observed in those manuscripts where the 'Balletto' survives in full score. In the 'Balletto' for Act I of *Archelao*, for example, the scoring ranges from two to six parts, with the six-part combination requiring violins 1 and 2, *corni da caccia* 1 and 2, viola, and bass: March (6 parts), Aria (6 parts), Aria (3 parts), Marche (initial dance repeated), Entrée (4 parts), Passepié (4 parts), and Rigadon (2 parts).

The Viennese custom of having dance music conclude an act of an opera can be traced back to Wolfgang Ebner (1625-65), one of the first to serve the court as a ballet composer. That tradition was admirably carried forth by his successors, Johann Schmelzer, Andreas Schmelzer, Johann Hoffer, and finally Nicola Matteis, who was appointed ballet composer when a vacancy arose during the period of reorganization of the Hofkapelle staff in 1712. This, of course, was not his initial appointment at the court. That occurred in 1700 when he was appointed a court violinist and subsequently earned the title 'Direttore della musica instrumentale', a position he held until his death in 1737. During his tenure at the court, Matteis achieved a considerable reputation, not only as a first violinist of the court orchestra but also as a ballet composer, writing music for many operas, including thirty-three by Caldara and the coronation opera *Costanza e fortezza* by Fux.[12]

According to several different contemporary sources, Matteis was responsible for writing all of the dance music for Conti's operas, though only a few of the extant opera manuscripts actually credit him as the composer. More often than not, it is the names of the choreographers with whom he collaborated that are listed on the prefatory pages of the scores rather than the name of the ballet composer. For example, there are dances that conclude each of the three acts of *Astarto* (1718): no one is credited with the 'Ballo di Pagodi e ridicoli Cinesi' that concludes Act I; 'Allessandro Fillebois' (Alessandro Phillibois) is credited with the choreography of the dances for Act II and 'Simon Pietro Levassori della Motta' (Pietro Simone Levassori della Motta) with that for Act III. Although both Phillebois and Levassori are here designated as a 'Maestro di Ballo', that is not how Phillibois is listed in the court financial records. There he is listed as a 'Hoff-Tanzer' and for this position he received an annual stipend of 1500 florins.[13]

The very first dances Matteis is known to have composed for Vienna were designed for three operas produced in 1714 – *Alba Cornelia* (with dances at the end of Acts I, II, and III), *I Satiri in Arcadia* (a dance at the end of Act I), and *L'Atenaide* (a dance at the end of Act III) – but the music for them has not survived. One of the manuscript copies of *Penelope* (A/*Wn*: Mus.Hs. 17226) has the 'Ballo' music at the end of the score, whereas another manuscript copy of this same opera (A/*Wn*: Mus.Hs. 17110) has no dance music. Neither manuscript includes the name of the ballet composer nor those of the choreographers.

Several operas limit the dances to a single act (*Griselda, Sesostri, Creso, Penelope*); others have dances at the end of two or three acts in the three- and five-act operas (*Il finto Policare, Don Chisciotte, Archelao, Alessandro in Sidone*).[14] The scoring for the dances is not necessarily confined to strings. In *Issipile*, the first dance that ends Act II is scored for four instrumental parts: two treble (presumably violins) and two bass instruments, with the uppermost bass part designated for 'violoncelli e fagotti'.

Aside from the overtures and dance music discussed above, other types of independent instrumental music are rarely included in the operas. This is in sharp contrast to many other secular dramatic works by his contemporaries, notably those by Handel, where dances, festal marches, and additional sinfonia-styled pieces can readily be found. By a curious paradox, the one Carnival opera by Conti to which no dance music is appended is the very opera that contains the greatest number of examples of instrumental music in any of his operas.[15] *Il trionfo dell'amicizia e dell'amore* has two scenes in which there was a dramatic necessity to add instrumental music. The festive nature of Scene xvi of Act I requires both a brief 'Sinfonia' (scored for six parts) and a sixteen-bar 'Minuet' with the stage directions 'dove si ballo' ('where they dance').[16] The music of this 'Minuet' is also used for the following chorus number. At the beginning of Scene ix of Act II, Conti inserts an 'Introduzione al Ballo' to allow the chorus of shepherds time to assemble on the stage. This 'Introduzione' is a substantial piece of fifty-one bars in triple metre and scored for six instrumental parts with 2 treble, 1 alto, 1 bass, and 2 (C) mezzo soprano clefs which are assigned to the *corni da caccia*. It is written in a *concertato* style with passages for the *corni da caccia* alternating with passages for the tutti ensemble made up of strings and *corni da caccia*. In the chorus number that follows, this same scoring is used for the accompaniment. Four other operas used the *corni da caccia*: choruses in *I Satiri in Arcadia* and *Don Chisciotte in Sierra in Morena* are accompanied by a six-part ensemble that includes this pair of instruments; *Archelao* and *Griselda* each have a tenor aria in which the string accompaniment is augmented by the *corni da caccia* ; some of the dances in *Archelao*, as described above, also include these instruments.

Conti also composed instrumental music that had no connection whatsoever with his vocal compositions. Examples include the 'Sonata al mandolino solo e basso', a 'Fugue', and the Sinfonia in A major, and all three are extant. There are also three works listed in the Herzogenburg catalogues that have since disappeared: 'Sonata à 2 violini, viola, e basso', 'Sinfonia à 2 violini, viola oblig., basso', and 'Sinfonia à 2 violini e basso'. Both of the works entitled 'Sinfonia' begin with movements in 3/8 metre.

The mandolin sonata is written in French tablature on a four-line staff and consists of four movements: [untitled], 'Allemande', 'Sarabande', and 'Menuet'. In a separate manuscript consisting of only four folios, there is a part for 'Basso per il mandolino' which represents an accompaniment for the mandolin part. In the first and fourth movements, this bass part functions more as a harmonic support, with notes tied over barlines to sustain the pitch; in the second and third movements, it participates in the presentation of melodic material. That the bass part was intended to be played by an instrument that could provide some harmonic realization (theorbo or violoncello and cembalo) is suggested by the presence of a few figures written above one or two bars in each of the four sections: namely, bar 13 in the first, bar 2 in the second, bar 25 in the third, and bars 9 and 11 in the fourth.[17] The mandolin part shows that it was written for an instrument using the standard tuning of e', a', d", and g".

The first movement functions as a prelude. It is through-composed, and is in duple metre and the key of C major. Each of the other three movements is constructed in an asymmetrical binary form, with the 'Allemande' and 'Menuet' in C major and the 'Sarabande' in G.

In a manuscript (D/*Bsb*: MS Dmb 366) containing six fugues by Gregor Joseph Werner (1693-1766), there is an additional fugue ascribed to a 'Sig^re. Conti'. Werner was organist at the Melk Abbey for a brief period around 1715 before entering the service of the Esterházy court in 1728, where his primary interest was in providing sacred music for services of worship. Werner's six fugues were originally written as overtures to six oratorios, which he composed between 1743 and 1749. They were published in 1804 by Ataria with introductory preludes composed by Joseph Haydn.[18] Another 'Allegro Fuga' in F minor is also ascribed to Conti (D/*Bsb*: MS Dmb 486). In neither work is a given name supplied with the surname, and therefore the ascription to Francesco Conti may not be correct.[19] Both fugues are for a four-part string ensemble, with the scoring specified in the fugue in the Werner manuscript and implied in the 'Allegro Fuga'.

These fugues, if they are indeed by Conti, may represent works he composed as studies in counterpoint. Certainly the structure of the 'Allegro Fuga' follows the standard pattern for fugal design for works of modest length. It has an exposition of the subject in the tonic tonality (F minor) by all four voices, a bridge passage, a second exposition in the related tonality of A-flat major, a more extensive bridge passage, a return to the tonic tonality with two statements of the subject, and a concluding coda. Although the subject reflects the Baroque style of fugal themes, the bridge passages are clearly reflective of the pre-Classical style which Conti had embraced in most of his other instrumental works.

The three-movement Sinfonia in A major survives in two manuscript sources.[20] One is a score and the other contains the instrumental parts. Although the score is written on four staves, the first and third movements show that violin 2 actually plays the same music as violin 1. This three-part texture of the outer movements contrasts with the middle movement, which is written in four parts, the lowest designated for 'Bassi pizzicati'.

The separate instrumental parts, however, make clear that a five-part scoring obtains in the outer movements, for Conti has written obbligato parts for oboe 1 and oboe 2. They augment the strings and play material similar to the violins. That this was indeed the composer's intention is confirmed by Conti's signature on the title page for the instrumental parts. In addition, the oboe parts together with the tempo and dynamic markings on many of the other parts are also in Conti's hand.[21]

No date is given on the title page of either the score or the parts, but several features such as the prevailing homophonic texture, the structural exploration of sonata forms, and most especially the style of the second movement suggest the sinfonia was composed during the last ten years of Conti's life. All three movements are in binary form, with the outer movements marked *presto* and the middle movement, *andante*. The design of sonata forms is operative in the first movement, with a change in texture and dynamics used to highlight a secondary theme area and a brief coda add to the recapitulation. Here and throughout the other movements, the appoggiatura plays an important role in shaping the melodic material. Emphasis is placed upon the exposition of a continuous melodic line in the uppermost string part or parts, while the lower strings are relegated to more of an accompanying role. As was true in the *Issipile* overture, the second movement of this Sinfonia in A major is of substantial length and interest, with the melodic interest concentrated in the first violin part. Those who claim overtures of the early decades of the eighteenth century lack middle movements of any substance need to reassess their opinions, for here is certainly one movement that could be aptly called 'an aria for strings'.

Notes

1   Modern editions of eight overtures and one independent Sinfonia in A major, together with a discussion of the same, are contained in *Italians in Vienna*, series B, in Barry Brook, ed., *The Symphony 1720-1840* (New York, 1983), II, xxi-xviii, 1-95. Performing editions (score and parts) of these and several other overtures by Conti have also been prepared by the author. Included are the overtures to *La colpa originale, Don Chisciotte in Sierra Morena, Alessandro in Sidone, Pallade trionfante, Il trionfo della fama, Griselda, Il contrasto della bellezza e del tempo*, and *Issipile*.

2   Egon Wellesz, *Essays on Opera* (New York, 1950), 57.

3   For more about the music borrowed from *Clotilda* for *Ormisda*, see chapter six.

4   For an important, but sometimes controversial, study of this terminology, see Charles Rosen, *Sonata Forms* (New York, 1980).

5   The facsimile of an overture that accompanies the Francesco Bartolomeo Conti entry in *Die Musik in Geschichte und Gegenwart*, II, 1642, is identified as the opening page from the overture to *Don Chisciotte in Sierra Morena*. The excerpt reproduced is not that of the overture to Conti's opera as performed in Vienna in 1719 nor as performed in a number of revivals outside of Vienna. In addition, the scoring shown in the reproduction also bears absolutely no relation to anything Conti ever wrote. Unfortunately, several scholars have been misled by this facsimile and have claimed on the basis of it that Conti used clarinets in his works. Colin Lawson, for example, mistakenly thought (on the basis of this facsimile) that Conti wrote for 'Clarinette in D' in 'one version of his popular comic opera Don Chisciotte . . . where the trumpet-like writing occurs at the beginning of the overture'. See his 'The Chalumeau in the works of Fux', in Harry White, ed., *Johann Joseph Fux and the Music of the Austro-Italian Baroque* (London, 1992), 90.

6   For example, the opening three-bar theme of the introductory 'spiritoso' section is stated in the tonic by the first violins and is immediately thereafter restated in the dominant by the continuo, in the manner of a fugal exposition, except here the texture is definitely not polyphonic.

7   Hugo Botstiber, *Geschichte der Ouverture und der freien Orchesterformen* (Leipzig, 1913), 82,; translation by Donald Jay Grout quoted *Italians in Vienna*, series B, in Barry Brook, ed., *The Symphony 1720-1840*, II, xix.

8   Guido Adler, *Handbbuch der Musikgeschichte* (Frankfurt am Main, 1924), 719.

9   A more complete list of these elements can be found in the author's introduction to Conti's overtures printed in *Italians in Vienna*, series B, in Barry Brook, ed., *The Symphony 1720-1840*, II, xx.

10   See chapter twelve for more about the *Sinfonia à 4* and the surviving instrumental parts.

11   See chapter eleven for a discussion of the 'Preludio'.

12   For an insightful article on the career Matteis had at the imperial court, see Andrew D. McCredie, 'Nicola Matteis, the younger: Caldara's collaborator and ballet composer in the service of the Emperor Charles VI', in Brian Pritchard, ed., *Antonio Caldara* (London, 1987), 154-82. See also Paul Nettl, 'An English Musician at the Court of Charles VI in Vienna', *The Musical Quarterly* 28 (July 1942): 323, and Alexander von Weilen, *Zur Wiener Theatergeschichte* (Vienna, 1901), 75.

13   Vienna, Finanz- und Hofkammerarchiv, *Kameral-Zahlamts-Buch*. Nr. 6, fol. 136, Nr. 869.

14   The facsimile edition of *Don Chisciotte in Sierra Morena* (New York, 1982), 368-72, provides examples of Conti's dance music in four-part scoring.

15   Other examples of instrumental music in Conti's operas can be found in *Penelope* and *Teseo in Creta*.

16   None of the six parts are assigned to specific instruments, but there are 2 treble, 1 alto, 1 bass, and 2 (C) soprano clefs.

17   The 'Sonata al mandolino solo e basso' is currently in the archives of the University of Prague (CS/*CSSR*: Pu II. KK. 36), but the cover for the volume containing this sonata indicates that the manuscript once belonged to the Prince Lobkowitz library in Roudnice. In addition to Conti's Sonata, there are six other mandolin works included by Filippo Sauli and anonymous composers, but none are supplied with an accompanying bass part. For more about this work, see chapter two. See also James Tyler, *The Early Mandolin*, (Los Angeles, 1989), 26-7, who mistakenly lists the title of the first movement of the sonata 'Arpeggio'. There is no title for the first movement. 'Arpeggio' is a directive to the performer to arpeggiate the first chord in the mandolin part. The dance titles for the other three movements appear in both the mandolin and bass parts.

18   Warren Kirkendale, *Fugue and Fugato in Rococo and Classical Chamber Music*, Margaret Bent, trans. (Durham, 1979), 279.

19   Robert Eitner, in his *Quellenlexicon*, III, 36, has ascribed both fugues to Francesco Conti.

20   The manuscript sources are located in Dresden's Sächische Landesbibliothek: D/*Dlb*: Mus. 2190-N-1, 1, Nr. 6 (score) and Mus. 2190-N-1, 2 Nr. 7 (parts; 2 oboe parts autograph). This sinfonia is attributed to Pietro Conti in Johann G. I. Breitkopf, *Catalogo delle sinfonie, partitie, . . . in manuscritto nella officina musica di Giovanni Gottlob Breitkopf, in Lipsia* (Leipzig, 1762-65); reprint, Barry Brook, ed., *Breitkopf Catalogo* (New York, 1966), Part I, 7.

21   The signature on these parts can be compared with Conti's signature on his testaments.

CHAPTER EIGHT

The cantatas

In the opinion of Johann Adolph Scheibe, expressed in 1739, the greatest masters of the cantata (in the chamber style) were Astorga, Marcello, Mancini, Conti, Handel, Heinichen, and Bigaglia.[1] What prompted this laudatory ranking of Conti among his contemporaries has yet to be discerned, for his contribution to this genre has attracted relatively little interest until the present decade.[2]

When Conti first arrived in Vienna in 1701, entertainment at the court consisted primarily of operas and oratorios. This preference for the spectacular and the dramatic, which had prevailed throughout the reign of Leopold I, minimized any need for more intimate forms of musical performance. Within a very short period of time, however, a noticeable shift in musical taste occurred, due in no small part to the preferences of the new emperor, Joseph I. During his reign there was a marked increase in the number of cantatas composed and performed for the Habsburgs.

Among the composers responsible for this renaissance of vocal chamber music were Ariosti, the brothers Bononcini, Ziani, and Badia. They were part of a new generation of musicians who came to Vienna from Italy in the opening decade of the eighteenth century and the corpus of chamber music they created was, according to Lawrence Bennett who made an in-depth study of their works, stylistically related to the musical training they had received in their respective native cities of Florence, Bologna, and Venice. Conti is mentioned in connection with this influx of Italians to Vienna, but Bennett does not discuss his cantatas because his study was limited to composers who had made 'significant contributions' to the genre in Vienna from 1700 to 1711.[3]

Few of the cantatas Conti composed are dated and therefore it would have been difficult, if not impossible, for Bennett to ascertain which works might have seen the light of day prior to the interregnum. A cantata by Conti in the British Library may well represent one of his earliest works in the genre. It is entitled *Il Rosignolo* and is included in a collection of cantatas composed by some of his contemporaries, among them Caldara, Giovanni Bononcini, and Nicola Fago. According to a note at the bottom of the first folio of the volume, the copying of manuscripts for the collection was begun 'P. F. An. Dom. 1706'. A further notation on the last flyleaf of the volume indicates the contents were copied by a 'Mr. Cousser who comes but twice a week'. An annotation by either the library's archivist or a former owner of the collection suggests that this 'Mr. Cousser' may be none other than John S. Cousser (1657-1727), 'who came first to England in 1705 and then to Ireland in 1710'.[4]

Il Rosignolo consists of two arias separated by a recitative, each aria presenting a different style of composition within the *da capo* form. The first is designed from a linear perspective, with voice and continuo having two melodically independent parts. The extreme brevity of the *B* section (less than half the length of *A*) produces an asymmetrical structure, noticeable more to the eye than the ear, since the two sections are so closely related thematically.

The second aria is based upon a vertically conceived design and symmetrical phrasing, with the thematic material for the vocal part derived from that initially presented by the continuo in the ten-bar introductory ritornello. In contrast to the previous aria, the *A* and *B* sections here are almost equal in length and even though similar thematic material appears in each, there seems to be a conscious effort to distinguish one section from the other. This is partially achieved by Conti's use of chromaticism to give expressive emphasis to the word 'dolor', which is repeated over and over in the *B* section.

Several other cantatas by Conti for soprano and continuo may also be from a period no later than 1713. 'Lasciami amor', 'Dimmi, ò sorte nemica', and 'Tento scuotere dal seno crudo' appear in a manuscript collection (A/W*n*: Mus.Hs. 17567) in Vienna, along with nine other cantatas by Caldara, Giovanni Bononcini, Astorga, and Fiorè. Of these, only the two by Caldara are dated (6 and 7 March 1712 respectively). Circumstantial evidence suggests that the contributions of some of the other composers represented in the collection may also have been written during the interregnum.[5]

Although Conti was not as prolific a composer of cantatas as Caldara, his contributions to the genre were no less significant. Further research is needed to determine the full extent of his vocal chamber compositions, but to date more than eighty complete cantatas are known to be extant.[6] Four are for two singers, divided equally between those for two sopranos and those for soprano and alto.[7] All of the other cantatas are written for solo soprano, a vocal part that could have been sung by either a male (castrato) or female.[8] While it is not unusual for a composer to favour the soprano voice in chamber works of this period, it is a bit of a surprise to find a total absence of solo cantatas for the alto voice.[9] Approximately one-quarter of the cantatas are scored for strings alone or for strings augmented by one or more obbligato instruments. The remaining works depend upon the realization of a *basso continuo* part for their accompaniments.

The overall structure of Conti's cantatas is governed by a predictable pattern of alternating recitatives and arias. In those accompanied solely by continuo, the number of arias is generally limited to two, resulting in a pattern of recitatives and arias that can be expressed as either R-A-R-A or A-R-A. An example of the former design is 'Mia bella Clori', the only composition by Conti among the thirty-two cantatas contained in the Osborn Collection manuscript.[10] Other composers whose works appear there include Ariosti, Giovanni Bononcini, Cesarini, Fago, Mancini, Sarri, and Alessandro Scarlatti, the last named credited with thirteen cantatas of which five are unique to this source.[11] No date or other details of provenance are visible on the oblong bound volume containing these chamber works.

After studying this collection of cantatas, Reinhard Strohm became convinced that the manuscript was in the hand of a Venetian known to have been a copyist of opera scores in his native city between 1710 and 1720. Strohm theorized that, given the overwhelming dominance of cantatas by composers with connections to Naples, a manuscript from that region may have served as the source from which the Venetian copy was prepared. He further speculated that Scarlatti may have brought the manuscript to Venice when he visited there in 1706-1707.[12]

Several cantatas in the manuscript are known to have been composed prior to 1710 (their dates confirmed from concordant sources), lending support to Strohm's suggestion that the whole collection may date from a period earlier than 1710. What does not seem wholly plausible is Strohm's attempt to link the contents of the manuscript with Naples, for if that were true, this would constitute the only known example of a work by Conti connected with that city.

Using the same criteria upon which Strohm based his conclusions, it is possible to suggest a different theory concerning the provenance of the manuscript. The names of several composers represented in the Osborn volume, including those of Scarlatti and Conti, also appear together as contributors to pasticcio works written and performed for the Medici in Florence between 1703 and 1708. It is therefore conceivable that this collection of cantatas was originally assembled for performance at the Florentine court before it was copied in Venice.

The opening *recitativo semplice* of 'Mia bella Clori' is only eleven bars long, a length that is slightly shorter than the average for recitatives in Conti's solo cantatas. It begins and ends in the key of B-flat, the tonality for each of the four numbers in this composition. The vocal line is segmented into short phrases of fairly equal length, many of them coming to rest on two crotchets, usually positioned on the first two beats of a bar. Multiple repetitions of this particular kind of rhythmic pattern slow the pace of the singer's declamation and accentuate the rhyme scheme of the text.[13] The continuo line is sparsely figured here and throughout the cantata.

Two very brief passages of *arioso* are interjected into this recitative to ornament the vocal line and draw attention to specific words. When this type of *arioso* passage occurs at the end of a *recitativo semplice*, as the second of these does, it imposes a strict tempo upon the final cadence (ex. 8.1). The resulting notation directs the vocal and continuo lines to cadence simultaneously. Obviously, this is in marked contrast to the performing ambiguities created by the most frequently used cadential formula, namely one wherein the final notes of the vocal line are positioned above the penultimate note of the continuo. This second type of $V^{4/3}$-I cadential pattern appears twice in the second recitative of this same cantata.

Example 8.1. 'Mia bella Clori': first recitative, bars 10-11

Arias in a cantata are most often differentiated by metre, tempo, and tonality. That is not the case in the Osborn Collection cantata. Both arias are in the same tonality and in triple metre (3/4). Although neither has tempo or dynamic markings, the nature of their respective thematic materials suggests they should be performed in an *allegro* tempo. What distinguishes them is the style of writing.

A four-bar theme played by the continuo alone begins and ends the *A* section of the first aria and from this initial theme are derived the motifs that pervade the accompaniment for the rest of the number. The initial vocal phrase also restates this opening continuo theme, with the final bar altered slightly to effect a transition to the dominant. Out of the primary melodic material is fashioned a related motif for the vocal part, used sequentially in an ascending pattern in the *A* section and in a descending pattern in the *B* section of this aria. Actually the descending sequence along with its attendant melodic extension appears twice in *B*, once in bars 21-5 and again in bars 25-8, and provides the greater part of all the vocal material of the second half of the aria. As a result, there is little to distinguish the *A* and *B* sections of the *da capo* form, for the two are nearly equal in length and use similar thematic material. It is therefore the shift in tonality, from B-flat major to G minor, that becomes the single most important factor in creating meaningful contrast.

The second aria in this cantata presents an entirely different approach to thematic organization, one that is associated with arias composed by an older generation of Conti's peers. The opening theme for the continuo is six bars long, the first three performed by the continuo alone and the final three heard as accompaniment to a vocal part which has completely contrasting material. All six bars are repeated before the aria unfolds with variants of its previously stated thematic ideas. As was true in the first aria, Conti relies here upon repetition to extend his material, only this time the repetitions are concentrated in the *A* section: the motto (*Devise*) opening of the vocal part is repeated as is the music of bars 18-25 which is restated in bars 26-32. Once again, Conti does little to make a sharp distinction between the *A* and *B* sections of the *da capo* form, save for the move from a major to a minor key.

'Mia bella Clori' is a very modest work but it offers one of relatively few examples from what appears to be an early phase of Conti's cantata composition. By way of contrast, his three cantatas for soprano and continuo contained in A/*Wn*: Mus.Hs. 17567 reveal a maturing of his compositional skills. Here the organization of the recitatives has become more flexible in response to a greater sensitivity to the dramatic nuances of the text. Conti achieves this by increasing the rhythmic and melodic variety of the vocal part and by exploring a wider range of harmonic resources in the continuo. The recitatives now adhere to the principle of concluding in a key related to, but not the same as, the arias which they introduce. Pairs of crotchets continue to be used as a way to conclude individual phrases, but they are no longer a dominant feature. In fact, the crotchet has disappeared altogether from the recitative in the 'Tento scuotere dal seno crudo' cantata. This same cantata also lacks the interpolation of brief *arioso* passages at points of cadential close. In this it differs from his other two cantatas in the same manuscript. The two-bar cadential pattern with an *arioso* passage also occurs in recitatives contained in 'Dopo tante e tante pene' and *Innamoramento*, two cantatas by Conti for which the dates and provenance are not known.[14] Its presence there suggests both works may bear a relationship with one or more of Conti's cantatas composed before 1713.[15]

While changes in the style of the recitatives are fairly subtle, those that pervade the arias of these three cantatas are considerably more visible. Most noticeable is the expanded length, especially in the *A* section. Conti achieves this by having longer ritornelli, by increasing the amount of vocal melismas, and most especially by creating thematic material that lends itself to fragmentation, repetition, and transformation. Tonality, metre, and tempo also begin to play a role in Conti's attempt to have some measure of contrast between the arias within a single cantata. Any contrast between the *A* and *B* sections of an individual aria, however, continues to be modest because the two tend to draw upon the same thematic material.

Each of the three cantatas contains a pair of *da capo* arias based upon a similar principle of organization. For example, the arias in 'Lasciami amor' open with a self-contained theme presented by the continuo (notated in both tenor and bass clefs), and those same eight (or nine) bars are heard again at the close of the *A* section. In both arias the continuo theme begins and ends on the tonic chord of B-flat and is composed of four motifs, each about two bars in length. When the voice enters, it restates the first two motifs of the ritornello before developing its own vocal material. The third motif of the opening theme is reserved almost exclusively for the continuo part. Only once, in a long melisma in the second aria, does the voice share in that particular motif. Conti still relies upon repetition as a way to extend the dimensions of his arias. For example, the opening six bars of the *B* section of the first aria are restated several bars later, but with different words. In the second aria the final seven bars of the vocal part in the *A* section are a repetition of the previous seven bars.

Both arias in the cantata 'Dimmi ò sorte nemica' open directly with the voice accompanied by the continuo. The only time the continuo has a passage independent from the vocal part is in the concluding measures of the *A* section. This does not mean, however, that this part is devoid of motivic interest or is divorced from presenting any of its own melodic material. For example, in the fourth bar of the first aria, an arpeggiated motif is initially presented by the continuo against a long-held note in the voice and then is restated by the voice immediately thereafter, the two statements respectively occurring on dominant and tonic chords. In the second aria, the continuo introduces a distinctive motif in the opening measures against the main theme in the voice, and this becomes the dominant motif for the entire number.

In the third cantata, 'Tento scuotere', Conti offers an entirely different approach to aria construction. Emphasis is placed on the linear rather than the horizontal structure, on the spinning out of melodic lines rather than the fragmentation of them into distinctive motifs. The relationship between the continuo and vocal parts here is akin to that of subject and countersubject in a fugal composition. The first aria, in an *adagio* tempo and in the key of C minor, opens with the continuo presenting a theme that consists of a single motif repeated several times sequentially in a descending pattern. At the conclusion of this three-bar statement, the continuo begins a restatement of the same theme as accompaniment to the vocal entry, but before more than one bar is completed, the material is altered to accommodate the harmonic underpinning of the vocal line. At bar 10, the continuo once again introduces its initial theme, this time restating two of the three bars, followed by a complete restatement (beginning in bar 17) to conclude the *A* section.

A similar design obtains in the second aria of this same cantata. The continuo's thematic material, presented in the eleven-bar ritornello, reappears throughout the aria as the accompaniment to a vocal part that maintains its own identity. Of particular interest here is the initial vocal phrase. The singer enters with the word 'fuggerò', sung to a triplet figure which, in its several repetitions, outlines the tonic chord of C minor. The thirteen-note range (c' to a♭") covered by this four-bar melsima on 'fuggerò' and the omission of the continuo in two of those bars produce a dramatic rendering of the text (ex. 8.2).

Example 8.2. 'Tento scuotere dal seno crudo': second aria, bars 11-16

If these three cantatas were composed during the interregnum, as the contents of this manuscript seem to suggest, then they may represent a stage in Conti's development as a composer which is best described as pivotal. 'Tento scuotere' reflects the style of Alessandro Scarlatti and an older generation of composers, while the other two cantatas point toward the style of a younger generation. All three suggest that Conti is experimenting with different forms and styles of composition.

In Bennett's study of the Viennese cantata, he found that 'the single characteristic that distinguishes cantatas in Vienna from those written elsewhere in Europe is the tendency to include obbligato instruments more frequently and to use larger groups of instruments in general'.[16] Of the one hundred cantatas in his study, more than thirty had this distinguishing characteristic, but they did not make use of as wide a variety of instruments as do those which Conti composed within this same category. The most extensive scoring Bennett reported was in Ziani's 'Cieco fanciul', a cantata composed for the *prima accademia* of 1706: violins 1 and 2, viola, oboes, bassoon, and continuo.

Eight of Conti's cantatas with orchestral accompaniment are in A/*Wn*: Mus.Hs. 17593. The others, with some exceptions, are in separate manuscripts. Of these, only a few can be dated with any certainty.[17] *Cantata allegorica* has the year 1720 on its title page and *L'Istro* can be dated by the event for which it was composed, namely, the festivities in Vienna accompanying the wedding of Maria Josefa and Friedrich August in 1719. In the case of *Nasce con fausti auspici* (soprano, strings, and continuo) and *Volate o lucciolette* (soprano and strings), their title pages state they were composed in 1726. The title page of *Cantata à due voci, Clizia, e Psiche* also provides a partial clue to its date by indicating that the work was composed to honour Empress Elisabeth Christina on her name-day (19 November). The year of performance, however, is not mentioned. Since the name 'Elisa' seems to be reiterated in the text more often than is usual in works honouring the empress, the cantata may have been written to greet her upon arrival in Vienna in 1713. It is also possible that this cantata was presented at the court in 1720, a year when all musical works of a festive nature were curtailed in deference to a period of mourning for the former Empress Eleonora Magdalena, whose death occurred on 19 January of that year.

Seldom do the title pages of Conti's cantatas give credit to the poets whose texts he set. Some exceptions to this statement, however, can be found among his cantatas with orchestral accompaniment. *L'Istro*, the wedding celebration cantata, is set to a text by Apostolo Zeno and *Cantata allegorica* has a text by Pietro Pariati. Four of the cantatas in A/*Wn*:Mus.Hs. 17593 set texts by F. Savallia, P. Savallia, C. Stella, and Silvio Stampiglia.

Of the cantatas selected for discussion here, seven are scored for an ensemble of violins (usually divided and doubled by oboes), viola, and a *basso continuo* part.[18] Three are in Mus.Hs. 17593 and one each in codices 17582, 17589, 17590, and 17651 (all located in A/*Wn*). For the remaining cantatas, Conti uses one or more of the following instruments to reinforce the basic string ensemble or to provide contrasting obbligato solos: flute, chalumeau, oboe, bassoon, lute, theorbo, trumpet, and tympani. In addition, Conti also makes use of the violins and violoncellos in an obbligato role.

Some of the cantatas have one or more arias with unspecified instrumental parts, a situation that poses a problem in determining the composer's intentions. Especially problematic are the continuo parts which rarely reveal what instruments are expected to play them. The *Cantata à voce sola con violini, e flauti* ('O nasca, ò muora il giorno') in A/*Wn*: Mus.Hs. 17589 is scored for six instrumental parts. The first four are for 'flauto primo', 'flauto secondo', 'violino primo', and 'violino secondo'; the final two are in the bass clef but are not designated. One of these is undoubtedly a typical continuo part, but the other remains a matter of conjecture.[19] Another cantata for which Conti wrote multiple instrumental parts in the bass clef is 'Lidia già mi vedesti', but here the parts are specifically assigned to bassoon, theorbo, and cembalo.[20]

In the manuscript A/*Wn*: Mus.Hs. 17593, the sum total of the various obbligato instruments is placed in the margin preceding the initial bar of each cantata. This usually results in the indications for the scoring of the first aria, if it is the opening number of the cantata, being far less specific than that for the subsequent arias. The eight cantatas that comprise this manuscript collection, together with the instruments (with the variant spellings retained) as indicated on the initial folio of each, are set forth in table 8.1.

The first five cantatas in Mus.Hs. 17593 include a part for the lute, notated in French tablature. The lute's role seems directed primarily towards reinforcing one of the other parts – the continuo, the treble line, or the vocal part – either by doubling it or by augmenting it through a realization of the harmonic structure. There are occasions, however, when these roles are reversed. One such example occurs in 'Lontananza dell'amato', where the lute's arpeggiated figure is doubled by 'violini sordini'.

One of these five cantatas, 'Con più luci', is extant in two versions, each giving a slightly different interpretation of what the instruments should perform.[21] In the version found in Mus.Hs. 17593, the initial aria is to be accompanied by four instrumental parts. Written down the side of the left margin of the score are the words 'Chalamaux e due violini, con leuto', with only the word *leuto* positioned directly in front of the part for this instrument. In the other version of this cantata

Table 8.1

Cantatas by Francesco Conti in A/*Wn*: Mus.Hs. 17953

Cantata Prima. 'Lontananza dell'amato': chaloumaux, flute allemand au hautbois, violini sordini, leuti francesi, [continuo]. Text by P. Savallia.

Cantata Seconda. 'Ride il prato e frà l'erbe': violini, leuti, flauto ò chaloumaux, [continuo].

Cantata Terza. 'Con più luci': chaloumaux e due violini con leuto, [continuo].

Cantata 4ª. 'Vaghi flagelletti che d'amor': violini e leuti con chaloumaux, [continuo].

Cantata 5ª. 'La beltà che il core adora': leuti e chalamaux e violini, [continuo]. Text by C. Stella.

Cantata 6ª. 'Gira per queste': violini e hoboa, [continuo]. Text by S. Stampiglia.

Cantata 7ª. 'Fugga l'ombra tenebrosa': violini e haubois, [continuo]. Text by F. Savallia.

Cantata à due voci con instromenti. 'Fra questi colli': violini e haubois, [continuo]. Duo for two sopranos [Lidia, Tirsi].

(A/*Wgm*: Ms. 1471), the initial aria is scored for three, not four, instrumental parts and across the top of the opening measure is written 'Chalamaux e un violino con leuto'. In addition, in the left margin directly in front of the uppermost part is written 'violino solo'; in front of the part on the second staff is written 'violini sordini'. Lacking is a separate part for the lute, even though the lute is expected to play in the opening aria and also in the concluding one, where 'Unisoni violini, chalamaux e leutti' appears over the opening measure and the only other instrumental part is the continuo. Thus, in the concluding aria, there is no question that violin, chalumeau, and lute are expected to play the uppermost part together.[22]

The middle aria ('I bei fregi') of this cantata presents no ambiguity in either source. It is scored for solo chalumeau, voice, and continuo. Here the obbligato instrument has a part that allows for a display of virtuoso skills. It should also be noted that this aria is in a minor key (E minor) and has a slow tempo (*adagio*), two elements composers in Vienna often incorporated into arias featuring the chalumeau as an obbligato instrument.[23]

Four other cantatas in Mus.Hs. 17593 include the chalumeau in their scoring. In 'Lontananza dell'amato' this instrument plays in unison with lute and violins and in 'Ride il prato e frà l'erbe' it is used as a solo obbligato instrument. For one of the four arias in 'Ride il prato', Conti offers a choice of 'Flauto ò Chaloumaux' for the obbligato part. It is conceivable that the substitution of the chalumeau was suggested simply because the flute already had an obbligato role in two of the other arias in this same cantata. In the cantatas 'Vaghi flugelletti che d'amor' and 'La beltà che il core adora', the chalumeau is not only combined with lute and violins, but it also has solo passages. For example, in the *A* section of the second of three arias in 'La beltà che il core adora', the obbligato part is assigned to 'violini unisoni', but in the *B* section (which is in a minor key) it is assigned to the chalumeau.

Conti composed very few works requiring the flute and therefore it is of special interest to observe his handling of this instrument in the cantatas. In *Cantata à voce sola con violini e flauti* ('O nasca, ò muora il giorno'), all three arias incorporate the flute into the scoring, but it is in the middle aria that a solo flute and the soprano, accompanied only by the continuo, share equally in presenting an ornately embellished melodic line. Given the *andante* tempo, the soloists are able to execute the florid passages in an introspective, rather than a virtuoso, manner. Three of the five arias in 'Ride il prato' also offer examples of Conti's writing for the flute. Here the emphasis is more on folk-like melodies, reflecting the spirit of the dance.

Woodwinds are also featured in 'Fra queste umbrose piante', one of thirteen cantatas in a collection (Mus.Ms. 1046) held by the Hessische Landesbibliothek in Darmstadt. This collection includes cantatas by Handel (1), Telemann (1), and Caldara (5), among others. On the opening folio of 'Fra queste umbrose piante' is written 'Sign: Conti'. Although no other qualifying name or initial is supplied, Francesco has been credited with its composition.[24] This cantata differs considerably from Conti's other works in the genre and therefore it is difficult to suggest a possible date of composition. The scoring calls for violins 1 and 2, oboes 1 and 2, 'chalumaux', 'flut' almande', 'basson' (chalumeau), and 'basso' (continuo).[25] The alto clef is not used for any part nor is a part designated for viola. The overall structure is as follows: 'Simphonia'-R(*stromentato*)-A-Ritornello-R-A-R-A-Instrumental Interlude-A-'Coro'.

The first and third movements of the 'Simphonia' are scored in three parts – unison violins, unison oboes, and a continuo line. The middle (*allegro*) movement is for five parts, four of which are in the treble clef, but since not one of the parts is assigned to an instrument, it is entirely possible that Conti wanted the same or similar scoring to continue, with the upper two parts taken by violins 1 and 2 and the lower two by oboes 1 and 2.[26] In any event, the oboes appear to be restricted to the 'Simphonia', for nowhere else in the cantata does the scoring call for this instrument.

In the opening recitative, the soprano soloist is accompanied by four instrumental parts, of which three are in the treble clef. The upper two parts have no instrumental designation, but the third one is assigned to 'violini', with arpeggiated chords as its primary material.[27] This is followed by an aria accompanied solely by the continuo, at the conclusion of which is a separate twenty-three bar ritornello for five instrumental parts: violins 1 and 2, 'chalumeau', 'flute almande' and continuo. After an intervening recitative comes a second *da capo* aria scored for woodwinds alone – its three parts designated for 'chalumeau', 'flute almande', and 'basson' (chalumeau) – which has substantial instrumental ritornelli and thematic material reminiscent of that found in the last aria of the cantata 'Con più luci'. Another brief recitative introduces the third aria, with its five-part scoring assigned to violins 1 and 2, chalumeau, flute, and 'basso' (not 'basson'). Separating this aria from the next is a twenty-seven bar interlude for solo chalumeau and continuo. It provides more of a virtuoso part for the obbligato instrument than is available elsewhere in the cantata. This solo interlude is in G minor but instead of cadencing on the tonic chord, it pauses on the dominant before leading directly into the fourth aria, which is also in G minor. This aria opens with an exceptionally long introductory ritornello for three instrumental parts, none of which are designated. The ritornello represents an asymmetrical binary form in which both sections are repeated. When the voice enters, the three-part scoring continues, but now the parts are indicated to be chalumeau, flute, and continuo. The vocal portion of the aria is closely related thematically to the ritornello. It is also in binary form, but only the *B* section is repeated. In the first half of the aria, the voice and chalumeau are in unison, but

Example 8.3. 'Lidia già mi vedesti': second aria, bars 32-3

in the second half, it is the flute that is in unison with the voice. The aria concludes with a *da capo* of the entire ritornello. Immediately thereafter the final number is introduced. This dance-like aria in B-flat major and 3/8 metre begins with a fifteen-bar ritornello scored for five instrumental parts (none of them are specified) and a single vocal part designated 'coro'. During the vocal passages, the scoring is considerably reduced. Sometimes only the continuo accompanies the voice; at other times the accompaniment is provided by the continuo and instruments are assigned to the third and fourth parts.

In only one of the cantatas under discussion here does Conti write a separate part for the theorbo. 'Lidia già mi vedesti' (D/*B*: Ms. 21206) is scored for seven instrumental parts: oboes 1 and 2, violins *unisoni*, violetta, fagotto, tiorba, and cembalo. Although the cembalo is the sole instrument specified for the continuo line, this does not preclude the doubling of the part by other instruments. The occasional insertion of *violoncelli soli* as a directive for the lowest part provides the evidence.

The overall design of 'Lidia già mi vedesti' is R-A-R-A-R-A. The first aria is in a minor key and *andante* tempo; the other two are in a major key and are marked *vivace allegro*. The first three bars of the first aria open with the woodwinds (oboes and bassoon); in the next three bars, all of the other instruments are introduced except the theorbo. When the voice enters in bar 13, so does the theorbo, its part consisting basically of a realization of the cembalo line. Apart from the arpeggiation of the chordal structure, the theorbo is not given obbligato status here. That is reserved for the solo violin in the *B* section.

In the second aria, the theorbo assumes a much more independent role. Its part is notated in both the bass and tenor clefs and consists of an almost incessant flow of semiquavers. When notes of a longer value do occur, the theorbo usually transforms them into arppegiated chords. The full beauty of the instrument is exposed in the *B* section where more than half of that part of the aria is scored for theorbo, voice, and violin and the continuo part is silent (ex. 8.3).

The third aria is written in a *concertato* style, with tutti passages marking the structural divisions. This time the theorbo's part is thematically shared with the violin and is therefore much more melodic in content. The theorbo tends to double the continuo line during vocal passages, but in the fifteen-bar ritornello that opens and concludes the *A* section and the numerous instrumental interludes, the theorbo is given an opportunity to be featured in an obbligato role (ex. 8.4).

Another of Conti's cantatas scored for seven instrumental parts is *L'Istro*. Obviously the choice of instruments – two trumpets, timpani, violins 1 and 2 (doubled by oboes), viola, and continuo – was governed by the imperial celebration for which the work was composed. This particular cantata opens with

Example 8.4. 'Lidia già mi vedesti: third aria, bars 1-2, 6-7

Example 8.4. (continued)

a three-movement 'Introduzione', the outer movements of which use the full scoring while the middle movement is limited to strings.[28] Although the trumpets have a very active role in the overture, their use as obbligato instruments is reserved for the arias, of which there are three separated by two recitatives. The first and third arias are scored for the full ensemble; the middle aria is limited to four-part strings (doubled by oboes). The quality of writing in this cantata is such that it may well be one of the works that prompted Johann Scheibe to declare Conti to be one of the best cantata composers of his generation.

The text for the initial aria opens with the words 'Fra cetre e fra trombe' and, as might be expected, the trumpets have their most extensive exposure as obbligato instruments in this number.[29] In the exceptionally long ritornello, the trumpets, supported by the timpani, present thematic material which predictably remains anchored on the tonic and dominant chords (of C major). It is also this material that forms the opening phrase for the vocal part. Passages for trumpets and timpani alternate, in *concertato* fashion, with those for strings and woodwinds, the latter able to explore a wider range of the harmonic vocabulary. The antiphony between the two instrumental groups is carried to an even fuller dimension when the voice enters as a participant. In the course of the aria, Conti varies the orchestral colour and texture: duos for the trumpets, unaccompanied by any of the other instruments; a single trumpet paired with the voice, allowing both to display a level of virtuosity not possible with the full ensemble; violins 1 and 2 (doubled by oboes) unaccompanied by other instruments; trumpets accompanied only by the continuo; and passages for tutti. Since the *A* and *B* sections of this first aria are thematically related, Conti has to find other means to provide contrast between them. He does this by modulating to a minor key, focusing attention upon the singer rather than the instruments, and limiting the orchestra's participation (minus the timpani) primarily to brief interludes that separate individual vocal phrases.

In the second aria of *L'Istro*, Conti reduces the basso continuo to *violoncelli soli* during the vocal sections and returns to the tutti for the interludes. In the *A* section of the final aria, the singer is accompanied solely by the upper strings, the viola supplying the harmonic support.

In addition to the instrumental aspects of the fourteen cantatas under consideration here, other elements of their design are worthy of discussion. For example, the lively instrumental 'Introduzione' (in repeated binary form) which opens *Cantata allegorica* leads directly into an aria in a contrasting tempo (*Largo*), scored for strings with oboes doubling the violins. In the initial bar, the soprano sings (unaccompanied and *ad libitum adagio*) the word 'Fermate' and then continues (with orchestral accompaniment) with the *A* section of the aria. A self-contained *recitativo semplice* constitutes the *B* section, followed by a restatement, in an abbreviated fashion, of material from both the 'Introduzione' and the first section of the aria. The resulting scheme of the first two numbers is: 'Introduzione' (37 bars); aria: *A* (15 bars) - *B* (recitative) - *C* (12 bars of the 'Introduzione' and 10 bars of *A*). This asymmetrical structure, together with the various changes in tempo (*allegro assai, ad libitum adagio*, and *largo*), underscores the dramatic intensity of the text.

The third number in this same cantata would normally have been a recitative, but the expected pattern of alternation is not observed. Instead a second aria immediately succeeds the first, resulting in the following scheme: Intro/A-A-R-A-R-A. As unusual as the opening of *Cantata allegorica* may seem, precedent for similar variants in design can be found in a few cantatas composed for the court between 1700 and 1711. Examples include the opening of Antonio Bononcini's cantata, 'Vorrei, pupille belle', where a recitative occupies the *B* section of the first aria and the second aria immediately succeeds the first.

There is yet another aspect of the Bononcini cantata that bears comparison with Conti's *Cantata allegorica*. It concerns the use of dynamic colouring to aurally define structural divisions. In the first aria of 'Vorrei, pupille belle', Bononcini has the *A* section move in a dynamic range from *forte* at the beginning to *piano* in the concluding phrase. For the written-out *da capo*, however, he reduces the dynamic level proportionally, marking the beginning *piano* and the final phrase *pianissimo*. Coincidentally, a similar dynamic plan obtains in the first aria of *Cantata allegorica*. In addition, Conti couples the *pianissimo* of the final vocal phrase with a reduction in the instruments assigned to the continuo, signalled by the words 'senza cimbalo'. Given the unconventional treatment of the opening numbers and the similar handling of the dynamics for structural reasons, it raises the possibility that Conti knew Bononcini's cantata and used it as a model for his own.[30]

Rarely does Conti include sudden changes of tempo within an aria in his cantatas, but two such examples can be found in *Cantata allegorica*. In the second aria, 'Da un amor tutte innocente', both the eleven-bar introduction and the initial vocal phrase are to be performed *non allegro*. Then in bar 14, at the end of a vocal melisma on 'innocente', the tempo shifts briefly to *adagio* before moving back again to *allegro* for the instrumental interlude separating the vocal phrases. Since these changes in tempo occur in the *A* section, the *da capo* form brings them into special focus through a restatement of the material.

In the last aria of this same cantata, 'Contente ad altra riva', a change in tempo is used to accentuate the meaning of the text. The *A* section (bars 1-15) begins immediately with voice and continuo in an *allegro* tempo and triple (3/8) metre. It is followed by a *B* section of identical length for instruments alone, the three parts presumably performed by violins ('con haut.'), viola, and continuo. The next section begins with the first five bars of the initial *A* theme for voice and continuo, giving the impression that a *da capo* is taking place. By the sixth bar, it is clear that a different scheme is planned for this through-composed aria which, with respect to its design, may be unique among Conti's aria compositions. This *C* section presents the material of the two previous sections, phrase by phrase, with one phrase from *A* (modified) alternating with one from *B*. Approximately all of the *B* material is restated in its original form, including the triplet figure for the violins, played *senza haut.* and unaccompanied, whereas the *A* material is considerably transformed to accommodate the alternating pattern. At the beginning of the final sixteen-bar vocal phrase, Conti has inserted the words *non tanto allegro*, and then ten bars later he has reduced the tempo again to *adagio*.

Table 8.2

Internal structure of the aria 'L'aura dolce'

a	1-8	voice, lute, basso continuo
a		voice, lute, basso continuo (repeat signalled by sign)
b	8-16	voice, lute, basso continuo
b		voice, lute, basso continuo (repeat signalled by sign)
a'	16-32	violins, lute, basso continuo
a'		violins, lute, basso continuo (repeat signalled by sign)
b'	32-40	violins, lute, basso continuo
b'		violins, lute, basso continuo (repeat signalled by sign)
c	40-44	voice, tutti
c	44-48	voice, tutti (repeat written out)
d	48-56	voice, tutti
d	56-64	voice, tutti (repeat written out)
e	64-66	violins, lute, basso continuo (repeat of bars 17-18)
a'''	66-74	voice, tutti
a'''	74-82	voice, tutti (repeat written out)
b'''	82-90	voice, tutti
b'''	90-98	voice, tutti (repeat written out)
	98-102	voice, tutti (repeat of bars 94-98 of b''')

By so doing, he has caused the pace of the singer's phrase to gradually slow to a tempo that coincides with the last word she sings, which is 'andante'. As soon as the singer has completed her phrase, the tempo shifts abruptly to *allegro* for the seven-bar instrumental coda.

Basso continuo arias followed by brief instrumental ritornellos for a tutti ensemble were a commonplace feature of works composed prior to 1700. After that date, they became more the exception than the rule. Although examples can still be found in the cantatas composed by Badia, Ziani, and Bononcini between 1700 and 1711, they certainly are not numerous. Of Conti's cantatas selected for discussion here, only 'Fra queste umbrose piante' and *Cantata à due voci con instromenti* include ritornellos. The former cantata was described above; the latter has the design of Duet-R-A-Rit-R-A-R-A-Rit-R-Duet. In this particular work, the two arias given to the soprano are accompanied by the continuo. Both are followed by separate ritornellos, which are scored for a four-part string ensemble and are thematically related to the arias to which they are appended.

Four cantatas in Mus.Hs. 17593 conclude with arias that modify the *da capo* form by having a four-part (*AABA*), rather than a three-part (*ABA*), structure. This particular variant in the *da capo* form was achieved by having the instruments repeat the *A* section originally scored for voice and continuo. This general description, however, does not adequately describe the internal organization of material in the arias in question and therefore a diagram of one of them, 'L'aura dolce', the final aria of the second cantata in the manuscript ('Ride il prato'), is provided in table 8.2.

Although recitatives occupy relatively little space in the cantatas, they nevertheless present aspects of Conti's style that should not be overlooked. Those in 'Lidia già mi vedesti' show how he alters expected patterns of declamation to more effectively convey the emotional content of his text. Among elements used to achieve this are a series of vocal phrases outlining seventh chords in the opening measures of the first recitative and the use of chromaticism in both continuo and vocal parts to depict words such as 'martire' in the third recitative.

Symmetrical phrasing, clear tonal design, motivic development – all contribute to making Conti's cantatas effective compositions for twentieth-century performance. Whereas Scarlatti's melodies more often than not defy the barlines, Conti's seem to adjust well to the periodic framework in which they are positioned. Not only are his melodies created with distinctive rhythmic components, but they also are adaptable to either vocal or instrumental parts.

Notes

1   Johann Adoph Scheibe entered this assessment of Conti's cantatas on 23 June 1739 in his *Critischer Musikus*. Quoted in translation in Otto Eric Deutsch, *Handel: A Documentary Biography* (New York, 1979), 485.

2   See Stefano Mengozzi, ed., *Archivum musicum*, vols 28/29 for a recent facsimile publication of eight cantatas by Conti comprising A/*Wn*: Mus.Hs. 17953, along with recordings and performances of Conti's cantatas at events such as an early music festival in Austria.

3   See Lawrence E. Bennett, 'The Italian Cantata in Vienna, ca. 1700-1711' (diss., New York University, 1980) and his essay with a similar title in Brian Pritchard, ed., *Antonio Caldara* (London, 1987), 183-211. His study was limited to 100 cantatas by the five composers cited.

4   *Il Rosignolo* is contained in GB/*Lbm*: Ms. Add. 38036. *Innamoramento*, an undated cantata (R-A-R-A) by Conti for soprano and *basso continuo*, also appears to be a very early work. It is extant on fols 141r-146v of MS 697 in the Royal College of Music, London. Syncopated rhythms are to be found in both arias, but the vocal line in the first aria is considerably more complicated rhythmically than is normally the case in Conti's works.

5   See chapter three, for an explanation of this evidence.

6   Multiple manuscript copies of certain cantatas complicate the process of ascertaining the number Conti composed.

7   Three of these cantatas have orchestral accompaniment. The fourth, 'Per tacer il mio tormento', is for soprano and alto with *basso continuo* accompaniment. It exists in an incomplete handwritten copy in the Uppsala University Library (VMHS 53:15). Available are the first six numbers of what was most likely a nine-number work: D-R-A(soprano)-R-A(alto)-R-[A(soprano)-R-D]. At the conclusion of the third recitative, the soprano clef is cued for the forthcoming number, which presumably was an aria.

8   Not even the character being portrayed in the cantata text provides a fail-safe measure by which to determine the gender of the singer, though the shepherd would most likely be male and the nymph, female.

9   A possible exception to this statement may be offered by a *Cantata con 4 voce* attributed to 'Sigr. Conti' (Rheda Ms. 159), owned by the Universitäts- und Landesbibliothek of Münster. Although the title implies that four different solo voices are involved, there is no way to verify this, since the manuscript survives in an incomplete state. The extant portions of this cantata are limited to two arias: the first ('Mio cor tradito') is for solo soprano, 'violino primo', viola, and continuo; the second ('In certe dubbioso') is for solo alto, 'violino primo', and continuo. The vocal parts are notated with the *basso continuo*; the string parts are notated separately. It is possible that the cantata was scored for additional instrumental parts given the fact that the extant violin part is specifically designated as a 'primo' part.

10 'Mia bella Clori' is contained on fols 65r-70v in the Osborn Music MS. 22, so named for its presence in The James Marshall and Marie Louise Osborn Collection, The Beinecke Rare Book Library, New Haven, CT. In the upper right corner of the initial folio is written 'del Sigr. Conti', the basis for the attribution by Reinhard Strohm to Francesco Conti.

11 For a detailed description of the Osborn Ms. 22, see Reinhard Strohm, 'Scarlattiana at Yale', in Nino Pirrotta and Agostino Ziino, eds, *Händel e gli Scarlatti a Roma* (Florence, 1987), 113-52.

12 Ibid., 125.

13 The second recitative of 'Mia bella Clori' opens with two crotchets, a quaver rest, three quavers, and then two more crotchets. This distinctive rhythmic pattern also can be found in the opening bars of several other cantatas by Conti and may represent an element by which some of his vocal chamber works could be dated or at the very least grouped together. See, for example, the recitatives in 'Dopo tante e tante pene' and 'Lidia già mi vedesti'.

14 'Dopo tante e tante pene' is extant as a separate manuscript in Berlin (D/*Bds*) with the shelf number of Ms. 9065. *Innamoramento* is on fols 141r-146v in a collection of cantatas (CM-MS 697) in the Royal College of Music, London.

15 *Arioso* passages are not confined to Conti's early works. See his *Cantata allegorica* (1720) which introduces a brief (three-bar) *arioso* passage for the final cadence of the opening

recitative. The vocal line in this particular example, however, is considerably more melismatic than in the examples cited above.

16 Lawrence Bennett, 'The Italian Cantata in Vienna, 1700-1711' (1987), 189.

17 Fragments of some of Conti's cantatas with orchestral accompaniment survive. See, for example, his *Cantata con 4 voce*, cited above in note 9.

18 The viola part is usually signalled by the presence of an alto clef rather than by the name of the instrument. These seven cantatas represent only about a third of the extant cantatas which Conti scored with string accompaniment. Some of his other cantatas in which the accompaniment is limited to strings include 'Sventurata Didone!' and 'Già la stagion d'amore'. In August 1996, the Freiburger Barockorchester Consort performed both of these works at the Early Music Festival in Innsbruck, Austria.

19 Bennett cites 'Un guardo solo' by Badia as an example of a cantata with two undesignated parts in the bass clef and he theorizes that the lower one is for the continuo and the other, slightly more elaborate part, is for 'cello obbligato'. See his 'The Italian cantata in Vienna, 1700-1711' (1987), 193.

20 The fact that one part is for 'cembalo' is significant because it is the only example among these particular cantatas where the continuo line is so designated. In all other instances, it is merely assumed that the lowest part is to be played by one or more continuo instruments. Only the occasional directive, such as *senza cembalo, senza fagotto*, or *violoncelli soli*, offers a clue about the make-up of the continuo part. On page 258 of their study of the obbligato instruments in Conti's cantatas, Efrim and Caroline Fruchtman incorrectly indicate the continuo part for *Cantata à 2 soprani con instromenti* (A/*Wn*: Mus.Hs. 17582) and *Cantata à due voci, Clizia, e Psiche* (A/*Wn*: Mus.Hs. 17590) as 'Continuo à 2'. Neither the word 'continuo' nor the directive 'à 2' are found with the continuo parts in these cantatas (nor in any of Conti's other cantatas in this category). In both cases, the Fruchtmans misread the 'à 2' that appears in the margin of the initial and final numbers which are duets. The 'à 2' refers to the singers and appears directly below their names. The positioning of the 'à 2' happened to coincide with an area directly in front of the continuo part and therefore was interpreted by the Fruchtmans to mean that two instruments were needed to realize the continuo line. See their essay, 'Instrumental Scoring in the Chamber Cantatas of Francesco Conti', in James W. Pruett, ed., *Studies in Musicology: Essays in the History, Style, and Bibliography of Music in Memory of Glen Haydon* (Westport, CT: 1976), 250, 258.

21 'Con più luci' appears both as *Cantata Terzo* in A/*Wn*: Mus.Hs. 17593 and as a single self-contained cantata A/*Wgm*: Ms. 1471. It also has been published in Karl Schnürl, *Wiener Lautenmusik*, vol. 84 of the *Denkmäler der Tonkunst in Österreich*.

22 In those places where the instrumental melody goes as low as middle C, notes are supplied an octave higher with upward stems and the letter *c* positioned above them, indicating those notes are to be played by the chalumeau.

23 For a discussion of how Conti used the chalumeau in his dramatic works, see chapter nine.

24 The attribution of works to Francesco and Ignazio Conti made by Robert Eitner in his *Biographisch-bibliographisches Quellenlexicon* (III, 36) 100 years ago have, for the most part, stood the test of time. This particular cantata represents a copy made in haste and seems to have served both as a source from which performance parts were prepared and as the score

from which the continuo was realized by the cembalist. Evidence of this comes in the *B* section of the third aria, where a partial realization of the cembalo part is written out.

25 The term 'basson' has been used by Conti in connection with the word 'chalumeau' to refer to the bass register of this instrument. It has also been used without the attendant word 'chalumeau', but is meant to refer to the same instrument. The incipit for this cantata in the Darmstadt catalogue mistakenly shows bassoons (fagotti) are required for the scoring. Bassoons may have supported the continuo line, especially in the overture, but the score does not specify this instrument.

26 On the basis of the five-part scoring found in two of the vocal numbers, a different reading might also be argued for this particular movement, namely, violins 1 and 2, chalumeau, flute, and continuo.

27 In his opera *Penelope* (1724), a treble instrument (undesignated) is given similar material to perform, including chords that are to be arpeggiated.

28 The way the copyist prepared the manuscript suggests the first movement consisted of two sections, the fanfare and the fugue. Given the length of each section, however, it is arguable that they could be considered as two separate movements. It is this latter interpretation that appears in Efrim and Caroline Fruchtman, 'Instrumental Scoring in the Chamber Cantatas of Francesco Conti', 254. For a fuller discussion of this overture in relation to other overtures by Conti, see chapter seven.

29 Many of the arias in Conti's cantatas exist as separate manuscript items in libraries outside of Vienna. Seldom, if ever, are the original sources from which the arias are taken indicated. Such is the case with this opening aria from *L'Istro*, which is in the Staatliche Museen in Meiningen.

30 In 'The Italian Cantata in Vienna 1700-1711' (1987), 197, Bennett discusses dynamic colouring in cantatas written for Vienna by some of Conti's colleagues, noting that the cantata by Antonio Bononcini and several cantatas by Badia contain examples of the *A* section of an aria concluding with a final phrase performed *piano*.

CHAPTER NINE

The operas

Francesco Conti composed twenty-six secular dramatic works for the imperial court. Of that number, sixteen are full-scale operas (table 9.1). All but two of the operas in this category were presented during Carnival and therefore the productions usually took place in the opera house that adjoined the Hofburg, the winter residence of the imperial family. As mentioned in a preceding chapter, the Carnival season provided members of the court with various kinds of entertainment, including an opera which, if well received by the emperor, was performed three or four times during that same season. Usually only one full-scale opera was performed during Carnival and therefore few composers had an opportunity to become involved in this festive occasion. Caldara, for instance, was a court composer for ten years before one of his full-scale operas was brought to the stage as Carnival entertainment. His opportunity came in 1726, the year when illness forced Conti to relinquish his monopoly on this event. For that year and several years following, he composed the operas for Carnival, but as soon as Conti was able to resume his court duties, Caldara once again found himself without an opportunity to provide the Carnival opera. This occurred in 1732, when Conti brought forth *Issipile*, his final contribution for the Vienna stage.

Two of Conti's full-scale operas, *Il trionfo dell'amizia e dell'amore* and *I Satiri in Arcadia*, were not intended to be Carnival operas. Both are pastorales and were commissioned to celebrate the birthday of Empress Elisabeth Christina. They differ from the other full-scale operas in one important respect: each concludes with a *licenza*, a textual and musical appendage used to praise the life of the person in whose honour the opera was being performed. The form of the *licenza* could vary from opera to opera, but Conti's *licenza* usually consisted of three components: recitative, aria, and chorus. Whereas the choral number of the *licenza* is often nothing more than a repetition of the music (and even the words) of the final number of the main opera, the aria is invariably a newly composed number and is sung by one of the principal characters.

Table 9.1

Operas by Francesco Conti for Vienna in three or five acts

Year	Title	Acts
1706	*Clotilde*	?
1711	*Il trionfo dell'amicizia e dell'amore*	3
1714	*Alba Cornelia*	3
1714	*I Satiri in Arcadia*	3
1715	*Ciro*	3
1715	*Teseo in Creta*	5
1716	*Il finto Policare*	3
1717	*Sesostri, rè di Egitto*	3
1718	*Astarto*	3
1719	*Don Chisciotte in Sierra Morena*	5
1721	*Alessandro in Sidone*	5
1722	*Archelao, re di Cappodocia*	5
1723	*Creso*	5
1724	*Penelope*	3
1725	*Griselda*	3
1732	*Issipile*	3

Although other court composers frequently marked a birthday or name-day celebration with a full-scale opera, Conti preferred to offer shorter dramatic works based upon myths and allegories. His works in this category for Vienna, noted in table 9.2, can best be described as one-act operas, even though they lack the customary scene divisions. An exception to this description is *Il contrasto della bellezza e del tempo*, which is little more than a cantata for two voices. Its smaller dimensions were perhaps dictated by the occasion for which the composition was written, namely, the name-day celebration of Maria Theresa who was at the time only nine years old.

The three terms which appear as subtitles for the works listed in table 9.2 imply that they are descriptive of three distinct types of dramatic works. In actual practice, these terms are used somewhat arbitrarily to refer to the same types of compositions. The distinctions among them is tenuous and often impossible to

Table 9.2

Secular dramatic works limited to a single act and the *licenza*

Year	Title	Subtitle
1713	*L'ammalato immaginario*	? (see intermezzos)
1713	*Circe fatta saggia*	Serenata
1718	*Amore in Tessaglia*	Componimento da camera
1719	*Galatea vendicata*	Feata teatrale
1721	*La via del saggio*	Componimento da camera
1722	*Pallade trionfante*	Festa teatrale
1723	*Il trionfo della fama*	Serenata
1724	*Meleagro*	Festa teatrale
1726	*Issicratea*	Festa teatrale
1726	*Il contrasto della bellezza e del tempo*	Componimento da camera

discern. Indeed, there are examples of the same work bearing different subtitles. When it was first presented at the Hofburg theatre on 19 November 1719, *Galatea vendicata* was called a 'festa teatrale'. A slightly different musical version of the same libretto was performed at the Favorita on 1 October 1724, the birthday of the emperor, and upon this occasion *Galatea vendicata* was called a 'serenata'. Conti may have changed the subtitle to indicate that the score had undergone revisions or perhaps he wanted to differentiate the manner in which each version was presented. A report in the *Wienerisches Diarium* for Sunday, 1 October 1724, mentions that a 'serenata' was given in either the imperial dining room or gallery ('in dem Kaiserl. Speiss-Saal oder Galeria'), whereas the 1719 performance took place in the Spanish room of the Hofburg.

The musicians who participated in Conti's opera productions remained fairly constant throughout his tenure at the court. He used the same singers over and over regardless of whether the work being performed was a full-scale opera or a *serenata*, an indication that no less importance was attached to the shorter dramatic works. The cast for operas of the *festa teatrale* type varied from five to seven singers; the Carnival operas usually required as many as nine to eleven singers. Judging from the stipends of the musicians, it is apparent that Conti tended to limit his choice of singers to the highest paid and thus presumably the most talented of those available to him.

The librettists

The success Conti achieved as a composer of both serious and comic dramatic material was due to a number of factors, not the least of them being the close partnership he established with two of the court poets, Apostolo Zeno and Pietro Pariati. Zeno succeeded Silvio Stampiglia as court poet and court historian in 1718. Prior to this appointment, he had resided in Venice and from there his influence as a dramatist pervaded the opera productions for all of Europe. He was also a literary critic, as exemplified in his *Storia de' poeti italiani* and *Dissertazioni Vossiane*, and in his founding of the *Giornale de' letterati d'Italia* in 1710. Such diversity of interests brought Zeno into contact with a wealth of literature. It is not surprising, therefore, to find that Corneille and Racine influenced him even more than they did the poet Pietro (Pier) Antonio Bernardoni. Zeno drew heavily upon the French dramas as a source for his own librettos. Adaptation and literal translation were not beneath the dignity of the Italian master nor did he attempt to conceal his borrowing, as shown by one of his letters dated 27 September 1735 in which he acknowledges his debt to the French tragedians. One of Zeno's finest melodramas is *Astarto*, a work based upon two dramas by Philippe Quinault, *Astarte, Roy de Tyr* and *Amalasonte*.

Zeno also drew from Greek and Roman history for the subjects of his dramas. In no sense, however, were the resulting poetical works mere re-enactments of historical events. In the preface to the tenth volume of his collected works, he makes clear that it is the poet's 'privilege' to blend together history and fiction in such a way that it is no longer possible to distinguish what is true and what is false.[1]

Most of Zeno's dramas are organized into three acts, though there are a significant number that are in five, reflecting his acquaintance with the French tragedians. Zeno was more concerned with the action of a drama than with those contemplative moments which were to be expressed in music by the aria. The recitative was so central for his dramas that he exercised great care in writing those passages to the extent that little or no corrections appear in the manuscripts. In contrast to this, the text for the arias display haste in composition, and hence those portions of his manuscripts underwent many corrections.[2] Even more important is the fact that many scenes in his dramas make no provision for an aria, especially those that coincide with the apex of the dramatic action. This no doubt resulted from Zeno detaching the textual aspect of his dramas from the musical, a characteristic of the 'reform' libretto to which he and Metastasio, his successor at the imperial court, subscribed.

Conspicuously lacking from Zeno's dramas is the comic element, even when his librettos include the role of a servant. For instance, Elpino is a servant in *Griselda*, but here he is called a 'servo faceto di Corte', a term used to describe a character who was intended to be 'not humorous, merely weak'.[3] To what can this lack of comedy be attributed? Zeno offers a simple explanation. In a letter written to the Marchese Giorgio Clerici in Milan on 4 January 1717, he professes not to have the vocation ('non ho vocazione') for writing comedy.[4]

Zeno's dramatic works were collected in ten volumes and published by Giambattista Pasquali in Venice, the tenth volume appearing in 1744. Not all of the dramas in this collection were written by Zeno alone. In the preface to both the ninth and tenth volumes, he acknowledges that some of the works represent a collaborative effort with 'il Signor dottore Pietro Pariati'. The man with whom Zeno admits collaboration is a relatively little-known figure in the literary world. That he has been forgotten in the main stream of events does not mean that his contribution was insignificant, for as the chief librettist for both Francesco Conti and Johann Joseph Fux, his influence on the history of Viennese opera was considerable.

Pietro Pariati was born in Reggio, Italy in 1665. After earning his doctorate in 1687, he entered the field of government. By 1695, Pariaiti held the post of secretary to the Marchese Taddeo Rangone of Modena. When the latter was called to Madrid in 1697, he took Pariati with him.[5] The description of Pariati's sojourn in Madrid reads much like a libretto, for he caused no end of trouble for himself and his superiors while in that city. His drawing of the sword against the servants of the governor's household, his refusal to enter the church to hear the Easter gospel, his love affairs with chambermaids and with the daughter of his host, Pietro Paolo Divi di Garfagnana, were but a few of the scandalous escapades that did not go unpunished by the authorities. Thus, only six months after he had made his notorious presence felt in Madrid, Pariati was back in Modena, serving a prison term, first in the palace dungeon and then in the citadel. Conditions in the dungeon were so intolerable they caused Pariati to become very ill. His jailer took pity on him and wrote a letter of complaint on his behalf to the Duke of Rinaldo of Modena. This letter of 29 May 1699 was instrumental in having Pariati transferred to the citadel and, more importantly, in having the length of his sentence reduced.

By November 1699, Pariati was released from prison, but this did not mean he had redeemed his reputation. The Modena officials permanently expelled him from the duchy. This action brought serious hardship to his mother, two sisters, and a brother whom Pariati had supported since the death of his father. Forced to leave his native soil, he set out for Bologna, but finding nothing there to interest him, he continued on to Venice, where he settled down and attempted to make his living as a writer. Whether or not he had had previous experience as a writer remains unknown, but his initial efforts in Venice brought him little by way of financial gain. In fact, even after several years of living in Venice, he was still unable to fully support himself by writing. The financial stress, however, was not in proportion to the merits of his abilities, for his talent was recognized by none other than Apostolo Zeno.

It is difficult to believe that Zeno took an interest in this renegade from Modena; yet, early in 1703, he recommended one of Pariati's dramas for performance at the Regio Teatro in Milan. Four years later, in a letter to Federico Piantanida of Milan, he acknowledged that he and Pariati had established a working relationship. During the fourteen years Pariati resided in Venice, he produced a number of works, either in collaboration with Zeno or independently, that brought his poetic abilities to the attention of audiences far beyond the Venetian republic. Even before receiving an appointment to the imperial court, the Habsburgs had commissioned him to write *Ercole in cielo* (1710/1713), a *serenata*, and *Il voto crudel* (1712), an oratorio.

Zeno wrote several of his best dramas with Pariati, but the nature and extent of Pariati's contribution is often difficult to determine. There is also conflicting evidence about the authorship of some of the dramas published in the ninth and tenth volumes of Zeno's collected works.[6] Because of this uncertainty, it is of interest to study the respective careers of these two poets between 1714 and 1718, the period when they worked independently, the one in Venice and the other in Vienna. During this four-year period, Zeno wrote but one drama, *Alessandro severo* (1717), while Pariati wrote more than ten new dramas, several of which even contradict dramatic and poetic principles characteristic of Zeno's works.

Before Pariati left Venice, he requested permission from the Duke of Modena to return to his native city so that he might visit his relatives. Not only was the request denied, but the Duke of Modena also wrote to his Minister of State in Vienna in an attempt to raise objections to Pariati's appointment at the court.[7] Those objections went unheeded and Pariati assumed his official role as court poet in July 1714. The first collaborative work after this date that he and Conti produced for the court on 28 August 1714 was *I Satiri in Arcadia*, a 'favola pastorale'. It is surprising that Pariati would have offered a 'pastorale' for his official debut at the court. He had had little experience with this type of libretto, because Zeno had abandoned the 'pastorale' after creating three such works at the beginning of his career. Furthermore, *I Satiri in Arcadia* has no comic servants playing an integral part of the drama and no intermezzos interpolated between the acts. In other words, comedy has been omitted from this libretto. Why Pariati suddenly abandoned the kind of librettos he had been writing for Venice may never be fully understood, but this particular work certainly signalled that he was asserting his literary independence from Zeno. The *I Satiri in Arcadia* performance was but the first of a long run of successful operatic productions which Pariati and Conti brought to the imperial stage. *I Satiri in Arcadia* was almost as unusual for Conti as it was for Pariati, for this was only the second and final time that he set a 'favola pastorale'.

In 1715, Pariati wrote *Teseo in Creta*, a *dramma per musica* type of libretto, to honour the empress on her birthday. The text is divided into five acts, restricts the comedy to two intermezzos, and includes a *licenza*.[8] Equally as popular as the *dramma per music* at the Habsburg court were two other types of librettos, the *festa teatrale* and the *tragicommedia*, both known to the Viennese by the beginning of the eighteenth century. The *festa teatrale* was usually composed of many loosely connected scenes which provided ample opportunity for musical and spectacular elements. The Habsburgs were particularly fond of the *festa teatrale* because it had the potential to mirror the splendour and majesty of the court. Pariati, wishing to please his patron, chose to write a *festa teatrale* upon several occasions. Two of his best known creations of this type are *Angelica vincitrice d'Alcina* and *Costanza e fortezza*, both set to music by Fux.

The *tragicommedia* type of libretto had become well established at the court during the reigns of Leopold I and Joseph I, mainly through the efforts of Stampiglia and Bernardoni. Unlike the *dramma per musica*, the *tragicommedia* permits the servants, and hence comedy, to be a part of the drama. The comic element, therefore, can exist in varying degrees throughout the opera and need not be relegated to interpolated intermezzos. The first *tragicommedia* libretto for Vienna to credit Pariati as the author was *Il finto Policare* (1716). Included in the cast of nine characters are two comic servants who form an integral part of the drama. The development of the comic intrigue is confined, in this case, to the final scenes of Acts I and II, and to one scene near the end of Act III, positions that are analogous to those occupied by the intermezzos.

That Pariati may have been involved as early as 1714 with the writing of *Alba Cornelia,* a *tragicommedia*, for a Vienna production has been suggested by those who have studied his works. An early version of *Alba Cornelia* was staged at the Regio Teatro in Milan in 1704, but neither poet nor composer is mentioned in connection with that performance.[9] The Vienna version of *Alba Cornelia* has traditionally been assigned to Stampiglia and perhaps with good reason, for this is the very type of *tragicommedia* that was the hallmark of his libretto style, not only for Viennese audiences but also for audiences in the major Italian cities as well.[10] Moreover, Stampiglia was an official court poet, residing in Vienna at this time, whereas Pariati was still in Venice and had not yet assumed his position as a court poet. If Pariati did supply the libretto for *Alba Cornelia*, then it seems strange that so little attention was given to his contribution to the 1714 production.

The 1714 libretto for *Alba Cornelia*, as published by the Vienna firm of Cosmerovius, does not indicate the author of the work. The title page states the place, year, and occasion for the performance; it also gives the name of the composer of the opera, Francesco Conti, and the composer of the dance music, Nicola Matteis. Those who claim authorship for Stampiglia cite as their authorities the *Wienerisches Diarium*, which recorded performances of the opera on 5 and 7 February 1714, and Lione Allacci's *Drammaturgia*.[11] Those who attribute the libretto to Pariati do so on the basis of his possible involvement with the 1704 version of *Alba Cornelia* as well as with the 1726 Breslau and 1728 Brussels revivals of Conti's *Alba Cornelia* for which he is acknowledged to be the librettist. In the 1726 and 1728 versions, Pariati retained the essential format of the 1714 libretto, but he eliminated one of the characters, Lentulo.

The Milan libretto for *Alba Cornelia* had comic scenes added in the absence of the unnamed librettist. These consist of two scenes for the comic servants, Lesbina and Milo. The first is intended to be inserted as the sixth scene of Act I, placed immediately after a change of scenery; the other is for the ninth scene of Act III, the normal location for this type of scene in a final act. Both of these comic scenes are long and elaborate, resembling an intermezzo, for each consists of two arias, a duet, and the intervening recitative passages. A third comic scene, consisting merely of a recitative and a duet, is contained within the libretto at the end of Act II.

The 1704 and 1714 librettos of *Alba Cornelia* are similar, with two notable exceptions: the comic scenes appended to the 1704 libretto bear absolutely no relation to the comparable scenes in the 1714 libretto, and the two scenes at the beginning of Act III of the 1704 libretto are omitted in the later version. Other differences between the two librettos concern the number of changes of scenery, of which there are seven in the 1704 libretto and three in the 1714 version, and the manner in which the text is divided into scenes. Where the earlier version has a sequence of R-A-R-A for a single scene (Act III, Scene iv), the later version subdivides that sequence into two scenes, each containing a recitative and an aria. In other words, the 1714 libretto limits the number of arias in a scene to one, thereby creating seven additional scenes. The one exception to this principle of organization occurs in the comic scene (Scene xiii) for Act I. Here the sequence of R-A-R-Duet is similar to an intermezzo.

The 1714 libretto of *Alba Cornelia* represents a pivotal work wherein old and new concepts of design coexist. *Tragicommedia* works that Pariati produced for the court's entertainment beginning in 1715 are consistently anchored in the new style, wherein each comic scene is restricted to a recitative and an aria or an ensemble number in conformance with the ideal of the 'reform' libretto. Between 1715 and 1718, Pariati supplied Conti with five opera librettos: *Ciro*, *Teseo in Creta*, *Il finto Policare*, *Sesostri, rè di Egitto*, and *Amore in Tessaglia*. After 1718, he contributed *Galatea vendicata*, *La via del saggio*, *Creso*, *Archelao, rè di Cappadocia*, *Penelope*, and *Meleagro*.

As soon as Zeno was appointed court poet and took up residence in Vienna in 1718, the partnership of the two poets was activated once again and resulted in them creating several interesting works: *Astarto*, *Don Chiscotte in Sierra Morena* and *Alessandro in Sidone*.[12] Of these, *Don Chisciotte* was one of Conti's most successful operas. The title page of the score refers to the text as a *tragicommedia*; it fails, however, to mention the author of the text. The identity of the poets was certainly not intended to be kept a secret. One month before the performance when three of the five acts had already been set to music, Zeno wrote to this brother in Venice to tell him that Pariati had satisfactorily accomplished the creation of the 'ridicolo'.[13] Two days after the initial performance, 13 February 1719, Zeno sent a report to Andrea Cornaro in which he described the incredible applause given the opera production. He then mentions that Pariati deserves more of the praise for this success than himself.[14] Even Pariati could not resist letting some of the musicians know that the success of this comedy was in large part due to his effort. In a letter to Francesco Borosini, the tenor who sang the title role in the Vienna productions, he mentions that several serious scenes ('alcune scene serie') were written by his colleague Zeno, but that it was he who wrote the major part of the libretto ('la maggior parte cioè il restante è tutto mio lavoro').[15]

No one needs the letters cited above to be convinced that Pariati deserves credit for the major portion of *Don Chisciotte*, for here is a work that is essentially a *dramma eroicomico*, embracing a mixture of the comic and the pathetic.[16] The libretto is a faithful adaptation of various episodes from part I of Cervantes' *Don Quixote*. Included are three *buffo* characters – Rodrigues, Grullo, and Sanchio –

whose scenes are structured in a manner similar to intermezzos. Although the libretto was published in Vienna by Van Ghelen, it does not appear in the complete editions of Zeno's works.[17] This opera was destined to become one of Conti's most popular works in Vienna. It was equally popular in several other cities, with productions in Breslau, Hamburg, and Braunschweig-Wolfenbüttel.

Alessandro in Sidone is a five-act libretto but, unlike *Don Chisciotte*, it is written in a more conventional style of the *tragicommedia* in which the comic events are of lesser importance than the serious ones. Two comic characters – one a gardener, the other a slave to the philosopher Crate – participate in the drama and also develop their own intrigue in the concluding scenes of Acts II and IV. This opera required five and a half hours to perform, a fact noted in a letter Zeno wrote on 8 February 1721.[18] The manner in which he calls attention to the excessive length suggests that his operas were usually of much shorter duration. *Don Chisciotte in Sierra Morena*, however, required a five-hour performance.[19]

No doubt the success the *tragicommedia* had achieved at the court encouraged Pariati and Conti to continue to produce this type of entertainment for the Carnival operas of 1722 (*Archelao*), 1723 *(Creso)*, and 1724 (*Penelope*).[20] In the first two of these works, Pariati retained the five-act arrangement found in *Don Chisciotte* and *Alessandro in Sidone,* but he reduced the number of characters from eleven to nine. *Penelope* is divided into three acts and requires eight characters. In all three librettos, Pariati allowed the comic element to assume a more prominent position. He achieved this by increasing the number of characters involved in the comic intrigue and by augmenting the number of scenes in which these characters appear. Moreover, the position occupied by the comic scenes is not restricted to any one act or portion of that act. Therefore, in *Archelao* one finds two consecutive comic scenes at the conclusion of Act II and comic scenes at the beginning and end of Acts III and IV. Comparable situations exist in *Creso* and *Penelope.*

There is no question that the Vienna audiences were delighted by Pariati's librettos, for these operas enjoyed several performances within the same season. His natural affinity for using the libretto as a means for caricature and derision produced inherently funny and delightfully entertaining material. Pariati's works also seem to have had an influence upon the contemporary Viennese theatre, particularly upon the Wanderbühne who held forth at the Kärntnertor-Theater with plays which are sometimes termed 'Haupt- und Staatsaktionen'. The Wanderbühnen were touring companies who frequented market places and fairs. These companies wandered from town to town, entirely dependent upon the goodwill of the civil authorities and upon the generosity of their audiences. It was not until the opening of the Kärntnertor-Theater in 1708 that the Wanderbühne found a permanent home in Vienna, thus marking a new era for the popular play in that city.[21] The repertory of the Wanderbühne during the seventeenth century had been based upon plays of the English stage.[22] By the end of that same century, however, a new source for the German popular play was beginning to make its appearance, destined to overshadow all other models – the Italian opera libretto.

The manner in which librettos were adapted for use as popular plays was studied by Mary Beare.[23] She investigated, in particular, the sources for *Der Stumme Prinz Atis*, one of the 'Haupt- und Staatsaktionen' performed in Vienna during the month of August 1723. In brief, the history behind this manuscript is as follows: in the year 1678, Nicolò Minato wrote a libretto entitled *Creso* for which Antonio Draghi composed the music. In the same year, Johann Albrecht Rudolph made the first German translation of Minato's libretto. Six years later, Lucas von Bostel and Johann Forsch prepared *Der Hochmüthige, Bestürtzte und Wieder-Erhobene Crosesus* for performance in Hamburg. The libretto for this German 'Singspiele' was a direct adaptation of Minato's Italian libretto, a fact which Bostel acknowledged by the words 'nach d(em) Ital(ienischen)' written under his own title.[24] It is this 'Singspiel' which is believed to have been the direct source for the *Stumme Prinz Atis* manuscript in Vienna, which has the following information concerning two performances: 'Finito d. 27 March 1708, M. Dorcheus; Hoffman, Direc. Comicus., August 1723'.[25]

Mary Beare interpreted the above information in this way: in 1711 both the Velten and Elenson-Haacke companies were in Frankfurt-am-Main for the coronation of Charles VI. The Elenson-Haacke company proved so superior in its productions that many of the Velten troupe deserted to the rival company. One of these deserters may have been Doreheus and with him could have come a copy of the play given in 1708. Since the Elenson-Haacke-Hoffmann company was in Vienna from 1722 to 1724, it would have been possible for the 1723 performance to have taken place as indicated in the notation to the manuscript.

What was not taken into account in her interpretation is that earlier in this same year of 1723, Pariati and Conti had produced for the Carnival season an opera entitled *Creso*. It treats the same material which had been used by Minato for his *Creso* of 1678. The coincidence of Conti's opera and the aforementioned 'Hauptaktion' appearing only eight months apart leads one to conjecture that just as Bostel's 'Singspiel' was a parody upon Minato's libretto, so *Atis* may well have been a parody upon Pariati's text. If so, there may be a direct link between the court operas written by Conti and Pariati and the farcical entertainment of the popular stage. Of course, it is also possible that the impromptu stage influenced the work of Pariati, for parody plays a role in some of his librettos, such as *Archelao*.

Another possible link between Pariati and the 'Haupt- und Staatsaktionen' is to be found in the fact that the tenor role for the opera *Creso* was sung by Francesco Borosini, a singer who was not only cast in the title role of *Don Chisciotte* but had also appeared in almost every opera and oratorio composed by Conti after 1714. This fact becomes significant when it is noted that in May 1726 Borosini, along with Karl Sellier, took over the management of the Kärntnertor-Theater. As a result of this, a new dimension was added to the theatre repertory. Borosini was instrumental in introducing to the theatre a kind of Italian opera that ultimately became known as the Wiener Volksoper. According to Robert Haas, this Volksoper was really 'Parodieoper'; it derived its particular attributes from a combination of court opera and improvised farce. Borosini, who was undoubtedly acquainted wiht the work of the Wanderbühne as well as that of the court poets and composers, may well have combined elements of both to produce the parody opera at the Kärntnertor-Theater. If he did, then this would lend credence to the idea that the Volksoper was closely related to the tradition of the *tragicommedi*a developed by Pariati and Conti at the court.

Pariati and Zeno supplied almost all of the librettos for Conti's secular dramatic works performed in Vienna. The four other librettists whose names appear in connection with Conti's operas are Francesco Ballerini, (Giovanni) Claudio Pasquini, Pietro Metastasio, and Francesco Fozio.[26] Conti set two of Pasquini's librettos and one by each of the other three librettists.

The recitative style of the musical settings

The stylized attributes of *recitativo semplice* are responsible for the many tedious and dull passages of recitative that so often occur in a Baroque opera. This is especially true whenever the recitatives are excessive in length. The fault for this tedium does not rest solely with the composer. Often the text is completely devoid of action and emotion, offering no opportunity to the composer for variation of the monotonous *parlando* style. A case in point is the final scene of Act III of *Il finto Policare*, where the complications of the plot are untangled and resolved. The text is therefore concerned primarily with the revelation of mistaken identities and the uniting of several pairs of lovers. No new action is introduced; dramatic tension is at a minimum. As a result, Conti was faced with a text that had considerable length and little emotion in proportion to that length. In the ten folios of the manuscript where this text is set in a *semplice* style, Conti clearly demonstrates that he was as capable of turning out pages of uninteresting and uninspired recitative as were any of his contemporaries.

Had the Italians been less generous with the amount of recitative in their librettos, they might have remedied the sameness that continually plagues this aspect of the opera. At least this was the consensus among dramatists and composers associated with the Hamburg stage during the eighteenth century. They advocated brevity in order to heighten the effectiveness of the recitative.

Conti was capable of writing effective passages of recitative, as exemplified by the *licenza* to *Pallade trionfante*. Here the effectiveness is not contingent upon the brevity of the passage, but rather upon the internal design. This *licenza* opens with Giove addressing the assembled members of the court in *recitative semplice*. His text has one purpose – to extol the name of the Empress Elisabeth Christina – and since the text is very short, it can be declaimed within the space of twenty bars.

At first glance, there seems to be little here to distinguish this particular recitative from any other monologue written by Conti, for the individual phrases exhibit the conventions of the *semplice* style.[27] Closer examination of the passage reveals that this recitative has a tightly organized musical structure. It is divided into four distinct sections, each marked by a different type of harmonic progression in the continuo and by a different cadence pattern. The design is also articulated by the repetition of rhythmic patterns. Of the various combinations present among the vocal phrases, all but one are repeated at least once during the course of the recitative. Sometimes Conti repeats a pattern when it is to fulfil an identical function, as in the cadence patterns. At other times, the pattern is repeated immediately for special emphasis of the text or for purposes of continuity. Even more interesting is the manner in which Conti organizes the rhythmic and melodic details within an individual section. He emphasizes the rhetorical beginning of the recitative by setting the text with three musical elements which are not to be found anywhere else in this recitative. They include the highest note of the recitative, the singular use of an upward leap of a fifth, and a two-note motif with its repetition. Here then is a recitative that is limited to the stylized phrases and yet evolves into much more than a stereotypical piece of writing. The absence of dialogue and the conciseness of the text have permitted the composer to exercise greater control over the music, a further manifestation of Conti's preoccupation with formal design that was exhibited in the overture to *Pallade trionfante*.

It is in Conti's handling of the dramatic exigencies that arise from changes of mood, situation, or emotion that reveals his originality and imagination in setting the recitative texts. Act III, Scene vii of *Alba Cornelia* provides one such example.

This particular scene represents the climax of the drama, for here the tragic dilemma is brought into full view. The title character is confronted with the fateful decision of either being loyal to Rome or saving the person whom she loves from death. She reacts to this conflict with a whole gamut of emotions, from her pleading with Silla to her outburst of despair, and ultimately to her resignation. To express increased dramatic intensity, Conti uses a device which consists essentially of a rising bass line against a quasi-sequential figure in the vocal part. Twice he uses this device within the space of a few bars: first with the words 'Silla, Signor sospendi, odimi ancora' and then with the words 'Oh Amor! Oh Onor! Oh Patria! Oh Laberinto!'. Conti sustains the intensity of Alba's outburst of emotion by extending the musical phrase beyond the conclusion of her words. To avoid a cadence on 'Laberinto!', he overlaps the musical phrase so that the harmonic resolution coincides with Silla's 'Pronto risolui'. The use of the rising bass line against a sequential vocal part is found throughout Conti's operas. This device was not only characteristic of his recitative style but was also cultivated by later eighteenth-century composers such as Hasse and Jommelli.

The passage cited above also exemplifies how a change in mood can be effectively conveyed in the musical setting. Silla's demand for an immediate decision calls forth in Alba an abrupt change of attitude. Her ambivalence becomes resolution; her hesitancy resignation. Conti, therefore, must contrast the excitement of the first half of the recitative with the tranquillity of the second. He expresses the change by reducing the harmonic motion and by reversing the direction of the bass line. In addition to the descending progression in the continuo, further emphasis of Alba's submission and resignation is expressed in the vocal line that slowly descends through an octave from the words 'hai vinto' to 'morte'.

Another means for expressing a change in mood in recitative passages can be found in Act III, Scene v of *Il trionfo dell'amicizia e dell'amore*. In this scene, Tirsi is so overcome with passion for Licori that he vacillates between moments of sanity and insanity. Conti delineates these polarities of emotion by juxtaposing two contrasting passages of recitative. The first has a conjunct, well-organized melodic line and slow harmonic rhythm in the continuo while the second has a disjunct melodic line, consisting of wide and uncommon leaps and constant changes in direction, accompanied by a chromatically altered continuo line. Here Conti departs from the conventions of the *recitativo semplice* in order to call attention to a particular dramatic situation, whereas in the previous example he retained the conventions to create a similar effect.

Conti knew how to turn the stylized conventions of recitative into effective dramatic passages, for he recognized that any deviation from the norm could produce remarkable results. For example, sometimes he emphasized an important word or idea by having the vocal line exceed the range of an octave. To those who were accustomed to hearing the vocal line confined within the limits of an octave, such a procedure would call attention to the importance of that particular dramatic moment. This is undoubtedly why Conti composed the vocal lines for the title role of *Don Chisciotte* in the way that he did. He intentionally circumvented the conventions of the recitative style for the purposes of word emphasis and characterization. In Act III, Scene viii of *Don Chisciotte*, the recitative concludes with a striking drop in the vocal line that encompasses the distance of almost two octaves (ex. 9.1). Since the text does not seem to invite word-painting, one has to look for another reason for this special treatment. The most plausible explanation is that Conti is attempting to depict the deep bow so characteristic of Don Chisciotte's chivalrous manners. Whether the music was meant to accompany or anticipate this gesture is impossible to say. In either case, the music communicates to the audience, in a rather conspicuous way, the courtly deportment of the leading character.

Example 9.1. *Don Chisciotte in Sierra Morena* (Act III, Scene viii): recitative, bars 61-2

In Act V, Scene vii of this same opera, a similar treatment is in evidence, but here the music expresses a general attitude rather than a simple gesture. Conti uses Don Chisciotte's proclamation of his identity as an excuse to characterize the knight-errant's grandiose conception of himself. The stylized patterning of the vocal line in the recitative is modified with the introduction of an ascending and descending triadic melodic line that exceeds the range of an octave and the hint of a martial rhythm at the point of cadence. (ex. 9.2). Twice in the course of this recitative Conti interpolates two bars for a choral-type response by four of the characters, accompanied by the tutti ensemble, in support of Don Chisciotte's endeavour to defend his honour. At the conclusion of this recitative, the score directs that the trumpets should sound and the duel begin ('Suonano la trombe, e segue il combattimento').

A second, and perhaps more innovative, way in which to modify the conventional recitative is through the occasional use of tempo marks. Conti found this type of modification to be especially effective, for it contrasts noticeably with the normal performance style of recitative in which the singer is guided by the natural rhythm of speech. One such example can be found in the final scene from Act IV, Scene ix of *Archelao*. Here Sinopio, the comic servant, attempts to parody

Example 9.2. *Don Chisciotte in Sierra Morena* (Act V, Scene vii): recitative, bars 32-8

events that have taken place in the preceding scenes by pretending to be the king, Ariarate. Therefore when Mirena, the other servant, addresses him as Sinopio, he admonishes her to show him the respect due his royal position: 'First begin by saying, Sire!' ('Prima d'incominciar si dice Sire!'). She obeys by mimicking him, but then hastens to berate him for his roguery. Conti dramatizes this comic moment by directing both performers to sing the word 'Sire' *adagio* in order to assure the full effect of Mirena's mimicry. The verbal onslaught which follows is accentuated by an abrupt change in tempo from *adagio* to *presto*. Here, then, is an example where a momentary deviation from the normal pace of the *semplice* style dramatically heightens a few bars of the recitative. For the remainder of the passage, Conti simply relies upon the text to communicate the comedy.

Act V, Scene vi of the *Don Chisciotte* score provides one of the rare examples where Conti introduces obbligato instruments into a recitative. This scene consists of a recitative, a through-composed number for four-part chorus alternating with solo passages sung by Dorothea and accompanied by a six-part ensemble of strings and *corni da caccia*, and finally a brief recitative in which Conti has the *corni da caccia* (unaccompanied) restate the opening bars of the choral section to frame one of Don Chisciotte's utterances. The *corni da caccia* help to create the atmosphere that will prevail in the following scene where Don Chisciotte prepares for battle (ex. 9.3).[28]

Example 9.3. *Don Chisciotte in Sierra Morena* (Act V, Scene vi): second recitative, bars 3-6

Conti can also set an entire recitative in such a way that the whole number rather than a few bars of it evokes the desired reaction in the audience. At the beginning of Act III, Scene ii of *Il trionfo dell'amicizia e dell'amore*, Batto bursts upon the stage, full of news concerning Delmira. Before he can actually relate his news, Silvandro interrupts him and he continues to interrupt so that the news the audience is waiting to hear is never forthcoming. Batto is never given a chance to speak. He is interrupted again and again as he tries vainly to proclaim what he knows. The basis for the comedy, of course, is found in the text; yet, the comic suspense is complemented by a series of half cadences and motivic sequences. Conti distinguishes between the positiveness of Batto's entry and the confusion of the interruptions by the type of harmonic progression with which each is accompanied. The I-IV-V-I progression of Batto's opening words contrasts with the succession of diminished seventh chords and their half-cadence resolutions which accompany the flurry of questions asked of him. Moreover, the excitement which the interruptions cause is highlighted by the repetition of motifs outlining the notes of a single harmony and by the brief four-part choral interjection (bar 16) sung by the four characters in a recitative style, just two bars before Batto concludes the recitative.[29] Here Conti weaves together text and music to produce an artistic unity of musical design and animated dialogue.

Other means Conti uses to enliven his recitatives include the use of unusual intervals to express violent emotions. One such example occurs in the recitative in Act I, Scene ii of *Il finto Policare* where Conti pairs chromaticism in the continuo with an abrupt leap of more than an octave on the word 'crudelissimo' to convey the feeling of rage. A more unique manner of expressing a similar kind of emotion is to be found in Act I, Scene iii of *Il trionfo dell'amicizia e dell'amore*, where Conti simply eliminates the continuo for one and a half bars to dramatize Silvandro's despair. A third means he uses upon rare occasion to guide the performance of dramatic passages of recitative is the addition of dynamic markings.[30]

The characteristics of Conti's *recitativo semplice* remained fairly constant in his secular dramatic works until his last opera. In *Issipile* there is a noticeable change in the frequency with which this type of recitative is used. In his setting of Metastasio's text, Conti greatly reduces the amount of *recitativo semplice* and increases the use of *recitativo stromentato* to set dramatically intense sections of the libretto. In his other operas, the *recitativo stromentato* is either not used at all or is reserved for isolated passages of extreme emotion.[31] That is not the case in *Issipile*. Rather than reserving the *stromentato* for one or two climactic scenes, Conti moves freely from one style of recitative to the other according to the exigencies of the text. It is significant that this change in style is also evident in the only other work Conti composed in 1732, the oratorio *L'osservanza della divina legge nel martirio de' Maccabei*. Why Conti suddenly altered his manner of setting the recitatives in 1732 is difficult to explain. Perhaps the change can be attributed to the influence the Metastasian drama exerted on his style of composition or to the influence his peers may have had on him, for coincidentally this change in Conti's approach to the recitative mirrors the general trend of the period.

Another way Conti varies recitative passages is to interpolate sections into an *arioso* style. One rather unique example of the *arioso* style being injected into a *recitativo semplice* number occurs in Act II, Scene vii of *Griselda*. In this passage of intense emotional conflict, a zealously confident Ottone offers Griselda two equally unacceptable choices: either she must marry Ottone and thus betray her fidelity to her rightful husband, the king, or she must suffer the death of her son at the hand of her suitor. The dialogue focuses on the word 'crudeltà'. Griselda, unable to resolve the fateful dilemma which confronts her, accuses Ottone of cruelty and pleads for mercy. Ottone returns the charge, claiming that her refusal of love and faithfulness is a cruelty that merits no mercy. Conti accentuates this seemingly unresolvable conflict by not only alternating passages in *recitativo semplice* and *arioso* but also alternating two different types of *arioso* passages to delineate the different emotions expressed by the two characters. To Ottone's caustic accusation, set in *semplice* style, Griselda responds in an *arioso* style.

Resolute, yet helpless, Griselda pleads for mercy. The tonality is minor; the tempo, *adagio*. The vocal line is angular and rhythmically intense, while the continuo descends with pulsating regularity. Conti contrasts Ottone's response to Griselda, for although it is given in an *arioso* style, he states it in a major tonality and an *allegro* tempo, with a rapid flow of notes in both the vocal and continuo parts. Conti further accentuates the contrast between the two characters by extending portions of their texts. In order to emphasize Griselda's quest for mercy he singles out 'pietà' for repetition. To convey Ottone's essentially selfish and demanding nature he repeats the final words 'anch'io da te' of the phrase 'Pietà voglio anch'io da te' ('Mercy I also want from you'). The dialogue then resumes in the *semplice* style.

There is another reason why Conti employed special means to delineate these two characters at this particular point in the drama. Their responses mark the turning-point in the opera. Griselda's virtue has withstood the temptation of Ottone and, since the consequences of the decision are irrevocable, Ottone's plans are doomed to frustration. It is clear, then, that the effectiveness of this entire scene does not depend solely upon the interjection of the *arioso* style into the recitative but rather upon the juxtaposition of two different interpretations of the *arioso* style itself. Conti's use of an *arioso* passage within the *semplice* style of recitative is, by this date, a well-worn convention of *opera seria*, but Conti takes up this convention and uses it creatively. It is in the adaptation that Conti reveals his merit as a dramatic composer.

The aria style of the musical settings

The majority of the arias in Conti's operas begin with an instrumental ritornello. Since the thematic material of this introductory ritornello is usually repeated during the course of the aria in the vocal part or the accompanying parts, it is the orchestra rather than the voice that normally establishes the mood and basic affection. Conti adopted a basic pattern of aria organization: *A*: ritornello I, stanza I, ritornello I; *B*: stanza II; *da capo* of *A*. Superimposed upon this pattern are variants, one of which involves the repetition of the first stanza of text within the *A* section. Although the repetition of the text can occur immediately as in the aria 'Se in verra' in Act I, Scene vi of *Don Chisciotte in Sierra Morena*, it is more likely to occur after a mediant ritornello separating the two statements of stanza I. More than half of the arias in *Don Chisciotte* have this variant of the basic *da capo* design, with an abbreviated form of the introductory ritornello providing the thematic material for the mediant ritornello.

Another variant of the basic pattern involves a repetition of the mediant, rather than the introductory, ritornello at the conclusion of the *A* section. This asymmetrical design occurs most often in those arias where two distinct thematic ideas are expressed in the initial ritornello. From these two, Conti selects one, usually the second, as the thematic material for the mediant ritornello and then restates that same ritornello in the tonic key to conclude the section. An excellent example of this variant is Tisaferne's aria 'Sei per noi quell' aura' in *Archelao* (Act IV, Scene ii). Here the orchestral introduction consists of seven bars with bars 1-3 containing one thematic idea and bars 4-7 a second. The similarity of the thematic material in these seven bars requires Conti to further distinguish them by their scoring. The first theme is scored for violins and viola; the second is for the full ensemble of strings, woodwinds, and continuo.

In arias with instrumental introductions, thematic material presented by the violins in the opening bars is frequently restated and developed by the vocal part. Whenever the violin theme is figurative rather than melodic, as in Nettuno's aria 'Se senza sdegno' from *Pallade trionfante*, the vocal part introduces material that is independent of the opening ritornello. A slightly different relation between introduction and voice obtains in Tisaferne's aria 'Sei per noi quell'aura' cited above. Here it is apparent that Conti does not utilize the introductory material presented by the violins for precisely the same reason as in Nettuno's aria from *Pallade Trionfante*. He does, however, use material contained in the initial three bars of the viola part for the opening vocal phrase. In so doing, he transforms what was merely a rather banal instrumental part into a stately vocal line.

An example of an even more complex relation between introduction and vocal part obtains in Cardenio's aria 'Con la fedel' from *Don Chisciotte* (Act II, Scene vii). Conti neither repeats the introductory instrumental material nor does he create a vocal line divorced from the ritornello. Within the fourteen-bar ritornello to this aria there are seven or more motifs, any one of which could be used by the vocal part. Conti does, indeed, use several of them, yet neither their original order nor their original function is preserved in the vocal part. Instead of starting with the initial violin phrase, Conti creates the head motif for the vocal part by repeating the final three notes with which the viola concludes the ritornello. He follows this with a motif derived from the violin part in the third and fourth bars of the ritornello. By continuing the process of adapting motifs from the introduction for use by the voice, Conti is able to create a vocal line that is at once related to, and independent from, the instrumental material. In other words, even though he draws virtually all of the thematic material used by the voice from the orchestral introduction, he combines the material in such a way that a contrasting melodic pattern is produced.

In the majority of Conti's arias, the *B* section is proportionally shorter than the *A* section. There are, however, a significant number of arias in which the two sections are nearly equal in length. The arias in *Meleagro*, for example, exhibit this type of symmetry. Seldom, however, is there much by way of contrast between the *A* and *B* sections, save for a shift in tonality. If contrast does exist, it usually arises in response to the requirements of the libretto. Such is the case with the aria 'Numi eterni, a voi prostrato' in *Pallade trionfante*, with the text of the *A* section assigned to a single character and that of the *B* section to a chorus. The aria 'Crudo amore' which concludes Act I, Scene xiv of *Issipile* offers yet another type of contrast. The heroine, torn between her love for Giascone and her filial duty toward her father, expresses extreme anguish over this dilemma which is nothing less than the essential conflict of the entire drama. Conti dramatizes this inner conflict of emotions by contrasting the tempo and orchestration of the *A* and *B* sections: *A* is marked *adagio* with only *basso continuo* accompaniment; *B* is marked *presto* and has a four-part string accompaniment. A third type of contrast appears in 'Qui sto appresso' from *Don Chisciotte* (Act IV, Scene x). The *A* section is accompanied by a *basso ostinato* figure; this ground bass pattern, however, is relinquished in the *B* section where the vocal part is accompanied by a non-repetitive bass line.

So consistently does Conti begin his arias with an instrumental introduction that any deviation from this norm can produce strikingly dramatic effects. Evidence of this can be seen in *Issipile* which contains only one aria that begins immediately with a vocal phrase. It is to be found in the penultimate scene of Act I, where Issipile, in order to save her father's life, informs Giascone falsely that she participated in the mass slaughter of men on the island and killed her father, the King of Lenno.[32] Giascone, who had already sworn revenge upon her father's murderer, reacts with horror, then with silent disbelief, as he stares at his wife. Issipile breaks the silence and asks 'Perchè mi guarda e taci?' ('Why do you gaze at me in silence?'). Instead of continuing the recitative dialogue with his wife, Giascone responds immediately with the opening line of his aria 'Ti vo cercando in volto di crudeltade un segno' ('I seek thro' all that lovely face some marks of cruelty to trace').[33]

Conti's arias often defy classification for, unlike some of his contemporaries who were apt to wed certain affections with specific types of arias, his do not seem to adhere to any underlying schematic arrangement. A stock aria in Conti's operas is primarily a musical phenomenon, divorced from the exposition of a specific affection. In his operas there are a surprisingly large number of arias requiring a *largo* tempo.[34] Some, of course, are related to dances such as the saraband. In fact, many of his opera arias are strongly influenced by dance music. Sometimes the derivation from a specific dance type is acknowledged with the labelling of the aria as a *menuetto* or a *sarabanda*, but more often than not Conti incorporates into his aria style stereotypical patterns of various dances without regard for authentic ascription to any specific type. One of the most frequent types of dance arias in his operas is characterized by an *allegro* tempo, a 3/8 metre, a folk-like melody, and a purely homophonic accompaniment. Although this type is often designated *menuetto*, it nevertheless seems more related to the Italian *corrente* or French *passepied* than to the more stately minuet in 3/4 metre. Among the other dances represented in his arias are the *gigue, gavotte*, and *siciliano*. Of these, the *siciliano*, with its 12/8 metre, slow tempo, and 'siciliano rhythm', is particularly distinctive. It is found in nearly every one of his operas, but is found most frequently in the works written before 1716. Each of his pastoral operas contain several examples.

Madrigal-style arias, which Van der Meer considers a distinctive feature of Fux's opera style, are also present in Conti's operas.[35] This type of aria, which generally lacks any indication of tempo, is in duple metre, has a time signature of 2/2 or a variant of the same, emphasizes crochet and minim motion in both the vocal and instrumental parts, involves some degree of polyphonic writing in the accompaniment, and is usually scored for a four-part string ensemble doubled by oboes and bassoon. There are only three examples of this type of aria in Fux's operas, the earliest occurring in *Psiche* (1720/1722). By contrast, Conti not only used this type much more frequently than Fux, but he also did much earlier, introducing it in *Alba Cornelia* (1714). The number of times Conti uses the madrigal-type aria varies from opera to opera. Generally there is one in every opera, with notable exceptions being *Astarto*, which has none, and *Il finto Policare*, which has five.

Although the *da capo* aria form prevails in Conti's works, it is important to note that some of his finest arias disregard this form entirely and are through-composed. Not every secular dramatic work by Conti includes a through-composed aria. Operas such as *Il trionfo dell'amicizia e dell'amore* and *Issipile* lack this type; several operas have only one through-composed aria. Nevertheless, Conti seems to write through-composed arias far more frequently than many of his contemporaries. For example, only one aria of this type is to be found in all of Fux's operas. The decision to set an aria text in a through-composed manner, however, was not made by the composer. It was the librettist who determined when and where the stanzaic form and usual rhyme scheme would be abandoned in order to accommodate a particular dramatic situation, such as that found in *I Satiri in Arcadia* (Act III, Scene iii). In this scene, Mirtella relates a story to Damone and Egisto as she sings her aria 'Entrate il Lupo'. If a *da capo* form were used in this situation, Mirtella would find herself retelling the beginning of her story.

'Entrate il Lupo' presents a highly organized structure based upon an alternation of vocal and instrumental phrases of approximately equal length; each vocal phrase introduces new melodic material while the instrumental interludes restate material presented in the initial three bars of the aria. The introductory ritornello, therefore, not only establishes an idyllic mood with its siciliano thematic material but also provides a unifying element for the entire number.

The unemotional quality of this aria's non-strophic text and the repetitive nature of the interludes might have produced, at the hands of a lesser composer, a monotonous number. Conti, sensing the danger of unrelieved sameness, modulates in a chromatically ascending pattern in order to increase the dramatic intensity. Not only does he devise a tonal scheme to heighten the text, but he also constructs the aria so that the shift from one tonality to the next coincides with the beginning of each new interlude.

Obviously the through-composed aria is most appropriate for the narration of a story, but it is by no means limited to this kind of dramatic situation. For example, the mounting dramatic tension developed during the first four acts of *Teseo in Creta* culminates in the through-composed aria 'Foschi orrori' which begins the fifth and final act. In order to accentuate the critical nature of this dramatic moment, the scene opens not with the expected *recitativo semplice* but with a through-composed aria in which Arianna expresses her anxious contemplation of Teseo's horrible fate in the Labyrinth. In contrast to the aria in *I Satiri in Arcadia* cited above, Arianna's aria, because of its emotional intensity, is fragmented and amorphous. Moreover, it ends inconclusively as Arianna moves into a *recitativo semplice* passage, followed by an extended passage of *recitativo stromentato*, the very style which one might have expected to find used for this entire scene.

One the finest examples of Conti's through-composed arias is to be found in *Griselda* (Act II, Scene ix).[36] The heroine, having been banished from the palace, returns to the forest where she had lived before her marriage to King Gualtiero. The ninth scene of Act II opens with Griselda seated upon a bed in a rude hut. Exhausted from despair and disillusionment, she addresses the words of her aria to sleep ('sonno'), to which she gradually succumbs. The means Conti uses to portray Griselda falling asleep are conventional – the descending chromatic line, the gradual shortening of the vocal phrases, the increasing number of rests between vocal phrases, and the cadencing of the final vocal phrase upon the dominant rather than the tonic – but the manner in which Conti moulds these conventions into a dramatic and musical unity is noteworthy. In the first two-thirds of the aria, the vocal line, characterized by conjunct melodic motion and phrases of approximately equal length, is doubled by the first violin part. In the final third, as Griselda shows signs of fatigue, the vocal part no longer shares in the exposition of the melody and assumes a subordinate role as it descends chromatically to the lowest note Griselda sings in the aria. Not only is this aria descriptively effective. Its impact upon an audience is further heightened by the relief which it brings to the endless succession of *da capo* arias.

Among the various characteristics of Conti's melodic style that are of interest is the rhythmically distinctive figure which appears in the aria 'Con la fedel' from *Don Chisciotte* (Act II, Scene vii). It is characterized by a syncopated pattern in which the rhythmic stress is placed upon the second rather than the first beat of the bar and it reappears throughout the aria in various melodic guises. Conti's use of the syncopated figure in this particular aria, however, is not typical of his compositional style, for Conti generally exercises considerably more restraint in his incorporation of it into his melodic vocabulary than is evident here. In this regard, 'Sei per noi quell'aura' from *Archelao* would more accurately typify his use of this device, for in this aria the syncopated motif is introduced as the primary motif of the second vocal phrase and in this position creates effective contrast with the initial vocal phrase. Although Conti normally confines the use of this syncopated figure to melismatic passage or secondary motifs, he does occasionally permit it to form the basis for the initial vocal phrase of an aria. Two striking and almost identical examples are afforded by the opening bars of the arias 'Quel misto colore' from *Il contrasto delle bellezza e del tempo* and 'Fa ch'ei tolga al suo rivale' from *Archelao*, with the latter illustrated below (ex. 9.4).

Example 9.4. *Archelao* (Act IV, Scene vi): aria, 'Fa ch'ei tolga'

Not all composers were as discerning as Conti in the use of the syncopated figure within their arias. Reinhard Keiser, for instance, used it repeatedly in his opera *Croesus* (1730), but does so in a rather haphazard manner. Further evidence of Keiser's indifference to the possibilities which such a device could add to his melodic style if used with moderation can be seen in his opera *Der lächerliche Printz Jodelet* (1726). Here, instead of reserving the device for a particular melodic effect, he draws it into the melodic material for most of his arias and thus allows the syncopated figure to become a mannerism. Some of Conti's other contemporaries in Vienna and elsewhere in Europe also availed themselves of this same syncopated figure, so much so, in fact, that it was doomed to become a worn-out cliché before the end of the third decade of the eighteenth century.[37]

Another element of Conti's melodic vocabulary is the simple consecutive repetition of a motif three (or more) times on the same degree of the scale. Such motivic repetition seems not to have exerted an appreciable effect upon his vocal style in the operas until 1719, for although he occasionally introduced it into his arias composed prior to that date, he did so primarily as an element of the instrumental, rather than the vocal, material. It is with the opera *Don Chisciotte* that the reiteration of a motivic pattern at the same pitch becomes associated as much with the vocal as with the instrumental parts and occurs frequently enough to be considered a characteristic of his melodic style. Sometimes this repeated motif appears as a self-contained unit, detached from the subsequent phrase by a rest. At other times, it is directly connected to the material that follows. In the opening vocal phrase of 'Care selve' from *Griselda* (Act II, Scene v), the repeated motif becomes a means to build a climactic phrase, for the tension which steadily increases at the beginning of the melodic line is released on the long-held note and resolved by the succeeding vocal melisma (ex. 9.5). By forming an integral part of a much longer phrase, this device can achieve quite a different effect from the simple reiteration described above.

Example 9.5. *Griselda* (Act II, Scene v): aria, 'Care selve'

ca - re __ sel - ve a voi ri - tor - - - - no

In some of Conti's early operas, there are long instrumentally conceived melismatic passages for the voice in both the *A* and *B* sections of an aria. In the later operas, such passages tend to be extremely limited and are usually confined to the *B* section. Whenever melismatic passages do occur in the later operas, they tend to be well controlled, motivic in design, and with their intricate marks of embellishment and complex rhythmic patterns may even resemble a written-out example of how a singer might have improvised the ornamentation of a melodic line. This kind of melismatic writing can be found in the *B* section of the aria 'Tu non sai' from *Issipile* (ex. 9.6). There is at least one notable exception to the use of extended vocal melismas in the later operas. It occurs in *Il trionfo della fama*, which has more melismatic vocal passages than any of his other operas, not only in the arias but also in the duet. The melismatic type of writing permeates the uppermost instrumental part, be it violin or bassoon, for the instrument and voice present much of the same material, either in dialogue or in unison.[38] It is conceivable that the occasion upon which this opera was performed, namely the coronation festivities in Prague in 1723, dictated this type of melodic writing to display the vocal talents of his cast.

Example 9.6. *Issipile* (Act II, Scene vii): aria, 'Tu non sai', *B* section

The gradual reduction in the number of melismatic passages in the later operas appears at first glance to be a contradiction of Conti's intention to glorify the virtuoso powers of his singers. Upon closer examination, it is apparent that what changes is the appearance of the score and not the opportunity for a singer to ornament the vocal material. Conti replaces the extensive vocal melisma with a single note prolonged by the voice for several bars against which the orchestra provides some melodic figuration. In actual performance, the singer no doubt embellished these long-held notes. His scores also provide opportunities for vocal cadenzas, signalled by the word *adagio* above the final cadence of one or both of the aria's two sections. Occasionally the vocal part will begin with a phrase that is to be sung *ad libitum*, a phrase which contrasts in tempo and melodic contour with the thematic material that follows. Usually this *ad libitum* phrase is very short, giving the singer merely the harmonic framework in which to extemporize a cadenza-like passage. On rare occasions, Conti even suggests to the singer the way in which he expects the *ad libitum* passage to be performed.

One of the most consistent features of Conti's operas is his use of interesting bass arias. With *Sesostri, Il contrasto della bellezza*, and *Issipile* notable as exceptions, almost all of his operas and shorter dramatic works have at least one bass soloist included in the cast. One might conclude from a cursory glance at the *dramatis personae* of *I Satiri in Arcadia* and *Teseo* that these operas should also be listed as exceptions, for the only male singers listed as performers, not counting the castrati, are the tenors Silvio Garghetti and Francesco Borosini. The arias in these two operas assigned to Borosini, however, are written in both the tenor and bass clefs, and although his arias are slightly higher in range than those usually sung by the bass soloist, they are, nevertheless, similiar in style to the serious bass arias found elsewhere in Conti's operas.

The scores of Conti's secular and sacred works confirm that Borosini was indeed a most gifted and versatile performer. He, of course, sang an exceptional number of regular tenor roles in Conti's operas and oratorios; yet, he was equally adept at singing a true bass role, for such was the role of the general which he portrayed in *Ciro*. From this, it becomes apparent that Conti created the baritone roles in order to exploit rather than to accommodate the range of Borosini's voice. This singer's versatility as a performer is further revealed by the fact that the characters he portrayed were as varied as the vocal parts he sang. Since he was cast in both leading and supporting roles, he was never identified with any specific type of character. One can find him playing the part of a king (*Archelao*), a philosopher (*Alessandro in Sidone*), a tyrant (*Sesostri*), and a god (*Pallade trionfante*). Perhaps his most outstanding stage appearance at the court was his portrayal of the title character in *Don Chisciotte in Sierra Morena*. His part was designed for a baritone in what was undoubtedly the most dramatically demanding role conceived by Conti. The character of this knight-errant, Don Chisciotte, is not easily positioned into a specific category. He is strictly speaking neither a comic nor a heroic character. His role is used to parody medieval chivalry in a way that, because of its very ludicrousness, borders upon the tragic. Is it not possible that in this case Conti chose to have the leading role sung by a baritone because he saw that the singer's range, which spans the tenor and bass clefs, mirrors the tragicomical nature of the character?

In contrast to the baritone roles which occur in less than half of Conti's operas, the roles created specifically for a bass voice are to be found in nearly all of his secular dramatic works. Of these, the serious bass roles were generally sung by Christoph Praun (also spelt Braun in the opera manuscripts), who appeared in Conti's operas between 1718 and 1732. Unlike Borosini, who portrayed various character types, Praun was generally cast in a supporting role, often as a confidant to the leading character. Occasionally, in some of the shorter dramatic works, he was given a role dramatically equal to those sung by the rest of the cast, as in *Pallade trionfante*, where he portrays the god Neptune, and in *Il trionfo della fama*, where he represents the allegorical figure Valore. Only in the oratorios, such as in *Naaman* and *L'osservanza della divina legge*, is the bass singer apt to be cast in a leading role.

In addition to the roles performed by Praun, some of Conti's operas also include comic bass roles. These were usually assigned to Pietro Paolo, whose name appears in Conti's manuscripts between 1715 and 1724. The comic bass roles, however, are far less numerous, since only a few of the Carnival operas incorporate comic servants into the plot rather than reserving them for the intermezzos. In several of the Carnival operas, baritone, serious bass, and comic bass roles are included within the same work, namely in *Il finto Policare*, *Don Chisciotte*, *Alessandro in Sidone*, *Archelao*, and *Creso*.

Conti exercised great care in the composition of his numerous bass and baritone arias. Frequently, they serve as vehicles for some of his more creative and distinctive musical ideas. He was sensitive to both the character being portrayed and to the dramatic situation, and therefore tended to be flexible in his handling of the internal design of these arias. It is precisely for this reason that it is difficult to generalize about his arias in this vocal range. Indeed, if one were to examine carefully all of the various forms and techniques used in these bass/baritone arias, one would be able to comprehend the total scope of his aria style, for not only does he employ here nearly all of the devices and forms found elsewhere in his operas, but he also introduces new musical ideas into them. The fact that the bass singer was cast in supporting roles, therefore, does not mean that his arias were secondary in importance or mediocre in musical design. On the contrary, there are occasions when the bass singer, although portraying the role of a minor character, may sing arias which are far more important, dramatically and musically, than his supporting role would seem to allow.

The aria 'Spento il foco', which immediately precedes the dramatic turning point in *Il finto Policare* (Act II, Scene iii), exemplifies this point well. In this opera, the bass singer plays the role of Aristone, a minor character; yet, because the text of his aria reveals to the audience the ultimate solution of the dramatic conflict, he has one of the most important arias in the entire opera. In addition, his aria happens to be musically one of the opera's more elaborate numbers. Conti underlines the significance of this dramatic situation by introducing the madrigal-type of aria discussed above in which the voice functions as one of the imitative parts in the contrapuntal texture. From this it is evident that the bass arias can be as important and well crafted as any accorded a prima donna.

Although there need not be any appreciable differences between an aria for a bass singer and those for the other voices in the cast, there are inevitably certain elements of the melodic style which are generally associated with arias for this vocal range: the repetitive use of a descending scale pattern, the double-cadence pattern, and above all the disjunct contour of the melodic material. In the example cited from *Il finto Policare* and in the bass aria 'Sei per noi quell'aura' from *Archelao*, one can find these features, but here they seem almost incidental to the creation of the vocal material. In many other bass arias, especially those in the shorter dramatic works, these same features are far more prominent. The excessive angularity of the vocal line and the extreme range demanded of the singer suggest a somewhat less than noble character. Conti uses these means of exaggeration to accentuate the pomposity of the god, Nettuno, in *Il finto Policare*, and to depict the grotesqueness of the giant, Polifemo, in *Galatea vendicata*. Almost invariably the nature of the character to whom such an aria is assigned borders upon the ridiculous; yet Conti is always in control of the mood to be communicated and manages to draw a fine line between the demonic and the comic. This is particularly significant in the shorter dramatic works, for they do not include *buffo* characters in the cast.

Another type of aria which a bass or baritone might sing is the heroic aria. The text for such a number generally involves either a call to, or a reflection upon, combat and acts of bravery. Those elements of musical style which are characteristic of the heroic aria include long melismatic passages with instrumental-like figuration, considerable repetition of individual words in the text, and an 'all' unisono' accompaniment of the vocal part. Conti's interpretation of the heroic style differs noticeably from that of other contemporary composers because he does not include obbligato trumpet parts in the orchestral accompaniment. Sometimes the martial character of the trumpet is imitated by the violins with a tonic-dominant motif repeated in the manner of a trumpet fanfare. More often, however, there is no suggestion of the brass instruments which play a colourful and descriptive part in the heroic arias by Alessandro Scarlatti and Handel. Although the heroic aria is found occasionally in Conti's operas, it is less common here than in the works of some of his contemporaries; this is because his librettist gave him few opportunities for its use. It should be noted that even when the text does lend itself to this type of aria, Conti does not always manifest great care in composition. For example, the bass aria 'Se al riposo' which opens Act I of *Ciro* is one of the weakest arias in that opera. Actually Conti's best arias in the heroic style are those he created for the title role in *Don Chisciotte*: 'Corro incontro' (Act I, Scene iii) and 'Sono un fulmine' (Act III, Scene x). Both arias were meant to be, or at least had the effect of producing, a parody upon the heroic type of aria. According to Hellmuth Christian Wolff's study of the Hamburg version of *Don Chisciotte in Sierra Morena*, these arias are but two instances of the sustained satire which pervades this entire opera.[39] Admittedly, the ambivalent and paradoxical character of Don Chisciotte makes it difficult for one to discern what is meant to be a parody and what is not. Nevertheless, that this was Conti's intent seems to be indicated by arias in some of his other works.

In 1718, the year before *Don Chisciotte* had its initial performance in Vienna, Conti set the text 'Sono un fulmine' for a bass aria; it appears as the opening number of the Intermezzo I which was performed with *Astarto*. In this intermezzo, Terremoto's aria was meant to be a comic parody. Since it probably served as the basis for the 'Sono un fulmine' aria sung by Don Chisciotte, its function was undoubtedly the same in both cases, despite the fact that in the later work it appears in a serious rather than a comic context.

Another aria that exemplifies Conti's parody of the heroic style is 'Uh! Che guerra', sung by the *buffo* base in *Penelope* (Act I, Scene ii). In this particular case, there is no ambiguity about Conti's intentions, for the text itself constitutes the parody. Tersile, instead of lauding the power of war and the honour of combat, presents a coward's version of battle. In order to communicate the comic nature of this text, Conti uses several obvious, yet very effective, musical devices. At the outset, the orchestra, through exaggerated use of motivic repetition, indicates to the audience that the aria to follow will be far from serious. In the course of the aria, the comedy is accentuated with word-painting in the vocal part designed to simulate gun fire and the noise of battle, and in the orchestral accompaniment to simulate the firing of a cannon (ex. 9.7). By these devices, Conti allows the orchestra to become a participant in the dramatic action. He also removes one of the features common to regular heroic arias, namely the excessively long melismatic passages. Through this omission he again signals to the audience that this aria is nothing less than a parody.

Conti achieves considerable variety in the instrumental accompaniments for his arias. The opera *Il trionfo dell'amicizia e dell'amore* (1711/1723) reveals his penchant for experimenting with instrumental combinations, a trait that prevails

Example 9.7. *Penelope* (Act I, Scene ii): aria, 'Un che guerra!' bars 25-41

in the only other major works he composed prior to his official appointment as a court composer, *Il Gioseffo* (1706) and *Il martirio di S. Lorenzo* (1710/1724). In these three works it is the number of different instrumental combinations rather than the combinations themselves that accounts for the marked difference between the accompaniments for arias written before and after 1714.

In *Il trionfo dell'amicizia e dell'amore*, the continuo aria predominates, with approximately one-third of the arias limited to this type of accompaniment. This same proportion of continuo arias to other types of accompaniments continues until the composition of *Teseo di Creta* in August 1715. From that time until October 1724, continuo arias can be found in Conti's operas, but they are few in number. With the second version of *Galatea vendicata* (1724), continuo arias disappear completely from Conti operas. This sudden change in Conti's style was probably not just the result of personal preference, but was instead symptomatic of the era in which he was composing. Alessandro Scarlatti and Handel also gradually abandoned the continuo aria during this same period. Why the change in Conti's style occurred so abruptly in 1724 is a difficult question to answer; it may simply be one facet of a more general change in his concept of aria accompaniment that manifested itself after October 1724.

The next most frequently used instrumental combination for the aria accompaniments in *Il trionfo dell'amicizia e dell'amore* is the full ensemble scored for three or four parts, and although rarely specified, the instrumentation was presumably for strings reinforced by oboes and bassoon. The viola part in Conti's scoring does not serve merely as a harmonic filler. It often plays a fairly independent and active role in the presentation of the melodic material, as illustrated by the aria 'Quel bel core' from *Meleagro*. Here the viola part is the prime expositor of the instrumental melodic material, as indicated by the three-part scoring for 'viole, violoncelli', and *basso continuo*. Conti's use of either the three- or four-part accompaniment is governed essentially by his need to vary the texture of his *da capo* arias. It is also governed by his desire to accentuate the importance of certain singers by reserving the four-part accompaniment for their arias. With this rudimentary means of characterization, Conti is able to differentiate between an aria sung by the prima donna and one sung by a lesser character such as the comic servant. He does not, however, use the four-part texture to enhance the growing intensity of dramatic situations. In this he differs from Alessandro Scarlatti who, in his operas composed before 1705, frequently delayed the introduction of this instrumental combination until the final aria of Act I, increased the use of the combination in Act II, and then concentrated upon its use throughout Act III – all to graphically portray increasing dramatic tension. As the continuo arias decrease in number throughout the succession of Conti's operas, those accompanied by the four-part tutti increase proportionally as the predominant type of orchestral accompaniment, becoming by 1724 virtually the sole type for his arias.[40]

A wide variety of textures and instrumental combinations appear in the operas composed prior to 1724. Often Conti is able to achieve this variety without introducing any instruments that are foreign to his basic string–woodwind orchestration. While his two-part accompaniments tend to be primarily composed of some combination of violins and continuo, they can also exhibit a more imaginative scoring. For example, the aria 'Spiega quel aquila' from *Circe fatta saggia* is scored for 'violoncelli unisoni' and 'violone, fagotti, e cembalo'. Even more striking is the accompaniment for the aria 'Se senza sdegno' from *Pallade trionfante* in which the strings are divided into a seven-part texture which produces a *concerto grosso* orchestral combination: 'Tre primi violini', 'Tre secondi violini', 'Violini primi', 'Violini secondi', 'Viole', 'Viole', and *basso continuo*. This interest in the manipulation of the strings to produce interesting orchestral effects had already been expressed by other composers writing for the imperial court. Antonio Maria Bononcini's oratorio *Il trionfo della grazia*, to cite but one example, has an aria scored for four solo violins, two cellos, and a string bass.

Conti provides additional orchestral colour through the introduction of instruments not normally contained within the regular tutti ensemble. Seldom, however, does he include more than one or two of these obbligato instruments within a single opera. Only *Il trionfo dell'amicizia e dell'amore* possesses an exceptional amount of instrumental colour, for Conti has added as many as eight different instruments to the basic scoring. As diverse as these accompaniments are, they do not include the trumpet. Conti introduces this instrument in three other operas – *Ciro, Don Chisciotte,* and *Il trionfo della fama* – but not in connection with an aria. Instead, the trumpet appears in the scoring of an overture, an instrumental interlude, and several choruses. This is in stark contrast to the way the trumpet was used in many contemporary operas, as discussed above. Although a few martial scenes and a significant number of heroic arias can be found in Conti's operas, none of them are scored with trumpets. Whenever Conti wanted to achieve a trumpet-like effect, particularly in those scenes involving a crowd (chorus), he did so with two *corni da caccia*. He also incorporated the *corni da caccia* into the six-part accompaniment for the heroic aria 'La bella nemica' from *Griselda* (Act II, Scene viii) and into the five-part accompaniment for 'De le fere', an aria sung by the title character in Act I of *Archelao*.[41]

Oboes and bassoons are included within the normal tutti ensemble, but seldom does Conti feature either of these instruments in obbligato roles. One of the more prominent positions accorded the oboe is in Act III, Scene xii of *Il finto Policare*. Here the comic servants sing a duet in which the accompaniment consists of an alternation between the tutti ensemble and a woodwind trio (oboes [1 and 2] and bassoons). The bassoon is given slightly more recognition as a solo instrument, and is not merely relegated to the performance of a continuo line. For example, in *Il trionfo della fama*, the aria 'L'Asia crolla' is scored for three parts: 'fagotti [1 and 2]', and 'violoncello e contrabassi senza cembalo'.[42]

Only once did Conti include the flute in one of his operas. He did so in an aria in *Il trionfo dell'amicizia e dell'amore*, where it is scored with chalumeau, viola, and bass chalumeau doubled by violoncello. By contrast, the chalumeau holds a prominent place as an obbligato instrument for aria accompaniments. Since Conti associates the chalumeau with introspective and quiet moods, such as might prevail in contemplative or pastoral scenes, he tends to use this reed instrument within the context of a thinly-scored texture. Hence, one is apt to find the chalumeau acting as the primary instrument for either a two- or three-part accompaniment with the lowest part scored for continuo or for 'basson chalamaux senza cembalo' as in *Teseo in Creta* (Act IV, Scene ii).[43] From 1706 to 1717, the chalumeau can be found in both Conti's opera and oratorio scores, but after 1717 it completely disappears from his dramatic works, except during the revival of earlier works which originally included the instrument. Its disappearance coincides with the general trend in Conti's operas away from the use of instruments not contained within the tutti ensemble.

Given the fact that Conti was a stellar theorbist, it is surprising that he incorporated the theorbo as an obbligato instrument in only three of his operas: *Il trionfo dell'amicizia e dell'amore*, *Galatea vendicata*, and *Archelao*. A typical, yet outstanding, example of the theorbo used in this capacity can be found in the aria 'Se mai dal crudo' from *Archelao* (Act IV, Scene vii). Particularly characteristic are the long instrumental introduction, the alternation of melodic and chordal passages for the theorbo, and the comparative neglect of the singer. Conti uses no single type of instrumental combination or texture with the theorbo, although he does seem to prefer using the theorbo in dialogue with the violoncello and omits the *cembalo* from the continuo line.

It is curious that Conti's use of the theorbo has been emphasized in writings about his music, but there is seldom any mention of his use of the mandolin, which appears in the accompaniment of four arias. While the theorbo, in its solo passages, is confined to a range that extends from one octave above middle C to two octaves below, the mandolin range is centred within the two octaves above middle C. The style of the arias accompanied by either mandolin or theorbo was established as early as *Il Gioseffo* in 1706. The difference between arias accompanied by the mandolin and those accompanied by the theorbo lies essentially in the range of the solo material performed by the instrument, and not in the nature of the material itself nor in the relationship between the obbligato and vocal parts. One of the most unusual orchestral combinations Conti created

Example 9.8. *Il trionfo dell'amicizia e dell'amore* (Act II, Scene ix): aria, 'Dei colli nostri'

was for the accompaniment of 'Dei colli nostri', an aria in *Il trionfo dell'amicizia e dell'amore* (Act II, Scene ix): '2 Mandolini accordati un tuono più basso, et Arpe, Primo Baridon, Secondo Baridon, Senza Cembalo, Contrabasso, e Violoncello'.[44] The mandolins are divided into first and second parts, doubled at the unison with parts for two harps and at the octave below by two barytons (ex. 9.8).[45] Twice Conti uses theorbo and mandolin within the same opera. In *Il trionfo dell'amicizia e dell'amore*, mandolins are introduced in the aria cited above and the theorbo accompanies an aria in Scene xiii of this same Act II. In the 1719 version of his *Galatea vendicata*, mandolin and theorbo appear together in the final aria of the opera which which is preceded by a separate 'Introduzione'. In the 1724 version of this opera, Conti scores the entire aria for a regular four-part tutti ensemble. This change in instrumentation reflects a broader stylistic change noticeable in the operas he composed after 1724, namely, the scoring is basically restricted to the instruments of the tutti ensemble and to a four-part texture.

The ensemble style of the musical settings

The importance of the vocal ensemble (duets, trios) in a Conti opera is directly related to the length of the work. In the shorter dramatic works, where the chorus plays a significant role, the ensemble has a relatively small part or no part at all. For example, there are no duets or trios in *Pallade trionfante*, *Meleagro*, or *Issicratea*. In the full-length operas, which contain few choruses, there may be as many as six ensembles. Most of these are either duets or ensemble finales. Both the frequency and the position of duets within the context of an opera are governed by the librettist; yet even he is somewhat restricted by the conventions of *opera seria*. The duet is usually introduced at that moment in the dramatic action when two characters, especially a pair of lovers, express a union of affection, but since both characters must exit immediately thereafter, the number of times when the duet can be used is rather limited. Furthermore, although comic duets are commonly placed at the end of an act (particularly at the end of the first and second acts of a three-act opera), the serious duet seldom occupies this position.

Conti's ability to write a dramatically moving duet in which the characters are well defined is nowhere better illustrated than in the oratorio *Il Gioseffo*, his earliest extant work. The famous biblical conflict between the virtuous Joseph and Potiphar's voluptuous wife is beautifully expressed by the duet 'Un ciglio sereno'. The struggle implicit in the text is projected into the musical setting and reveals Conti's ability to delineate musically a conflict of sentiments. The serious (as opposed to the comic) opera duets seldom present any such conflict between the characters. In fact, the opposite effect, harmony of thought or purpose, is normally the *raison d'être* for the creation of this type of duet. As a consequence, there is little need to contrast the two vocal parts and therefore they frequently move together in parallel thirds. Some duets seem to be little more than a single melody divided between two voices. Others give the impression of differentiated vocal parts by having one imitate the other, especially at the beginning of a phrase.

A very effective example of Conti's duet style is to be found in *Griselda* (Act II, Scene x). In this scene, Costanza discovers Griselda asleep. When she awakens, they engage in conversation, each describing the fate that has befallen her. Evidence points to the fact that Costanza is the daughter of Griselda, but the coincidence is so perfect that they dare not believe what seems to be the truth. Although the characters do not draw the obvious conclusion from their conversation, the music reveals to the audience the relationship which actually exists between the two apparent strangers.

While most of the serious duets in Conti's operas emphasize the accord which exists between two characters, his comic duets generally express conflict, because the basis for the comedy is frequently a genuine or feigned argument in which each person is given an opportunity to reveal his or her own distinctive character. To delineate these distinctions, Conti generally assigns different melodic material to each vocal part. Throughout the entire duet 'Guarda che insolenza' from *Il finto Policare* (Act I, Scene xv), the delicate and lyrical vocal phrases of Serpilla, who pretends to be a princess, contrast with the reiteration of a conventional *buffo* motif based upon octave leaps, sung by the servant, Volpastro. Conti's comic duets also exhibit several other features which tend to set them apart from his serious duets. Perhaps the most obvious difference concerns the excessive repetition of the text. In both his arias and serious duets, Conti prefers to repeat an entire stanza rather than individual words or short phrases. In the comic duets, instead of stressing the unity of the stanza, he fragments it by repeating over and over again small segments of the text. Particularly characteristic is his persistent reiteration of such words as 'si', 'nò', and 'oh' to contrast the two sides of an argument, and his rapid alternation of phrases which makes one singer appear to be interrupting the other singer. This treatment of the text inevitably produces a comic duet that is considerably longer than a serious one. Two striking examples of the extreme length of these duets are to be found at the conclusion of the second and fourth acts of *Alessandro in Sidone*.

Sometimes a duet represents the culmination of a sequence of musical numbers that are all based upon the same music. One such example occurs in Act V of *Teseo in Creta*: Piritoo's aria in binary form and accompanied by continuo is followed by Carilda's aria based on the same music but scored for three instrumental parts *senza continuo*, and this in turn is followed by a duet sung by Piritoo and Carilda which again is based upon the music of the first aria, only this time scored for four instrumental parts.

One of the most interesting duets created by Conti can be found in the final scene of Act II of *Don Chisciotte in Sierra Morena*. At this point in the opera, Sanchio, recently appointed governor of Nicomicon, takes leave of Maritorne, whom he no longer considers worthy of his love. Conti has given this duet the form of a chaconne based upon the 'Folia d'Espagno' theme. It is presented first in the introductory ritornello, then sung successively by Maritorne and Sanchio, and finally, when both characters join together to sing, the 'Folia' theme is used to accompany their vocal parts. Variations upon the chaconne theme are effected through changes in tempo (*allegro, presto, largo*) and texture, and through embellishment by both the voices and the orchestral accompaniment. Wolff considers this duet to be one of the greatest musical parodies in Baroque opera.[46]

Conti's librettists provided him with many occasions when a duet could be used, but they seldom included a situation which would call for a trio. In fact, only two trios are to be found in Conti's operas, whereas four appear in his intermezzos. In almost every case, little distinction occurs among the three vocal parts with respect to the thematic material. At the same time, the trios are organized so that two voices are paired against the third. An interesting example is the trio from *La via del saggio*.

The practice of concluding a dramatic work with a choral finale is observed by Conti. In most of his full-scale operas, the finale is an ensemble performed by the main singers of the cast. Unlike the finales by some composers which merely bring the 'Scene ultima' of an *opera seria* to a close with a few measures in chordal style, the concluding 'coro' in Conti's operas assumes the proportions of a well-defined number, usually composed in *da capo* form. Generally his finales are scored for a four-part vocal ensemble (SATB) with the vocal parts doubled by instruments. Exceptions to this occur in *Sesostri* and *Issipile*. Here the final 'coro' for each is limited to three vocal parts (SAT) because neither opera includes a bass singer (excluding the *buffo* bass). With chordal texture and triple metre, Conti's finales produce a gay, dance-like mood for the inevitable happy ending.

In his full-scale operas, Conti avoids having a choral number open an opera except in *Teseo in Creta*. This exception can perhaps be explained by the fact that *Teseo* was performed for a birthday celebration of the empress. For such an occasion, an opening chorus was undoubtedly expected because it served, as did the prologue in a French opera, as a vehicle for the expression of homage to the imperial family. This explanation is also borne out by the fact that most of Conti's shorter dramatic works, which were designed for the same type of imperial celebration, begin with a choral number, the exceptions being *Pallade trionfante* and *Il contrasto della bellezza*. In both *Teseo* and the other shorter dramatic works, the choruses are sung by a separate group of singers instead of by the soloists of the opera cast. In some of the shorter works, the chorus is used only to open and/or conclude the opera. In a few, it may also appear at other places in the work. *Galatea vendicata* offers one of the best examples to illustrate the varied ways in which Conti constructs and uses the chorus. Not only does the chorus function here as a kind of prologue and epilogue; it is also used several times in the course of the opera as a commentator upon and a participant in the dramatic action. Nor does Conti confine himself to the use of a four-part (SATB) chorus or to the usual tutti orchestral accompaniment. Perhaps the most unusual scoring occurs in the chorus 'Più non batta', which is scored for a 'Coro di Ciclopi' comprised solely of tenors and basses and a seven-part instrumental ensemble. Twice during this opera, Conti takes the material from one chorus to create another. The opening chorus, for instance, which features a 'tutti' chorus (SATB) and a 'solo' chorus (SAT), reappears in a modified and contracted form after two intervening arias. The music of the final chorus is also repeated as the concluding number of the *licenza*. This practice of reusing musical material from one chorus for another is by no means confined to *Galatea vendicata*; it is a feature common to his other shorter dramatic works.

One of the more complex examples of this practice is to be found in the opening chorus from *Circe fatta saggia*. The opera begins with what at first seems to be a *basso continuo* aria sung by Circe, but after eleven bars the aria cadences on a dominant chord and a chorus enters with tutti orchestral accompaniment. The whole number, which alternates sectionally between solo voice and chorus, can be illustrated as follows:

A:	solo voice and continuo	11 bars	C major
	chorus and tutti orchestra	22 bars	C major
B:	solo voice and continuo	7 bars	A minor
	chorus and tutti orchestra	14 bars	A minor
A:	(*da capo*)		

After this opening number, the opera continues with a recitative sung by Circe alone, followed by a repetition of the choral part from the *A* section of the initial *da capo* number. Circe again enters with a passage of recitative which is once more followed by the chorus, this time with a repetition of the choral part from the *B* section of the opening number. This rondo scheme created by the reuse of choral sections can also be found in Fux's operas.

The choral numbers in *Circe fatta saggia* are set for five vocal parts (SSATB) and, therefore, may have been sung by the five soloists in the cast rather than by a separate chorus. Moreover, there is no mention made of a separate chorus in the list of *dramatis personae*. If this is the case, *Circe fatta saggia* would be unique among Conti's shorter dramatic works, because all the others appear to employ separate choruses. This is, in fact, one of the ways in which the one-act and full-scale operas differ, since the choral numbers in most of the full-scale operas are written for the principals rather than a separate group of singers. *Il trionfo dell'amicizia e dell'amore*, *I Satiri in Arcadia*, and *Teseo in Creta* are exceptions to this statement, for their choral numbers are designed for a group of singers other than those in the opera cast. It should also be noted that Conti's use of the chorus in the full-scale operas need not differ greatly from his use of it in the one-act operas. In other words, the chorus does not have to be confined solely to the finale; instead, it can form a part of the drama itself. This is illustrated by Scene iii of Act II in *Il finto Policare*. Here the chorus is used as an integral part of the drama to express the approval of all the characters of Ladice's decision to marry Policare.

An interesting use of the chorus as a basic factor in the organization of an act is to be found in the opera *Don Chisciotte in Sierra Morena*. At the beginning of Scene iv of Act V, only two characters are on stage; as the next two scenes unfold, others are added so that almost all are on stage for Scene vi. At this point, Don Chisciotte is challenged to meet a giant in a duel. He accepts the challenge and the giant is summoned by the sounding of the *corni da caccia*. In order to convey a feeling of the passage of time spent awaiting the arrival of the giant, Conti introduces the chorus. In the remaining scenes of this act, the chorus is also used to convey the thoughts and emotions of the spectators who witness this duel. These interjected comments by the chorus constitute just a few bars of interruption in the flow of recitative each time they occur. Act V concludes with a grand choral finale in a *da capo* form.

It is clear from the preceding discussion that Conti's concept of the opera chorus did not differ appreciably from that held by Fux. Homophonic texture, dance-like characteristics, and a *da capo* or rondo form – all these features are present in opera choruses created by both composers. It is true that Fux appears to use the chorus more frequently, but this is undoubtedly because all of his extant operas were written expressly for birthday or name-day celebrations of the imperial family, the very occasions when Conti also emphasized the chorus.

Notes

1   Apostolo Zeno, *Poesie drammatiche*, Gasparo Gozzi, ed., vol. 10 (Venice, 1744).
2   Max Fehr, *Apostolo Zeno (1668-1750) und seine Reform des Operntextes* (Zurich, 1912), 88.
3   Nathaniel Burt, 'Opera in Arcadia', *The Musical Quarterly* (April, 1955), 162.
4   Apostolo Zeno, *Lettere* (Venice, 1785), II, 402.
5   Naborre Campanini, *Un precursore del Metastasio* (Florence, 1904), 7.
6   For example, *Costantino* (Venice, 1711) is included in volume nine and, therefore, is presumably by both Zeno and Pariati. Campanini, however, attributes this drama solely to Pariati and further claims that it was rewritten by Pariati for Vienna in 1731 under the title of *Massimiano*. Campanini, *Un precursore del Metastasio*, 30.

7   This was not the last time Rinaldo tried to exercise some control over Pariati. He continued
     his surveillance of the librettist by way of his representatives at the imperial court, as a letter
     sent to Guicciardi in 1720 confirms. See Naborre Campanini, *Un precursore del Metastasio*,
     30-31, 46-7. Pariati was aware of his actions, and his libretto for *Archelao* (1722) includes
     not-so-subtle allusions to various intrigues that plagued him and other Italians from Modena,
     including the singer Anna d'Ambreville, sister of Rosa d'Ambreville Borosini. After Anna
     d'Ambreville's marriage to Annibale Traeri was annulled in 1725, she married Giovanni
     Peroni, an imperial court violoncellist. For a discussion of this libretto and its relationship
     to the Duke of Modena, see Campanini (cited above). See also Herbert Seifert, 'Pietro Pariati
     poeta cesareo' and Giovanna Gronda, 'Il mestiere del librettista' in Giovanna Gronda, ed.,
     La carriera di un librettista (Bologna, 1990), 65-7, 161-5.

8   Giovanna Gronda, whose study of Pariati's works centres on his *Teseo in Creta*, considers
     Conti's setting of this libretto to be one of his best operas. Perhaps she arrived at this
     assessment solely on the basis of the libretto, for overall the musical score has little to
     distinguish it from Conti's other full-scale operas. In fact, *Teseo in Creta* might be best
     described as an adequate, but not an exceptional, score.

9   Giovanna Gronda, 'Il mestiere del librettista', 187-9. Gronda attempts to make a case for
     Pariati being the librettist for the 1714 *Alba Cornelia*, but her line of reasoning is faulty at
     best. She points out that in Act II, Scene xiii of the 1704 *Alba Cornelia*, Milo sings the same
     aria text given to Sosia in Act I, Scene ii of Pariati's 1707 *Anfitrione*. From this information,
     she suggests Pariati may have been responsible for at least the comic scenes of the 1704 *Alba
     Cornelia* and then, by extension, that he also wrote the 1714 version, never realizing that the
     comic scenes of 1704 have nothing to do with those in the 1714 libretto. In addition she
     makes two more assumptions: (1) Pariati was involved with a revival of Conti's *Alba
     Cornelia* for Breslau in 1726, and therefore he must have been the librettist of the 1714
     version. Gronda never took into account important differences between the 1714 and 1726
     versions of the librettos. (2) Pariati was the only official poet serving the court in 1714. This,
     of course, is not true. Stampiglia was an official court poet until his death in 1725; Pariati did
     not become an official court poet in residence until July of 1714, six months after *Alba
     Cornelia* was staged at the imperial court. (Gronda provides a list of Pariati's librettos in an
     appendix to her chapter on Pariati's works).

10   The surviving manuscript score of Conti's *Alba Cornelia* lacks a descriptive subtitle, but it
     should be listed as a *tragicommedia*, not a *dramma per musica* as has been done by at least
     one author. See Franz Hadamowsky, 'Barocktheater am Wiener Kaiserhof', *Jahrbuch der
     Gesellschaft für Wiener Theaterforschung 1951/52* (Vienna, 1955), 101. See also Ludwig
     von Köchel, *Johann Josef Fux* (Hildesheim, 1974), 530.

11   Alexander von Weilen, *Zur Wiener Theatergeschichte* (Vienna, 1901), 75; Köchel, *Johann
     Josef Fux*, 530; Lione Allacci, *Drammaturgia* (Venice, 1755), col. 19.

12   Robert Eitner, in his *Quellenlexicon*, III, 36, gives two dates for productions of *Alessandro
     in Sidone*, 1715 and 1722. He also indicates that a score for the 1715 production is in the
     Gesellschaft der Musikfreunde in Vienna, but this information does not correspond with the
     holdings of that institution where there is only a manuscript related to the 1721 production.
     There is also no evidence to suggest that Zeno and Pariati wrote the libretto prior to 1721.

13   Zeno, *Lettere*, II, 463.

14   Ibid., III, 11.

15 Letter quoted in Naborre Campanini, *Un precursore di Metastasio*, 44-5.
16 For a discussion of librettists' adapations of Cervantes' *Don Quixote*, see Stefan Kunze, 'Die Entstehung eines Buffo-Librettos: Don-Quijote-Bearbeitungen', *Deutsches Jahrbuch der Musikwissenschaft* 12 (1968): 75-95
17 When the works of Zeno (and Pariati) were collected for publication, the editor mistakenly published Claudio Pasquini's *Don Chisciotte in corte della duchessa* (set by Caldara, 1727) instead of the Zeno-Pariati *Don Chisciotte in Sierra Morena* of 1719. See this author's *Francesco Bartolomeo Conti: His Life and Operas* (diss., Columbia University, 1964), 105.
18 Zeno, *Lettere*, III, 245. He attributed the length to the inclusion of eleven characters and four *balli*.
19 Zeno, *Lettere*, III, 11.
20 *Archelao* is described as a three-act opera in Eitner's *Quellenlexicon*, III, 36. It also has not been included in Naborre Campanini's list of Pariati's works.
21 Joseph Gregor, *Geschichte des Österreichischen Theaters* (Vienna, 1948), 115.
22 The 'strolling players' from England were frequent visitors to the Continent and their presence exerted a strong influence upon the popular plays of the towns and cities where they entertained. See Willi Flemming, *Das Schauspiel der Wanderbühne* (Leipzig, 1931), III, 17.
23 Mary Beare, *The German Popular Play 'Atis' and the Venetian Opera* (Cambridge, 1938).
24 Ibid., 59
25 Ibid., 1.
26 The librettists for *Clotilde*, *Alba Cornelia*, and *Pallade trionfante* remain unknown.
27 The one-act operas contain many more monologues than the full-scale operas. This is especially true of *Pallade trionfante*, where the monologues far outnumber the dialogue recitatives.
28 The *corni da caccia* are introduced twice in the same recitative.
29 Unlike many of his contemporaries, Conti made considerable use of having a bar or two of recitative sung simultaneously by more than one character in a chordal fashion.
30 One such example occurs in Act III of *Archelao* in the recitative that introduces the tenor aria 'Fredda insensata e immobile'.
31 Conti does not make use of the *recitativo stromentato* in *Ciro* and *Amore in Tessaglia*.
32 A similar passage exists in the penultimate scene of Act I in *Griselda* where, in answer to Ottone's command, Griselda answers with a very simple aria which, like the preceding example, also lacks an instrumental introduction.
33 Pietro Metastasio, *The Works of Pietro Metastasio*, John Hoole, trans. (London, 1767), I, 267.
34 A classification of Conti's arias solely upon the basis of tempo is an impossibility because in approximately one-third of the arias for each of his operas, tempo marks are not provided.
35 John Henry van der Meer, *Johann Josef Fux als Opernkomponist* (Bilthoven, 1961), II, 80-82.
36 This and many other numbers from Conti's operas are available for study in appendix III of this author's *Francesco Bartolomeo Conti: His Life and Operas* (diss., Columbia University, 1964).
37 See, in particular, the works of Antonio Caldara and Giovanni Pergolesi.

38 See, for example, the alto aria 'Ecco il mare' where the melismas depict the waves of the ocean, and the bass aria accompanied by three parts assigned to *fagotti* (1 and 2) and *violoncelli and contrabass senza cembalo.*

39 Hellmuth Christian Wolff, *Die Barockoper in Hamburg 1678-1738* (Wolfenbüttel, 1957), 299-305.

40 Exceptions to this statement occur most noticeably in *Griselda* (Act II, Scene iv; Act II, Scene viii; Act III, Scene ix).

41 This aria is one of many that are extant in single copies in archives outside Vienna. This may indicate the popularity that some of Conti's arias had apart from their function within a dramatic work. In the original performance, 'De le fere' was sung by Borosini. The vocal part, notated in both the tenor and bass clefs, has a range of notes that span almost two octaves.

42 A similar three-part accompaniment appears in *Il Gioseffo* and in the Intermezzo III that was performed with *Sesostri, rè di Egitto.*

43 Bass chalumeau parts appear in the scores of other Viennese composers at the beginning of the eighteenth century. See, for example, *Julo Ascanio* by Fux and *Il trionfo della grazia* by A. Bononcini. The use of the chalumeau in operas performed in Vienna from 1706 (*Endimione* by G. Bononcini) until 1725 is discussed briefly by Colin Lawson in 'The Chalumeau in the works of Fux', in Harry White, ed., *Johann Joseph Fux and the Music of the Austro-Italian Baroque* (London, 1992), 84-5. He, however, puts forth an incorrect assessment of the use of the chalumeau when he writes: 'Fux included chalumeaux in *Julo Ascanio* (1708), the first of nine chamber operas written for special occasions which use the instrument. It was thus apparently excluded only from the large-scale operas, appearing consistently in shorter pieces (for an orchestra of 18 to 24 players) until 1725'. His statement is not correct as evidenced by Conti's large-scale operas which do include the chalumeau.

44 The use of mandolin, harp, and theorbo invites comparison with Handel's use of these instruments. See, for example, the aria 'Hark, hark he strikes the golden lyre' in *Alexander Balus* which is scored for harp, mandolin, divided cellos, and basses. See also arias in *Guilio Cesare* and *Esther.*

45 The combined range of the Primo and Secondo Baridon parts extends from C to g' requiring a seven-stringed baryton tuned to A', D, G, c, e, a, d'. See Daniel Frylund, 'Viola di Bardone' *Svensk Tidskrift för Musikforskning* IV (1922): 133, for a discussion of the seven-stringed baryton.

46 Hellmuth Christian Wolff, *Die Barockoper in Hamburg 1678-1738*, 304.

CHAPTER TEN

The intermezzos

Between 1706 and 1709, a new dimension in operatic entertainment took root in Venice, as separately published librettos for sets of comic intermezzos began to make their appearance in that city. These librettos were a welcome source from which composers could draw material to create a comic scenario totally independent of the opera with which it would be performed. Venice was ripe for the reintroduction of comedy into its operatic productions, for during the last quarter of the seventeenth century, *scene buffe* had gradually been eliminated from the *opere serie* librettos in response to the reform process advocated by Apostolo Zeno and his contemporaries.

For the most part, the intermezzo libretto is subdivided into two or three (rarely four) parts and is restricted to two or three singers, one of whom impersonates a female and the other, a male character. Typically these *dramatis personae* mirror the stock characters of the *commedia dell'arte,* such as the young servant girl (*servetta*) who wishes to advance her station in life by marrying a rich old man (*vecchio*).

Some of the best known sets of intermezzos, among them *L'ammalato immaginario*, were based upon the works of Molière. Since his comedies had been published in Italian translation shortly before the end of the seventeenth century, they were readily available for adaptation. Other sets of intermezzos were fashioned by usurping comic scenes from pre-existing opera librettos. For example, the comic scenes in Silvio Stampiglia's *L'Abdolomino*, which had its initial performance in Vienna in 1709 with music by Giovanni Bononcini, were extracted to create an intermezzo libretto known by the name of its characters, Ircano (a bourgeois gentleman) and Lidia (the king's gardener).

In contrast to the situation that existed in Naples, where a pair of singers was tenured specifically to perform the *scene buffe* and intermezzos, most cities in Italy were dependent upon travelling troupes to provide them with singers who had the specialized skills required for the comic roles. As these troupes moved from one opera centre to another, carrying their props and costumes, they brought along copies of their favourite sets of intermezzos which mainly derived from the core of the Venetian repertoire. They were free to stage these sets repeatedly and to revise them as often as needed. As a result, the repertoire was disseminated first in Italy and eventually throughout Europe. New sets of intermezzos were also designed for singers who had made a name for themselves in these *buffo* roles.

One of the most famous bass singers who for more than a quarter of a century performed the independent comic intermezzos in the major opera centres in Italy was Giovanni Battista Cavana from Mantua. He played opposite several well-known female singers, but perhaps the most famous of his partners was the soprano Rosa Ungarelli from Bologna. Although their professional relationship was of short duration, that which brought together Rosa Ungarelli and Antonio Maria Ristorini of Florence lasted for more than sixteen years (*c.* 1716 to *c.* 1732). The Ungarelli and Ristorini duo was no doubt the most celebrated of the intermezzo troupes of its generation. Since they gave performances which took them beyond the borders of their native land to Paris, Brussels, and Munich, they were responsible for fostering what amounted to an international repertoire of intermezzos. Admittedly, the repertoire they chose to perform was rather limited, for it centred on just a few sets which they staged over and over again. Among them were *Pimpinone* (Pimpinone annd Vespetta) and *L'ammalato immaginario* (Erighetta and Don Chilone).

Independent sets of intermezzos came to the stage in Vienna, Dresden, and Hamburg a decade or more after the core repertoire was developed in Venice. One of the composers associated with the introduction of the new genre in all three of these cities was Francesco Conti, whom Johann Mattheson regarded as having exceptional talent for the comic style.[1] According to various contemporary sources, a set of intermezzos entitled *L'ammalato immaginario* with music by Conti was given in Vienna on 23 February 1713.[2] If indeed this production took place, this intermezzo set most likely would have been performed without a host opera, for no three- or five-act operas were produced for the court during the 1713 Carnival season. That this sort of small-scale entertainment might have taken place is not outside the realms of possibility, given the fact that the regular schedule of theatrical productions had been curtailed during that particular season.

There does exist a libretto of *L'ammalato immaginario*, entitled *Intermezzi musicali*, that credits Conti with a production in Perugia during the Carnival season of 1727.[3] Interestingly, this same set of intermezzos by Conti was heard again some 100 years later in Vienna in association with productions sponsored by the Société des Cavaliers. Performances of *L'ammalato immaginario* took place on 26 May and 15 June 1748 and were under the direction of the composer, Christoph Gluck [4]

Although these later productions lend credence to the possibility that the intermezzos performed in 1713 were composed by Conti, no score or libretto associated with that performance has been found. That this early work may actually be preserved in a different guise, however, is suggested by the final set of intermezzos which Conti brought to the imperial stage in 1725 with the performance of his opera *Griselda*. The principal characters of that set are Erighetta (alto) and Don Chilone (bass), the very same who appear in *L'ammalato immaginario* cited above.[5] One of the first recorded settings of *L'ammalato immaginario* dates from 1707, when the 'Erighetta e Don Chilone' set of three intermezzos was performed with Francesco Gasparini's *Anfitrione* at the Teatro San Cassiano in Venice. A number of other performances of this text, either under the title *L'ammalato immaginario* or under the names of the *dramatis personae*, Erighetta and Don Chilone, were presented during Conti's lifetime, although the majority of them are recorded as having taken place after 1721.[6] If Conti did compose *L'ammalato immaginario* for Vienna in 1713, it would have been one of the few settings of this libretto that came to the stage between 1707 and 1721.

Listed in table 10.1 are the intermezzos composed by Conti which were performed with his own operas.[7] In addition to those listed, Conti also composed intermezzos for *L'Atenaide*, an opera performed on 19 November 1714 in honour of the name-day of Empress Elisabeth Christina. Zeno wrote the libretto of this three-act *dramma per musica* and Marc'Antonio Ziani (Act I), Antonio Negri (Act II), and Antonio Caldara (Act III) composed the music. The title page of the score cites Conti as the composer of the intermezzos and the *licenza*, but it fails to mention the librettist. Nevertheless, it has generally been assumed that the text was prepared by Pietro Pariati, who by this date held an appointment with the imperial court.[8] The intermezzos involve two characters named Dorimena (alto) and Tuberone (bass); the names of the singers who played these roles, however, are not indicated in the score. Based upon information about those who sang some of Conti's other intermezzo roles, it would be reasonable to suggest that Dorimena's (alto) role was sung by a castrato, for Vienna and Rome were two of the operatic centres where castrati were regularly cast in the female *buffo* roles. This particular set of two intermezzos constitutes the first ever performed in the imperial city that was wholly independent of the opera with which it was staged.

Table 10.1

Operas by Francesco Conti with intermezzos

Opera	Date	Intermezzos	Roles	Characters / Singers
Ciro	1715	2	3	Bagatella / soprano – D. Giulio Mamalucca / alto – Giovanni Pattalocco / bass – P. Paolo
Teseo in Creta	1715	2	2	Galantina / soprano – Giovannino Pampalugo / bass – P. Paolo
Sesostri	1717	3	2	Grilletta / soprano – La Faustina Pimpinone / bass – P. Paolo
Astarto	1718	3	3	Farfalletta / soprano – ? Lirone / alto – ? Terremoto / bass – ?
Griselda	1725	3	2	Eringhetta / soprano – ? Donchilone / bass – ?

These same intermezzos also may have been presented as an independent set in Hamburg in 1719, as will be discussed below.[9]

Conti's musical setting for the 'Tuberone e Dorimena' libretto is exceptionally clever. It gives the impression that the music he composed is an inevitable and spontaneous response to the text. At the same time, Conti does not compromise the characteristic components of his musical style. The end result is that he has created one of his more successful scores for portraying a comic situation.

The scenario that unfolds can be summarized in a few words. Tuberone is interested in marrying Dorimena, but instead of coming right to the point and proposing to her, he takes the circuitous route and describes to her someone who would make an ideal husband, someone just like himself. Dorimena's curiosity is aroused and she begins to ask some specific questions, such as what does the man do for a living and is he handsome and polite. Without hesitation, Tuberone supplies answers that are intended to cover all possibilities. Not until Dorimena asks him to reveal the name of the person he is describing does Tuberone's confidence falter. He is at first reluctant to tell the truth, but then begins to give out his name, syllable by syllable, in a halting, almost stuttering fashion, until he simply announces that it is he, 'Tuberone' (ex. 10.1).

Example 10.1. 'Tuberone e Dorimena' (Intermezzo I): recitative

In Intermezzo II, Tuberone realizes that the only way to win Dorimena for his wife is to capture her by means of magic. For the purpose, he acquires a magic wand, but, as luck would have it, the wand falls into the possession of Dorimena. She casts a spell over Tuberone and makes him dance while he sings the aria 'Ballarino saltarino', a delightful aria in 12/8 metre which no doubt caused much amusement for the audience. In the end, as expected, Dorimena and Tuberone put aside their *commedia dell'arte* tactics and come together in spirit and song to perform (*à due*) the concluding bars of the recitative that leads into their final duet. In both intermezzos, the attention of the audience is focused upon the *buffo* bass arias. This is true not only for this particular set, but for Conti's other intermezzos as well. Although the arias are often divided equally between the two characters, those for the *buffo* bass present some of the best examples of his comic aria style.

These intermezzos, of course, resemble the *scene buffe* Stampiglia wrote for Scarlatti and therefore it should come as no surprise that some of the musical means to set them are also similar. The first intermezzo has two arias and one duet: A(alto)-R-A(bass)-R-Duet; the second intermezzo has one aria and a duet: R-A(bass)-R-Duet. Within the recitative section that separates the aria from the final duet, there are two *stromentato* passages for Dorimena with four-part (tutti) orchestral accompaniment, the same scoring that pervades the accompaniment for all but one of the arias and duets. That exception involves Tuberone's aria in intermezzo I for which the scoring is reduced to unison violins and continuo.

Dorimena's first aria is marked *allegro* and is in the key of F major.[10] It opens with a thirteen-bar ritornello that is thematically interesting because it contains several different motifs, all of which have a significant part to play in the musical design of the entire aria. These motifs are made distinctive by their melodic contour and most especially by their easily recognized rhythmic patterns: one has triplets, another has dotted rhythms, and so forth. Dorimena sings her opening phrase to the initial motif of the first violins. She then introduces the words, 'stuzzicando' ('exciting') and 'pizzicando' ('pinching'), separating them into four syllables and singing them on the off-beat of each of the four beats in a bar. These same two words are repeated a few bars later, but here they are set in an entirely different manner. This time Conti introduces a four-bar motif that is not found in the ritornello to set this portion of the text and to provide the material for two of the intervening instrumental interludes.

Repetition is a key ingredient for creating a comic style. Conti prefers to repeat short phrases of text and individual words rather than whole sections of text and music, though there are some notable exceptions to this. Frequently, these textual repetitions are paired with the same music, as exemplified by a passage from the first duet (ex. 10.2). Another kind of repetition occurs in the fast-paced *parlando* style of Tuberone's aria in Intermezzo I. This patter-type of vocal style demands

Example 10.2. 'Tuberone e Dorimena' (Intermezzo I): duet

great skill on the part of both composer and performer to make it an effective vehicle for comedy. In this particular aria, Conti has wisely reduced the scoring so that the text, even though sung at a rapid tempo, is comprehensible to the audience. In the preceding recitative, Tuberone has just finished describing who the ideal man for Dorimena might be and now he tells her in his opening phrase of the aria, sung in an *adagio* tempo, that if she sees him, she will think him quite a handsome man. He then breaks into a *presto* tempo and rattles off the various professions – mathematician, astrologer, doctor – that he had previously

Example 10.3. 'Tuberone e Dorimena' (Intermezzo I): Tuberone's aria

mentioned to her, throwing in for good measure several words that rhyme with 'matematica' – 'estatica, paralitica, e lunatica' – all sung to many notes repeated at the same pitch (ex. 10.3). This entire opening section is accompanied by the continuo, at the conclusion of which the violins enter with figuration for a three-bar interlude. Tuberone repeats his opening two-bar *adagio* phrase, which is then followed by a *presto* section that begins with the same initial phrase as before, but moves on to embrace other thematic ideas. In the course of this second *presto* section, Conti chooses to repeat six or more times the words 'ch'egl'è Dottor' ('that he is a doctor'). While the rhythmic motif used to set these words remains unchanged, the melodic contour of that same motif changes slightly with each repetition, all the while supported by a rather static harmonic bass line.

Since Tuberone's aria is in the *da capo* form, the changes in tempo of the *A* section are again encountered on the repeat. This constant shifting of the musical pace from *adagio* to *presto* is, of course, an element frequently encountered in *buffo* compositions. Conti takes full advantage of it in this work, not only in this aria, but also in the duet that concludes Intermezzo I and in the accompanied recitative in Intermezzo II.

In two of the arias, both of which happen to be sung by Tuberone, Conti dispenses with an introductory ritornello and begins directly with the vocal part. This achieves a bit of realism as the plot unfolds, while at the same time providing variety in the way the individual numbers are constructed, for all of the other arias and duets have substantial introductory ritornellos which reappear, in whole or in part, at the conclusion of the *A* section. For example, in the first duet a full repetition of the instrumental introduction occurs at the end of *A* and a partial repetition occurs as a medial ritornello; in the second duet, an abbreviated form of the introductory ritornello concludes *A* and a brief medial interlude for the orchestra, thematically related to the ritornello, appears in that same section.

In general, a set of intermezzos ends with a duet that focuses on the resolution of whatever conflict has existed between the protagonists. Musically, this union of affection is expressed by having the singers share the same thematic material: the duet might begin with one singer introducing a complete melodic phrase, followed by the second singer repeating it; shorter (one- or two-bar) phrases are then tossed back and forth between the singers; finally, the two voices join to sing the final *A* section in parallel thirds or sixths. The *B* section is usually quite short, thematically related to *A*, and is treated variously with respect to the material assigned to the singers, although the tendency is to have them sing together in thirds. Such is the final duet in this set.

If a composer is going to differentiate the personalities and emotions of the protagonists in a duet, he will usually do so in the duet that is positioned at the end of the first intermezzo (and/or at the end of the second intermezzo, whenever the set is made up of more than two), for here the characters are more than likely to be in disagreement about some matter and their respective positions lend themselves to musical depiction. In the duet that concludes Intermezzo I, Conti does little to distinguish the personalities of Dorimena and Tuberone in the *A* section, which is in triple metre (3/8) and marked *allegro*. In the *B* section, however, the differences between the characters become clearer, and Conti achieves this by creating an unusual design for this portion of the *da capo* form. At the beginning of *B*, he alters the metre, tempo, scoring, and style of the musical material assigned to the vocal parts. Duple metre replaces triple metre; the tempo at the outset is marked *largo* but then shifts abruptly to *allegro* for the second half of *B;* and the instrumental accompaniment is reduced throughout *B* from a four-part ensemble to the *basso continuo*. The *largo* section begins with two long solo phrases sung by Tuberone. In between them, Dorimena interjects one brief question ('Che farai?'). Conti then reverses the procedure and gives Dorimena several long solo phrases, separating them with a brief remark ('O che sbizza') by Tuberone. In the *allegro* portion of *B*, the characters continue to be differentiated by their vocal material, Tuberone with his patter style of delivery using multiple repetitions of a single note to set forth his verbose text and Dorimena with her multiple repetitions of individual words such as 'via' sung to a wide range of pitches.

There is but one number in this set of intermezzos that involves recitative accompanied by the four-part strings. It occurs in Intermezzo II in a passage where Dorimena expresses her displeasure with Tuberone. Here the strings are used in an agitated, rather than a sustained, style to augment the animated vocal delivery of the singer. Conti, however, does not use *recitativo stromentato* throughout the whole of this number. He alternates it with passages of *recitativo semplice*, composing two extended passages in each style. The care with which Conti handled the text–music relationship in this number is indicative of the manner in which he dealt with the entire text. The result was the creation of an excellent example of the comic style, one which even he would have difficulty surpassing as he continued to compose several more sets of intermezzos.

For the 1715 Carnival season, Conti wrote the music for *Ciro,* a three-act opera based upon a libretto by Pariati to which is appended an independent set of two intermezzos. These intermezzos involve three characters: Bagatella (Giovanni – soprano), Mamalucca (D. Giulio – alto) and Pattatocco (Pietro Paolo – bass). Of the three performers, Pietro Paolo (Pezzoni) was among the most recent additions to the group of singers available to Conti for his productions.[11] This *buffo* bass began his official association with the imperial court on 1 January 1715 and thus his appearance in the *Ciro* production may have marked his debut in Vienna. Although Paolo's name is very prominent among Conti's scores produced for the imperial court that required a *buffo* bass, it is noticeably absent from the group of singers who regularly performed the music for the Hofkapelle. He earned a stipend of 1260 florins, which was somewhat less than the 1440 florins paid to some of his colleagues. Nevertheless, the mere fact that he held a virtual monopoly on the *buffo* bass roles suggests that he had little competition from any rivals who might have wanted to fill his position.

Giovanni Vincenzi was only sixteen years of age when he joined the roster of court singers on 1 January 1713. Perhaps this is why the diminutive form of his first name, Giovannino, is to be found in several cast lists, including that for *I Satiri in Arcadia* (1714), the first opera by Conti in which he had a role. Whereas Giovanni and Paolo appear in Köchel's listing of singers at the court, the name of the alto castrato D. Giulio does not, though he is known to have sung roles in a number of operas. His first connection with a work by Conti seems to have come in 1714 when he sang the *buffo* role of Lesbina, the servant of the title character, in *Alba Cornelia*.

The untitled set of intermezzos for *Ciro,* with the characters Bagatella, Mamalucca, and Pattalocco, has the following format: Duet-A-A-Trio; A-A-Trio. Pattalocco (bass) has two arias, one in each of the intermezzos, and both are accompanied by three instrumental (unspecified) parts. The other two characters are limited to one aria apiece; both of their arias are in a minor key and have *basso continuo* accompaniment. Bagatella's (soprano) aria is in the first intermezzo and Mamalucca's (alto) is in the second. There is little to distinguish this set from the expected comic style of the period. The spontaneity of expression found in the 'Tuberone e Dorimena' set is not as evident here, nor is it in the next set Conti composed in August 1715. The host opera this time is *Teseo in Creta* and again it is based upon a libretto by Pariati. The opera is in five acts and therefore could have accommodated three intermezzos, but the set that is provided in Pariati's libretto has only two because the production was staged in honour of the empress's birthday (20 August). The requisite *licenza* took the place of a third intermezzo.

The set of intermezzos staged with *Teseo in Creta* calls for two singers: a bass, cast in the role of Pampalugo, and a soprano, in the role of Galantina. Paolo sang the bass role and Giovannino sang the soprano. Intermezzo I opens with a composite group that contains an accompanied recitative, an instrumental interlude, and finally a *da capo* aria with three-part orchestral accompaniment. This initial group is sung by Pampalugo who is dressed as a parrot ('vestito da papagallo'). His aria is cast in a minor key and shows considerable attention to text–music relationships. This sometimes extends to word-painting, as shown by the chromatic scale used to set the word 'moro' ('I die'). The second aria, sung by Galantina, is in a minor key and has 12/8 metre and continuo accompaniment. A duet marked *allegro* and in a major key concludes the first intermezzo.

In the second intermezzo, the characters appear in the same sequence as in the first one. The initial aria sung by Pampalugo is rather unusual in that it is a through-composed piece. Galantina's aria follows and it contrasts with the previous one in form (*da capo*), key (minor), and accompaniment (continuo). For the final duet, Conti returns to a major key and orchestral accompaniment. The *buffo* style is effectively conveyed in this set of intermezzos, with the melodic material closely aligned with the inflection of the text. In addition, the musical inventiveness of Conti's writing in the host opera is carried over into the intermezzos, thereby making them of a quality worthy to be performed between the acts of the serious drama.

Conti's music played a part in yet another production that marked the first time *scene buffe* were staged independently of their attendant *opera seria*. The occasion was the inauguration of the Redoutensaal in Dresden, which was to be used as a provisional theatre while the new opera house was being constructed. It took place on 25 October 1717 and involved the production of Antonio Lotti's *Giove in Argo*. Performed with the opera was a set (untitled) of three intermezzos, the text of the first two by Silvio Stampiglia and that of the third by Francesco Ballerini.[12] The responsibility for writing the music was also shared by two composers; Alessandro Scarlatti composed the first two intermezzos, and Conti, the third. For this première, the roles of Vespetta and Milo were sung by Signori Livia Constantini 'La Polachina' and Lucrezio Borsari. The 1717 *Intermedi* libretto advertises both singers as the *virtuosi* of (Friedrich) August II, King of Poland and the Elector of Saxony.[13] Although the Dresden publication of the libretto survives, the score for the intermezzos does not. Charles Troy, in his study of the comic intermezzo, suggests that the first two intermezzos in this set may represent comic scenes from an as-yet-undiscovered opera by Scarlatti composed for Naples.[14]

The libretto for the *Intermedi* was published in two languages side by side, in Italian and in French. In the prefatory note to the reader, it is indicated that the arias, although translated into French, will be sung in Italian. The musical division of the three intermezzos is as follows: A(Vespetta)-R-A(Milo)-Duet; A (Vespetta)-R-A (Milo)-R-Duet; R-Duet. Obviously the third intermezzo, if indeed this is the way the text was set, offers Conti little opportunity to show the Dresden court his handling of comic episodes. There is, of course, the possibility that what appears to be a division into recitative and duet may not represent what actually took shape in the score, for given the way the libretto is printed, it is not always clear which lines were intended to be sung as recitative and which as arias. In any event, any impact Conti's music might have had on Dresden with this production would have been minimal.

Lotti's *Giove in Argo* was presented again in Dresden on 3 September 1719, this time to inaugurate the new opera house.[15] Presumably the same set of intermezzos that accompanied the initial 1717 production were staged with this one. Handel attended the 1719 production and if the 'Vespetta e Milo' set of intermezzos was included, this could have been his first encounter with Conti's music in a live performance.

Perhaps the most celebrated of the independent sets of intermezzos is *Pimpinone*, an anonymous work that was first published in Venice in 1708. Music composed for one of the earliest productions of *Pimpinone* is not only preserved but is also published in a modern edition. This is in sharp contrast to the situation with many other intermezzos, for seldom has the music originally composed for them survived. The earliest extant musical rendition of the 1708 text coexists in the same manuscript containing the host opera, Antonio Orefici and Francesco Mancini's *L'Engelberta*, with which it was performed in 1709 in Naples. Although the manuscript fails to indicate the composer of this set of intermezzos, it has since been determined, largely on the basis of circumstantial evidence, that Tomaso Albinoni was responsible for its creation. Revivals of the 1709 musical version of *Pimpinone* were facilitated by having the performance materials remain essentially the same regardless of where or when these independent *scene buffe* were staged. Another factor that contributed to the numerous revivals of *Pimpinone* was that more often than not the contralto (Vespetta) and bass (Pimpinone) roles were sung by the same one or two pairs of singers, thereby lessening the need for any changes in the score to accommodate the whims or talents of new performers.

Between 1708 and 1740, at least two dozen performances of Albinoni's version of *Pimpinone* have been documented, confirming that this particular musical rendition of the libretto had become a favourite among similar works which formed an internationally recognized repertoire of intermezzos.[16] So popular was Albinoni's version, that only two other composers bothered to try their hand at setting the same basic text. One was Francesco Conti in 1717 and the other was Georg Philipp Telemann in 1725.[17]

The very first time the name of a librettist was linked with the writing of *Pimpinone* came in 1717, when a libretto with this title was published in Vienna together with that for *Sesostri, rè di Egitto*, the host opera with which the intermezzos were staged. Pariati is the author credited for the combined libretto, and it is on the basis of this information that he has also been credited with the earliest version of the libretto for *Pimpinone* published in Venice in 1708. It is certainly not unreasonable to conclude that Pariati might be the author of the Venetian publication. After all, he spent a considerable amount of time writing librettos or portions thereof in Venice long before he accepted an appointment to the Habsburg court. Whether or not he was responsible for the 1708 version of *Pimpinone*, however, may forever remain a matter of conjecture. Since he worked for the greater part of his life in the shadow of Apostolo Zeno, the full extent of his contribution to the librettos they produced while living in the same city is often difficult, if not impossible, to determine. Those who argue for Pariati's authorship cite the fact that Zeno, by his own admission, was not one to write *scene buffe* and therefore the comic scenes and independent intermezzos most likely came from the pen of none other than his partner.[18]

That having been said, it should be noted that the text of Conti's version of *Pimpinone* differs considerably from the one found in the 1709 version by Albinoni.[19] Apart from a change in the name of the female character from Vespetta ('little wasp') to Grilletta ('little cricket') and variant readings that affect individual words and phrases, the primary differences concern the duet at the end of Intermezzo I and the two arias in Intermezzo III.[20] In the 1717 version of the duet, the final line of the *B* section, 'O felice Pimpinon', also appears as the final line of the *A* section and is directly preceded by two other lines, one of which differs from the 1709 version (line 86), with which it rhymes:

> Pimpinone: M'incammino. Tu hai ragion.
> Grilletta: Io mio umilo al mio Padron.
> Pimpinone: O felice Pimpinon.

Conti makes the most of this rearrangement of the text to enhance the humourous situation by repeating several times the phrases 'Il mio umili al mio Padron' ('I humble myself to my master') and 'O felice Pimpinon' ('O happy Pimpinone'). In fact, repetition of key phrases of text together with their musical settings is a characteristic of the way Conti handles the material in these intermezzos.

The textual variants in Intermezzo I are minor when compared with those that occur in Intermezzo III.[21] Except for the initial line of Grilletta's aria, 'Voglio far come fan l'altre' ('I want to do as others do'), both arias in this section are newly created.[22] Gone is Pimpinone's humorous impersonation of the ladies gossiping about their husbands. Instead, the substituted aria for Pimpinone adds a bit of stuttering, one of the stock-in-trade methods for injecting humour into a situation. In the 1709 version of the aria assigned to the female role, Vespetta professes her desire to play the part of a lady. She wants, among other things, to dress well and speak French. In the 1717 substitute aria, Grilletta expresses some of these same desires, but here she actually uses two of the French words, 'monsieur' and 'adieu' to show that she is already moving up the social ladder.

Michael Talbot, who has made the most extensive study to date of Albinoni's *Pimpinone*, notes that the lack of an aria for Pimpinone in Intermezzo I creates a certain imbalance, a situation that most other versions of the libretto created after 1715 attempt to remedy by inserting after line 58 of the libretto an extra aria, 'Ella mi vuol confonder'. This aria, however, does not appear in the version set by Conti. Talbot also notes that some versions of *Pimpinone* have substituted the aria 'Eh non giova l'esser buona' for 'Chi mi vuol?', the opening aria of Intermezzo I, but again this change does not occur in the 1717 libretto or score.[23]

Pimpinone focuses on the classic dilemma of the flirtatious servant girl who knows that the only way to advance her position in life is to marry a well-to-do gentleman. The librettist wastes no time in establishing the framework for this comic situation. He quickly draws the audience into the plot by having Intermezzo I open directly with a question posed as the first line of Grilletta's aria:'Chi mi vuol?' ('Who will want me?'). Grilletta then proceeds to enumerate her qualities, introducing herself as a sincere person with no ambitions, capable of performing every household task she is asked to do, and accepting the good with the bad as a fact of life. All she has to do is find someone who is in need of her services, someone who has enough money to pay a sum that will help her earn a dowry and thereby make her eligible for marriage. Along comes Pimpinone, whom Grilletta describes for the benefit of the audience as being wealthy and a bit foolish, but not of the highest social rank ('nobil non è'). Pimpinone continues with a description of his situation, explaining that he is tired of continually being taken advantage of by so many visitors in his house. What he would like to have is a maidservant and at the very moment he expresses that wish, he notices Grilletta. He believes she will be the perfect person to alleviate his domestic situation; she, in turn, considers him to be the perfect employer. After several exchanges in which Pimpinone tries to learn of her past and she, pretending to be discreet in discussing her previous employer, describes the perfect master for whom she is willing to work, Pimpinone takes the bait and hires her on the spot, willing to pay any price she demands.

Intermezzo II opens with a recitative and, similar to the previous intermezzo, this one also begins with a question: 'Grilletta, tu lasciarmi?' ('Grilletta, you are leaving me?'). From this point forward, the audience listens as Grilletta cleverly entraps Pimpinone into asking her to be his wife. She does this in a more subtle manner than might have occurred in a Neapolitan version of a servant ensnaring a husband. Grilletta uses the excuse that there is gossip in the neighbourhood about their relationship being somewhat less than honourable, and in order to quiet the wagging tongues, she has decided to depart. Pimpinone realizes he cannot live without her and instantly proposes, even agreeing to supply the requisite dowry. In return, she agrees to abide by the rules of conduct he has laid down for her.

Intermezzo III shows Grilletta has taken on the airs of a lady. She demands Pimpinone show her the respect and manners due her station, and that includes speaking some French. She also wants the freedom to come and go as she pleases. Pimpinone finds that demand very irksome, but when Grilletta threatens divorce if she cannot have her way, Pimpinone surrenders to her wishes. The final duet has Grilletta rejoicing in her ability to subject Pimpinone to her every whim and Pimpinone regretting that he is in this predicament of loving a person who has driven him to distraction.

The following represents the sequence in which the musical numbers occur: A-R-Duet; R-A-R-A-R-Duet; R-A-R-A-R-Duet. Of the eight set pieces, five are in major keys, but Grilletta's arias in the second and third intermezzos and also the final duet are in minor keys. Two numbers have triple metre (3/4, 3/8), whereas the remaining six make use of various duple metres (4/4, 2/2, 1/2). A variety of instrumental accompaniments can be found among these eight pieces. A simple *basso continuo* is used for Grilletta's aria in the second intermezzo and bassoons (1 and 2) and continuo *senza cembali* support Pimpinone's aria in the third intermezzo. The remaining pieces utilize different combinations of the strings, ranging from unison violins and continuo to the tutti ensemble divided into three or four parts. In the case of the aria and duet in Intermezzo I, oboes are directed to play in unison with the first violins. Throughout the three intermezzos, the instruments seem to have a more active role here than in some of the other intermezzos discussed above. This is true even for the viola part which, with only one or two exceptions, plays as an important role as the second violin.

Instrumental ritornellos of varying lengths (three to twelve bars) introduce all but one of the eight numbers. In only three of the eight numbers is the initial phrase for the vocal part related to the ritornello theme. In two of them, the restatement is confined for the most part to the first one or two bars of the violin's theme, but in Grilletta's final aria, the opening motif for the voice is taken from the first few notes of the viola part in the ritornello. Passages of accompanied recitative are lacking in this set of intermezzos, but the first recitative, which is exceptionally long, does include an *arioso* section.

The variety in tonality, metre, and scoring all contribute to making the intermezzos effective vehicles for the theatre, but the importance of these components pale in comparison to the more subtle means which Conti uses to transform Pariati's text into entertainment. Two examples may suffice to show how Conti achieves his goal. In Intermezzo II, Grilletta sings an aria in which she makes clear that she is not like other young women who spend time and energy trying to improve on what nature has given them. She sings: 'Io non sono una di quelle nate brutte e fatte belle' ('I am not one of those, born ugly and made beautiful'). In his setting of the text, Conti reinforces Grilletta's contention that she is indeed different from the other women Pimpinone has known, for the aria he creates for her to sing is also quite different from others he has composed, be they comic or serious.

This aria has no introductory ritornello. It opens directly with a four-bar phrase for the voice in A minor that presents the kind of tuneful melody that can be remembered long after the intermezzo has ended (ex. 10.4). This same melodic phrase is immediately repeated three times, each repetition at a higher pitch and with different lyrics. In other words, the same melodic phrase is used to set the first four lines of the aria's text. The first repetition of the melody is in C major and begins a third higher than the initial statement. The second and third repetitions revert back to the minor keys; they occur at the distance of a whole tone higher in D minor and E minor respectively. Only one more repetition of this

Example 10.4. 'Pimpinone e Grilletta'(Intermezzo II): Grilletta's aria 'Io non sono', bars 1-8

melodic phrase is heard in the *A* section; it is in the tonic key of A minor and occurs in bars 30-33, where the restatement of the entire text of the *A* section begins. New thematic material is introduced to set this second portion of *A* and out of it Conti fashions a concluding six-bar segment for the continuo alone to conclude the section. The *B* section is short and is closely related thematically to the second half of *A*.

Of particular interest is the way Conti begins the *da capo* of this aria. If he had introduced the *da capo* in exactly the same way the *A* section was initially presented, the final C major cadence of *B* (where voice and continuo end together) and the opening measure of *A* would have had only a half bar rest separating the two sections. To provide a much smoother transition into the A minor tonality, Conti has inserted four bars in which the continuo alone introduces the initial vocal phrase (in the bass clef) before the actual *da capo* begins. This, of course, adds yet another repetition of this tuneful melody, bringing the total to six in the course of the *da capo*. The multiple repetitions of the initial theme have the effect of reinforcing the words Grilletta sings.

The second example concerns Pimpinone's substitute aria, 'Gran Diavola' in Intermezzo III. The scoring offers the first clue that this aria is going to be somewhat out of the ordinary, for two of the three instrumental parts are played by bassoons and their very presence in obbligato roles signals that a comic situation is at hand. Pimpinone has just had a taste of how independent his bride can be and it is making him sick to his stomach. As he describes his malady, the bassoons either reinforce his vocal line by playing in unison with him, or provide contrast with it by introducing more melodic material whenever he rants and raves in a patter style. Conti varies the manner in which the bassoons present their material: sometimes they play together, in unison or parallel thirds; at other times they imitate each other's motifs; and occasionally they each have a solo passage. An example of the latter occurs in the *B* section where the first bassoon part plays a two-octave descending E minor scale mimicking Pimpinone's vocal line while also depicting the final word of that phrase, 'frenetico' ('frenzied'). Two bars later, the second bassoon reverses the process and plays a two-octave ascending E minor scale, but this time the inclusion of the scale seems more related to a balancing of the bassoon parts than to any word-painting of the text.

When the final duet begins, the audience is expecting a *lieto fine*, but what they are given is an ensemble in a minor key that is meant to reflect the rather ambiguous state of affairs in which the characters find themselves. Grilletta is indeed delighted with her blissful arrangement. Pimpinone, however, is decidedly unhappy with his fate and curses the day ('sia maledetto') that he became involved with such a devil ('con tal demonio'). The tables have been turned on him. Instead of being the ruler of his domain, he is now the slave ('schiavo') of his former servant. Conti's setting seems to focus more on the desperate situation in which Pimpinone finds himself and less on the victory won by Grilletta. His frequent injection of unprepared dissonance into the harmonic scheme underscores this unhappy turn of events.

Although the final duet is musically the weakest of the three ensemble pieces, it nevertheless provides ample opportunity for the two characters to fully express their respective differences in outlook on this marriage. Conti is never one to shy away from repeating segments of the text if it will help to highlight the situation at hand. One of the best examples of this occurs in the final bars of the *B* section where Pimpinone warns other men that they too will regret their married status if their wives are possessed by a devil. Here Conti uses a four-note descending sequence to set the two lines of text, and then he repeats the crucial 'si pentirà' ('he will regret it') nine times, with Grilletta interjecting her 'vò libertà' ('I want liberty') in between each repetition, as the first violins add their rather gleeful motivic commentary.

Conti's score for *Pimpinone* holds little in common with that composed by Albinoni. His style of writing for the comic characters has moved away from the Baroque figuration and has become firmly planted in the newer *galant* style. He balances melodic inventiveness with rhythmic variety to produce thematic material that is interesting and, more importantly, effective in communicating the subtleties of the text. One has to look no further than the opening bars of each of the set pieces to see how successful Conti is in avoiding a certain monotony that colours portions of the Albinoni setting. Another point worth noting is that there are relatively few melismas in any of Conti's solo or ensemble pieces; those that are included tend to be of fairly short duration.

The part of Grilletta in the 1717 production was sung by 'La Faustina'. Undoubtedly this was none other than Faustina Bordoni (1697-1781), who made a guest appearance at the court that season. She played opposite Pietro Paolo in the role of Pimpinone. As far as is known, this is the only work by Conti in which Faustina took part, even though she did return to Vienna during the 1725-26 season before her London debut. Faustina grew up in Venice, where she studied voice with Michel Gasparini and enjoyed the support of the Marcello brothers, Alessandro and Benedetto. She made her stage debut in the Venetian production of Carlo Francesco Pollarolo's *Ariodante*. This occurred in 1716, just one year before her appearance in the *buffo* role for Conti's intermezzos. It is perhaps ironic that Faustina was cast as Grilletta, given the fact that she was well acquainted with the part she was asked to portray. Her father earned his living as a domestic servant, which meant that she, too, had been raised in rather modest circumstances and perhaps longed for a way to better her station in life.[24]

Faustina is usually classified as a mezzo-soprano because her vocal range extended from a low b-flat to a high g". Conti, however, centred her vocal part at the high end of her range, primarily between a' and f". Evidence of how she might have embellished the final cadences of the *A* and *B* sections of her arias in this work, something she was famous for doing later in her career, is lacking.[25] Paolo's vocal part encompasses a very wide range of notes, but again it is the upper end of that range that is emphasized by Conti, with e' being the highest note he has to sing.

The Carnival season of 1718 provided yet another an opportunity for Conti to stage three intermezzos with his *Astarto*. The set requires three characters: Farfalletta (soprano), Lirone (alto), and Terremoto (bass), but once again the manuscript of the host opera offers no information about the names of the *buffo* singers.[26] These intermezzos have, in addition to the recitatives set in a *semplice* style, one fairly extensive *recitativo stromentato* for the bass. They also have three *da capo* arias and a composite musical number that consists of two short arias and a duet, with the first of these two arias, 'Vorrei amarti', sung by Farfalletta and in repeated binary form. Immediately upon the conclusion of her solo, Lirone, who plays the part of one who stutters, sings a second strophe to essentially the same music, only now it is in the key of the dominant. To these aria sections, Conti attaches a duet for both singers. Interestingly, the duet represents a return to the musical and textual material of Farfalletta's initial aria, and hence a return to the original tonality. Allowing, of course, for the difference caused by the presence of a second vocal part (which primarily moves in parallel thirds with the first one), the overall design formed by the two arias and duet is really a modified *da capo* (*ABA'*). The juxtaposition of two arias utilizing the same thematic material, but in different tonalities, can be found in opera scores by Conti's contemporaries; yet Conti himself makes little use of a design in which a duet is appended to a pair of related vocal numbers.[27]

In addition to the ensemble cited above, Conti uses a trio to conclude both the first and third intermezzos and a duet to conclude the second intermezzo. With the exception of the final trio, the arias and ensembles are in major keys. Some of the stock-in-trade elements of the *buffo* style such as rapid parlando passages, stuttering, and disguises are incorporated into this set, all of which inspired Conti to create a very entertaining bit of comedy.

The final set of intermezzos Conti brought to the imperial stage appeared with *Griselda*, his Carnival opera for 1725.[28] As indicated by the manuscript, Zeno was responsible for the opera libretto. The manuscript, however, is silent about who provided the libretto for the intermezzos and what singers were assigned to play the roles of Eringhetta (soprano) and Donchilone (bass). Although the spelling of their names differs, these characters are the same as Erighetta and Don Chilone of *L'ammalato immaginario* mentioned above.[29]

The 'Erighetta e Don Chilone' text was published in 1723 as part of a collection of some fifty-four intermezzos librettos. It appeared in volume I of *Raccolta copiosa d'intermedj* (fols 8-22) and seems to have sparked considerable interest, for musical settings of this comedy increased rapidly after that date. Some were designed to be performed independently of a host opera; others, such as the one staged with Leonardo Vinci's 1726 production of *L'Ernelinda* in Naples, were intended to be performed with a host opera. Conti's interpretation of the comedy involves three intermezzos which have the following design: A-R-A-R-Duet; R-A-R-A-R-Duet; Duet-R-A-R-Duet. Five of the nine set pieces are wholly or partially in triple metre and none are accompanied solely by the continuo, although the first aria Donchilone sings comes close to fitting this category because the scoring is for 'violini e violette al unisoni col basso'. Because of the low range of the bass line, the violins obviously had to play an octave above the continuo. Throughout all three intermezzos, the orchestra has a very active role, with participation by the full ensemble extended well beyond the usual introductory and mediant ritornellos. Here, more than in any of Conti's other sets of intermezzos, the continuo is often tacit during vocal passages, allowing the upper strings to provide the accompaniment.

Intermezzo I opens with Eringhetta singing a typical 'pathetic' aria in A minor, accompanied by three instrumental parts. Conti chooses this style to mirror Eringhetta's complaint about the sad state of affairs in which she finds herself. Her initial vocal phrase is a restatement of the first few bars of the ritornello and is followed by a brief orchestral interlude, after which Eringhetta restates her initial phrase and then continues on with new material. Here, then, is a rare example of Conti employing the old-fashioned *Devisen* or motto beginning. In the *B* section of the aria, Conti signals a change in Eringhetta's mood by shifting the metre from triple (3/8) to duple (2/4) and by altering the orchestral texture, wherein the continuo drops out during most of the vocal passages while the upper strings have the responsibility for the accompaniment.

Example 10.5. 'Eringhetta e Donchilone' (Intermezzo I): aria, bars 1-18

Eringhetta remains on stage to sing a brief recitative before the orchestra brings on Donchilone with the first notes of the ritornello introducing his aria. He is holding a piece of paper in his hand, and as he begins to sing, the audience hears him tallying up the figures on a pharmacist's bill. He starts the tabulation process slowly, but then picks up the pace as he computes the numbers in a quasi-*parlando* style – the whole section marked *presto assai* (ex. 10.5). Given the nature of the text, Conti does not wish to overextend this comic moment and therefore the aria is not only very short but also through-composed. In the course of the aria the entire text is stated twice, but on the repetition Conti varies the musical setting. One of the clever means he employs to extend the aria is to have Donchilone sing a phrase and then have the continuo part repeat it at pitch. By so doing he is able to have several internal repetitions of certain textual phrases that might otherwise seem out of place in an aria which is devoted solely to mathematical calculations.

Matheson, in his *Der vollkommene Capellmeister,* singled out Conti for having a special talent for communicating gesture through musical means. He wrote:

> Conti . . . was uncommonly experienced in the portrayal of gestures through musical notes (where is this a loss to art?) and his ideas have about the same charming effect merely on paper as if one were to see all sorts of pleasant, vivacious postures in the flesh.[30]

There are any number of examples in Conti's recitatives and arias that could demonstrate the aptness of Mattheson's comment. One such gestural example is contained in the opening bars of Donchilon's aria cited above. Here the composer has intentionally set the numbers *uno* and *due* to notes of a duration that are longer than the other notes in the vocal line, the reason being that he wants to give the singer enough time to act out his puzzlement of how to compute the numbers on the pharmacist's bill. Upon repetition of the text, however, Conti does not treat his setting of these first two numbers any differently than the rest of the vocal part.

When Eringhetta discovers that Donchilone is fretting over his various maladies and the ineffectual remedies for them, she decides to disguise herself as a doctor so that she can prescribe a cure for what ails him. Intermezzo II begins with 'Doctor' Eringhetta listening to Donchilone describe his ailments. After suggesting several remedies, she/he decides there is but one that will provide an effective cure for everything: 'il più certo rimedio è il matrimonio' ('the most certain remedy is marriage'). Eringhetta reinforces this prescription when she, still playing the role of a doctor, sings the aria 'Questo è il mio recipe'. The aria opens with an introductory ritornello in which the primary motif, repeated three times by the first violins, is echoed in the manner of a canon at the distance of one bar by the second violins. When the voice enters, the singer takes up this same primary motif of the ritornello and is accompanied, in canonic fashion, by the strings. The musical setting achieves its humorous intent by allowing the text to be projected clearly and succinctly, even to the point of having the final two bars of the *B* section sung *a cappella*. The simplicity of the harmonic support adds to the overall effect.

While Donchilone remains alone on stage to sing a brief recitative and an aria, Eringhetta is exchanging the doctor's outfit for her rightful costume so that she can appear as herself at the beginning of the next recitative. As soon as Donchilone sees her, he is quick to explain what the doctor has ordered him to do. Eringhetta's response is that he should marry a certain Zittella, knowing full well he is not in love with her. As expected, Donchilone rejects this idea, confessing he has someone else in mind. With much hesitation, he finally admits that the someone else is none other than Eringhetta.

The duet that follows is designed to portray this union of affections and to suggest that a blissful ending is about to be achieved. By using a four-part ensemble for the accompaniment, Conti seems to have intentionally elevated the status of this duet, for in all of the other arias and duets, the number of accompanying instrumental parts is limited to three. That the two characters are of one mind is made clear to the audience as soon as the voices enter. Their initial vocal phrase is sung *à due* and restates the opening bars of the introductory ritornello. Later on in the aria, Conti segments the opening theme into motifs defined by their distinctive rhythmic patterns. For example, out of the second bar of the ritornello theme, Conti fashions a separate motif recognizable by its short –long pulse. When Donchilone sings that motif, repeating it four times in succession, there is no mistaking its source. The reuse of motifs to recall thematic material that has a structural point of reference is characteristic of Conti's style of composition.

Intermezzo III begins not with an aria or recitative, but with a duet which happens to offer a good example of how Conti is able musically to delineate differences between two characters. The first words out of Donchilone's mouth, 'Maledetta la ricetta' ('Cursed be the prescription'), alert the audience that all has not turned out as planned. He curses the doctor for his predicament, unaware that he is actually cursing Eringhetta. She, for her part, is equally distressed with Donchilone, and this tension is reflected in the way Conti handles the vocal lines. Each singer has distinctive melodic material with which to express his or her thoughts, but when their individual vocal phrases are sung simultaneously, as they often are, the lyrics become less distinct as the frustration with their present situation increases. To further accentuate the disharmony that exists between the characters, Conti purposely avoids having them sing in parallel thirds or sixths.

There is but one aria in this third intermezzo. It is sung by Eringhetta and opens directly with a six-bar phrase for the voice in unison with the violins. In the next six-bar phrase, the viola is added to the vocal and violins parts, and finally in bar 13 the continuo joins the ensemble. Not until the conclusion of the *A* section is there an instrumental ritornello. Eringhetta has had second thoughts about her deception of Donchilone and reconsiders her plight in both the aria and the recitative that follows. A reconciliation eventually takes place, resulting in the need for yet another duet. Perhaps to suggest a more serious tone for the finale, Conti has composed this duet in A minor.

If Conti did indeed set this Molière comedy twice, once under the title *L'ammalato immaginario* and again in the untitled set of intermezzos discussed above, it is all the more unfortunate that the musical score for the former has not been located, for it would have allowed for a very meaningful comparison of the two versions.

The intermezzo, so common to the Viennese stage during Conti's career as a composer there, was rarely experienced in places such as the court of Braunschweig-Wolfenbüttel. According to Gustav Schmidt, only five different sets of intermezzos were staged there between 1716 and 1730. Of these, at least two were composed by Conti: 'Pimpinone e Grilletta' staged with the 1720 revival of *Sesostri* and 'Farfalletta, Lirone, e Terremotto' staged with the 1722 revival of *Astarto*.[31] A third set may also be by Conti, for the 1716 and 1721 performances of *Teodosio ed Eudossa* by Fux, Gasparini, and Caldara included two independent intermezzos, 'Tuberone e Dorimene', which were sung in German. Although any one of the three composers who created this pasticcio opera could have composed these intermezzos, it is probable that they were composed by Conti, inasmuch as he had already provided a similar set for the 1714 Vienna production of *L'Atenaide*. The plot of *Teodosio* is the same as that for *L'Atenaide*, for Eudossa's real name is Atenaide.

A question that needs to be raised at this point is this: did the sets of intermezzos composed by Conti continue to be staged with the same host operas whenever the latter were given additional productions, either in Vienna or abroad? Three of the host operas – *Astarto*, *Griselda*, and *Teseo in Creta* – are not known to have had revivals and thus they can be eliminated from consideration here. That leaves *Sesostri, rè di Egitto* and *Ciro* as two sources that might shed light on this question.

Sesostri reportedly had two revivals: one was in August 1720 at the court in Braunschweig and the other was in 1729 for Vienna's Carnival season. Manuscripts related to these productions are not extant, making it impossible to ascertain if the original set of intermezzos was ever revived or revised for either or both of the performances cited. *Ciro* may have had at least one revival, as suggested by a manuscript of the opera in the Marburg an der Lahn Staatsarchiv (D/*MGs*: Mus. 4072). This score differs somewhat from the manuscript (A/*Wn*: Mus.Hs. 18087) that is in the Österreichische Nationalbibliothek. Interestingly, the greatest degree of difference between them concerns Intermezzo I, for the Marburg score consists solely of a recitative and a duet, the two arias having been omitted. This difference suggests that the intermezzos were probably revived along with the opera for a production that has yet to be identified.

In 1719 the opera *Tigranes* (*Die über Hass und Liebe siegende Beständigkeit*) was produced for the Hamburg stage with a set of intermezzos involving the characters Tuberone and Dorimena. According to Mattheson, the opera represented the collaborative effort of several composers, including Conti, but since the score is no longer extant, it is not possible to determine the specific contribution he may have made to the production.[32] It is possible, however, to suggest that he was responsible for the intermezzos, given the fact that he had already contributed a 'Tuberone e Dorimena' set for a production of *L'Atenaide* in Vienna in 1714. In fact, the music for the 1714 and 1719 productions may have been one and the same. Since the performance of *Tigranes* marked only the second time that intermezzos were presented on the Hamburg stage, the first having taken place in 1708, 'Tuberone e Dorimena' can be credited with having played a significant role in providing a new form of entertainment for audiences in that city.[33]

Notes

1   Johann Mattheson, *Der vollkommene Capellmeister* (Hamburg, 1739), 40.
2   See, for example, Alexander von Weilen, *Geschichte des Wiener Theaterwesens* (Vienna, 1899), I, 74. Francesco S. Quadrio, in his *Della storia e della ragione d'ogni poesia* (Bologna, 1739-52), III, 506, also considers this work to represent a set of intermezzos, for he includes it with other similar sets (*Lesbina e Milo* and *Pimpinone e Vespetta*) in his inventory of volume one of *Raccolta copiosa d'intermedj*, published in Milan (imprint gives Amsterdam) in 1723. A different interpretation is set forth by Robert Eitner in his *Quellenlexicon*, III, 35, where he labels this work a *serenata* and indicates the manuscript is in A/*Wn*. Presently, no mansucript by Conti with this title is in Vienna. Curiously, Köchel also lists *Ammalato immaginario* as a *serenata* performed in February of the 1713 Carnival season. See his *Johann Josef Fux* (Hildesheim, 1974), 530.
3   Listed as Schatz no. 2204, in Oscar G. T. Sonneck, ed., *Catalogue of Opera Librettos Printed Before 1800* (Washington, DC, 1914), II, 1484.
4   Robert Haas, *Gluck und Durazzo im Burgtheater* (Zurich, 1925), 23, and *idem*, 'Die Musik in der Wiener deutschen Stegreifkomödie', *Studien zur Musikwissenschaft* 12 (1925): 7, 22, for a list of comic scenes and intermezzos performed in Vienna from 1714 to 1728.
5   Note, the characters' names in the score are spelled Eringhetta and Donchilone.
6   For performances in Venice, Florence, Pistoia, Brussels, Pergola, Ferrara, and Naples between 1721 and 1732 of intermezzos listed under the title *L'ammalato immaginario* or under the names of the *dramatis personae* (Erighetta and Don Chilone), see Charles Troy, *The Comic Intermezzo* (Ann Arbor, MI, 1979), 50-51, 143, and 161. See also *Raccolta copiosa d'intermedj*, I, 8-22, where one version of the text for these intermezzos is printed.
7   On page 46 of *The Comic Intermezzo*, Charles Troy lists Conti's intermezzos which had their premières with his own operas. Not included in that list are the three intermezzos played by the characters 'Eringhetta' [sic] and 'Donchilone' [sic], which were staged with *Griselda* (1725); yet, on p. 216, where the scores that Troy consulted for his book are cited, this set

of intermezzos appears correctly with its host opera, *Griselda*, along with the folios in the opera manuscript where the intermezzos are positioned. Also on p. 46, Troy mentions Conti's contribution of intermezzos to *L'Atenaide*, but he says nothing about his contribution of one intermezzo to the set that was performed with Antonio Lotti's *Giove in Argo* in Dresden, even though he does call attention (on p. 42) to the other two intermezzos of this set composed by Scarlatti .

8   In 1710, Apostolo Zeno was commissioned by Charles III, then King of Spain and residing in Barcelona, to write *L'Atenaide*; its musical setting involved the collaboration of three composers – Fiorè, Caldara, and Gasparini. Perhaps it was the emperor's enjoyment of the original production that prompted yet another in 1714, albeit with different music.

9   Hellmuth Christian Wolff, *Die Barockoper in Hamburg (1678-1738)* (Wolfenbüttel, 1957), I, 116.

10   This set of intermezzos begins and ends in F major, with all of its other arias and a duet also in major keys.

11   This surname of this singer is always listed as Paolo, not Pezzoni, in the cast lists for Conti's scores.

12   For a discussion of Ballerini's (Ballarini) association with Conti, see chapter two.

13   The libretto for the *Intermedi* was published separately from the opera libretto by Jean Riedel in Dresden, 1717. Copies of the libretto are available in several libraries, including US/LC.

14   Charles Troy, *The Comic Intermezzo* (Ann Arbor, MI, 1979), 42-3.

15   In his *The Late Baroque Era* (Englewood Cliffs, NJ, 1994), 223, George J. Buelow indicates that a production of *Giove in Argo* took place in 1719 in connection with the dedication of the new opera house, but since he does not mention that this was the second production of this opera in Dresden, he leaves the reader with the impression that it was the first and only production.

16   For a list of these productions and the casting, see Michael Talbot, 'Albinoni's *Pimpinone* and the Comic Intermezzo', in Iain Fenlon and Tim Carter, eds, *Con che soavità: Studies in Italian Opera, Song, and Dance, 1580-1740* (Oxford, 1995), 236.

17   For a comparative study of the Albinoni and Telemann settings of *Pimpinone*, see Hellmuth Christian Wolff, '*Pimpinone* von Albinoni und Telemann – ein Vergleich', *Hamburger Jahrbuch für Musikwissenschaft* 5 (1981): 29-36. Telemann's *Pimpinone oder Die ungleiche Heirat* was first performed in Hamburg in 1725. His version retains the text of the Italian arias and duets of the first two intermezzos as well as those of Intermezzo III as they appeared in Albinoni's *Pimpinone*, and it also contains the additional Italian aria 'Ella mi vuol confondere' that appears in versions created after 1715. The recitatives are in German and an aria with German text is added to Intermezzo I and two duets in German are supplied for Intermezzo III. While Telemann's setting is a delightful interpretation of the comedy, it is still anchored, for the most part, in a style that is similar to that exhibited by the Albinoni score. That he was acquainted with Conti's version is quite apparent in his writing of Pimpinone's aria 'Guarda un poso', even to the extent that he adopts one of the dominant motifs from Conti's aria for his own purposes. Compare bar 5 of Conti's score with bar 4 of the modern edition of Telemann's score (p. 38), ed. by Th. W. Werner and published as Georg Philipp Telemann, *Pimpinone* (Mainz: 1936).

18 Naborre Campanini held that the extant correspondence of Zeno and Pariati confirmed his opinion that Pariati was indeed responsible for writing the comic scenes that appear in connection with librettos credited to Zeno. See his *Un prescursore del Metastasio* (Florence, 1904), 22.

19 Michael Talbot discusses some of the differences between the text used in the 1709 score and the earliest printed edition, which he characterizes as the polished 'literary' edition. See his *Tomaso Albinoni, The Venetian Composer and His World* (Oxford, 1990), 223.

20 Some examples of the minor differences between the texts found in the 1709 and 1717 scores are indicated below, using as a convenient reference point the numbering of individual lines of the 1709 text as printed in Michael Talbot's edition of Tomaso Albinoni, *Pimpinone* (Madison, WI, 1983), xviii-xxv:

	1709	1717
line 43	discolpa ogni difetto	discolpa un tal difetto
line 86	Illustrissimo padron!	Io mi umilio al mio Padron.
line 164	dieci mille. Oh.	dieci mila. Andiamo. Oh.
line 178	(Per amore manca il core.)	(Per amore mi manca il core.)
line 181	Ora è il tempo del goder.	[omitted]
line 249	con la moglie	con le mogli
line 252	I dieci mille	I dieci mila
line 261	fa quel che vuoi	fa quel che brami

21 Giovanna Gronda, in her chapter entitled 'Il mestiere del librettista' contained in Giovanna Gronda, ed., *La carriera di un librettista: Pietro Pariati da Reggio di Lombardia* (Bologna, 1990), 124-5, mentions that Pariati retouched the earlier version of his work for Vienna and she prints side by side the two versions of the second of the two arias in Intermezzo III to demonstrate the changes. She, however, makes no mention that the first aria has also been changed. Michael Talbot, in the preface to his edition of *Pimpinone,* calls attention to the subsitution of 'Gran Diavola' for the first aria in the 1709 version of the libretto, indicating that 'only one aria is omitted'. He, however, seems not to have been aware of the substitution for the second aria. See his edition of Tomaso Albinoni, *Pimpinone,* xvii, note 31.

22 The text for the 1717 version of the arias in the third intermezzo, given below, is taken directly from the manuscript (A/*Wn*: Mus.Hs. 17210) of the host opera, *Sesostri, rè di Egitto*:

Pimpinone:

Gran Diavola!	Di Rabbia già son tiscio
Per collera nel ventre, e ne lo stomaco	Di smania già son etico,
Un fla, fla, fla, flato Ipocondriaco	E temo che fronetico
Mi sento a brontolar	Mi fascia diventar
E non si può parlar.	Ne' so che cosa far.

Grilletta:

Volgio far come fan l'altre,	Vo' saper cos' è l'odiglio
Darmi l'aria d'una Dama	Entro Passo-caseariglio
S'un mi chiama, dir monsieur	Dir mi dò' mi dò con leggradria
S'un mi lasica, dir Adieu	S'aggagne con bizzaria
E ad ogn'un far civiltà.	E far quel ch'ogni si fà.

The corresponding texts for the 1709 version of these arias can be found on p. xxiv in the modern edition of *Pimpinone* edited by Talbot cited above.

23 See Talbot's preface to his edition of Tomaso Albinoni, *Pimpinone*, xii.

24 K. Vlaardingerbrock's research corrects the long-held belief that Faustina was of noble birth. See his 'Faustina Bordoni Applauds John Alensoon,' *Music and Letters* (1991): 546.

25 For a discussion and an example of how Faustina may have ornamented her vocal lines, see George J. Buelow, 'A Lesson in Operatic Performance by Madame Faustina Bordoni', in *A Musical Offering: Essays for Martin Bernstein* (New York, 1977), 79-96.

26 The manuscript consulted was A/*Wn*: Mus. Hs.17242, with fols I, 93-132; II, 68-86; III, 87-115 containing the intermezzos. The libretto for *Astarto* represents the collaborative work of Zeno and Pariati.

27 For another example, see Act V of Conti's *Teseo*. This modified *da capo* begins with Piritoo's aria 'Tanto brama il fior' in binary form and continuo accompaniment. It continues with Carilda's aria sung to the same music as was used for Piritoo, only now the accompaniment is for three-part strings. The third segment is a duet for Carilda and Piritoo which again uses the music from the initial aria and expands the accompaniment to four-part strings.

28 Several manuscripts of *Griselda* are extant. The discussion here is based upon A/*Wn*: Mus.Hs. 17238.

29 The libretto may have been provided by Pariati. For performances of untitled intermezzos with the characters Erighetta and Don Chilone and of *L'ammalato immaginario* given between 1707 and 1732, see note 6 above.

30 Johann Mattheson, *Der vollkommene Capellmeister*, Ernest C. Harris, trans. (Ann Arbor, MI, 1981), 142-3.

31 Gustav Friedrich Schmidt, 'Zur Geschichte, Dramaturgie und Statistik der frühdeutschen Oper (1627-1750)', *Zeitschrift für Musikwissenschaft* VI (1923-24): 524.

32 Johann Mattheson, *Die musikalische Patriot* (Hamburg, 1728), 190.

33 Paul Alfred Merbach, 'Das Repertoire der Hamburger Oper von 1718 bis 1750', *Archiv für Musikwissenschaft* VI (1924): 355-6.

CHAPTER ELEVEN

The oratorios

Of the ten or more oratorios Conti composed, only nine had performances during his lifetime. At least one oratorio, and possibly as many as two others, were presented posthumously in 1736.[1] Nine of the extant scores are complete; one, *Il Gioseffo* (1706), is lacking Part II. Scores for the other two oratorios do not survive, but information about them, taken from the title pages of their librettos, indicates that they were commissioned by Johann Adam (Graf) Questenberg for performances in Bruna (Brno). One was *Il martirio della madre de' Maccabei*, an oratorio for six voices which was sung during the 1736 Lenten season at the church of San Michel' Arcangelo de' Padri Predicatore. The other was *Sant' Elena al Calvario*, a *componimento sacro per musica* sung in the parochial church of San Giacomo at an unspecified time in 1736.[2]

The number of solo roles in the surviving oratorios varies from four to seven singers, with the majority of scores requiring two sopranos, an alto, tenor, and bass. *Il martirio di San Lorenzo* does not have a second soprano role because its cast is limited to four voices (SATB). Two other oratorios, *Mosè preservato* and *L'osservanza della divina legge nel martirio de' Maccabei*, lack a tenor role and *Gioseffo, che interpreta i sogni* is the only one that includes a *testo* or narrator's part (for tenor). Since the singers who performed these sacred dramatic works for Conti were usually the very same who sang his operas, it is reasonable to assume that he was mindful of their personalities and musical skills and designed his vocal parts accordingly. The soprano roles were divided between female singers and castrati, whereas the alto roles were primarily assigned to three castrati. In *Mosè preservato*, however, the alto roles were shared by the castrato Pietro Casati and a female singer, Signora Forastiera. Maria Landini Conti, Francesco's second wife, sang at least two roles in her husband's oratorios: Eva in 1718 performance of *La colpa originale* and 'La madre di Mosè' in *Mosè preservato*. She also may have sung the role of Maria in *Dio sul Sinai*, but since the cast list supplied with the manuscript score for the 1719 performance does not include the names of the singers, there is no way to confirm this. For the revival of *La colpa originale* in 1725, the role of Eva was sung by Maria Lorenzani Conti, Francesco's third wife.

Conti has woven contrapuntal textures into the fabric of many of these works. His mastery of this compositional technique can be observed in the overtures, choral numbers, and in the so-called *doppelfugato* arias This type of aria, structured as a fugue with two subjects, can be found in Part I of each of his oratorios except *Il Gioseffo*. Whenever two or more *doppelfugato* arias are included, as in *Naaman*, *Il David perseguitato*, and *David*, one of them will appear in Part II.[3] Of the thirteen *doppelfugato* arias under consideration here, ten are for a bass soloist, two are for a soprano, and one is for an alto castrato.

Two or more choral numbers are in all but the *Il Gioseffo* score.[4] Usually they are positioned as the concluding numbers for the first and second parts of the oratorio. An exception occurs in *Il martirio di San Lorenzo*, where the first of the two choral numbers begins Part I. This particular chorus is also unusual in that the middle (B) section of the *da capo* structure is cast in a recitative – *arioso* style for the bass soloist.[5] Four of the oratorios have three choral numbers, but in only two of the four scores does this extra chorus appear at the beginning of a part. In *Il David perseguitato*, the chorus begins Part I and in *David* it begins Part II. *Dio sul Sinai* offers another variant. The choral numbers in this oratorio, which are labelled *madrigale*, conclude both parts of the score, but a portion of the first chorus from Part I is repeated in the beginning section of Part II.[6] Other types of vocal ensembles (duets, trios) are used sparingly. Some of the oratorios lack them completely; others have between one and three ensembles.

Obbligato instruments have an important role to play in most of the oratorios, as will become evident in the discussion of individual works. The most frequently featured obbligato instrument is the theorbo; it is given this role in seven of the oratorios.[7] Other obbligato instruments include the trombone, mandolin, flute, chalumeau, and bassoon, along with the instruments that comprise the basic string ensemble – violin, viola, and violoncello.

With few exceptions, Conti's oratorio librettos are drawn from the Hebrew scriptures. Those exceptions are *Il David perseguitato*, which has an allegorical text superimposed upon a biblical story, and the hagiographical *Il martirio di San Lorenzo* and *Sant'Elena al Calvario*. Despite the frequency with which some of his contemporaries, Fux and Caldara among them, set the *sepolcro* type of libretto based upon the stories related to Christ's crucifixion, it is curious that in his works for Vienna Conti never ventured into this special category of oratorio, designed primarily for performance during Holy Week.[8]

Whether or not any of Conti's oratorios could be viewed as vehicles for social and political commentary is difficult to assess; yet that possibility certainly exists. Since printed copies of the librettos were available for those who attended the performances, the librettists could have used them as an expedient means to communicate their ideas. One need look no further than England to observe the manner in which librettists coded their offerings to effect allusions well understood by their audiences but which today are difficult, if not impossible, to fathom.[9] A connection between Conti's oratorios and events related to the imperial realm has already been suggested for *Il Gioseffo* and *Il martirio di S. Lorenzo*.[10] No doubt there are similar connections between his other oratorios and court happenings, but at the moment they remain a mystery. Conti's choice of librettos may also reflect his own personal attitude towards religion, politics, and social issues. Themes relating to the moral integrity of a human being and to a person's steadfast devotion to a divine, rather than a temporal, power are prominent in his oratorios. He also set two different librettos for each of the biblical stories that pertain to Joseph, David, and perhaps also to the Maccabei massacre. Is any of this coincidental or is there an agenda here that awaits discovery?

The twelve librettos set by Conti represent the work of at least eight different authors.[11] Two were contributed by Apostolo Zeno and two, possibly three, by Antonio Maria Lucchini.[12] Surprisingly, Pietro Pariati contributed only one, *La colpa originale*.[13] This stands in sharp contrast to Conti's opera librettos, with the majority of them authored by Pariati alone or in collaboration with Zeno. Pariati and Zeno never collaborated in the writing of oratorio librettos, for this was a genre that Zeno wanted strictly reserved for his own creativity. He viewed the oratorio as an *azione sacra* and constructed his texts in a manner that allowed them to be performed independently of any musical accompaniment. Comments made by Zeno in his letters and in a dedicatory preface to a published edition of his oratorio texts reveal the high regard he had for his sacred, as opposed to his secular, dramatic librettos. His letters also set forth what he considered to be appropriate subject matter, structure, and style: texts should be based upon biblical material and avoid the inclusion of divine personages; the overall structure should reflect the unities of action, time, and place; and patriarchs, prophets, and apostles should speak in a style commensurate with that observed in the Bible.[14]

Naaman (1721) and *David* (1724) exemplify well Zeno's concept of what an oratorio should be. These two librettos closely parallel the biblical accounts upon which they are based.[15] They also are phrased in language that corresponds to the interpretative writings of the church scholars of the period. *Naaman* presents the story of the leper as told in the fifth chapter of II Kings; it requires a cast of seven characters (SSSAATB) and a chorus of servants.[16] In his setting of the text, Conti incorporates features that are commonly found in many Viennese oratorios. For example, fugal writing is present in the overture, in the choruses that conclude Parts I and II, and in the *doppelfugato* arias. Instrumentally accompanied recitative is used to underline those passages wherein events in the drama precipitate strong emotional reactions. Just such a situation occurs in Part II when Eliseo proclaims a curse on his servant. This is expressed in a recitative that moves from a section in *stromentato*, to one of *recitativo semplice*, and then back again to *stromentato* when the curse on Gesi actually takes effect.

Noticeably lacking from this oratorio are the obbligato instruments. Instead of adding instruments to the basic ensemble, Conti concentrates on varying the textures and placing one or more of the strings in an obbligato role. In other words, arias and choruses in *Naaman* are accompanied either by the *basso continuo* alone or by the string ensemble divided into two, three, or four parts. Only two of the arias are accompanied solely by the continuo and each is followed by a separate, but thematically related, ritornello scored for four-part strings.

One aria that stands apart from all of the others in *Naaman* is 'Fermati e dove, dove corri?', sung by Gesi (tenor), the servant of Eliseo, and accompanied by four-part strings. Its position in Part II coincides with the dramatic high point of the libretto, the very place where Conti frequently introduces an aria with a substantial obbligato part for either the theorbo or trombone. Instead of relying on an obbligato instrument to accentuate the importance of the aria, Conti depends here upon significant changes in tempo to achieve a similar goal. The opening bars (1-22) of the aria are in an *adagio* tempo, but following a strong cadential close in the tonic key in bars 19-22, the tempo abruptly changes to *presto* and along with that change comes new thematic material. These changes create the impression, from the listener's point of view, that the *presto* section of the aria constitutes the middle or *B* section of a *da capo* form. Not until the full *da capo* is sung, however, does it become clear that *A* contains two distinctly different sections. The *B* section of the aria opens with a few bars in an *adagio* tempo, then moves into a *presto* tempo for a number of bars before finally returning to the *adagio* for the final phrase. The *presto* portions of both *A* and *B* use similar thematic material for the instrumental accompaniment, further blurring the distinction between the two sections of the aria. Interestingly, each of the *adagio* portions in this aria has been paired with a question in the text. What is more, when the singer poses each of the three questions, he does so with virtually no accompaniment, which further heightens the contrast between the *adagio* and *presto* portions of the entire piece. In the première performance of *Naaman*, this aria was sung by Francesco Borosini.

Oratorio performances, as reported in the *Wienerisches Diarium*, traditionally occurred within the framework of a Thursday afternoon Lenten service. For example, an entry in the *Diarium* for Thursday, 30 March 1724, announces that *David* (with text by Zeno and music by Conti) will be sung at the Hofkapelle that afternoon and that there will be the customary sermon preached in Italian.[17] In a letter Apostolo Zeno wrote to Pietro Caterino Zeno in 1728, he explains that the sermon on these occasions was delivered between the first and second parts of the oratorio, a practice not unlike that observed in Lutheran services of worship in Germany during this same period where the sermon was framed by the two parts of a cantata or other musical composition.[18] In the Lutheran services the texts of the sermon and the musical work were related since both were based upon the lectionary readings prescribed in the liturgical calendar. Whether or not there was any correlation between the text of the Italian sermon delivered in the Hofkapelle and that of the oratorio being performed is not known.

David is one of Conti's finest oratorios.[19] Some contemporary accounts of this composition considered it to be on a level with Handel's *Saul*. It represents a mature work, the eighth oratorio Conti composed for Vienna. *David* retells the story of the title character as it is found in I Samuel 17:55-19:24. It requires a cast of six characters (SSAATB) and a chorus. The singers who participated in the 1724 performance were Rosa d'Ambreville Borosini (Micol, soprano), Domenico Genovesi (Gionata, soprano), Pietro Casati (Abner, alto), Gaetano Orsini (David, alto), Francesco Borosini (Saul, tenor), and Christoph Praun (Falti, bass). The principal character, David, has four arias, Micol and Gionata have three, and the remaining characters have two arias each. David and Saul also have significant passages in *recitativo stromentato*. A mere reckoning of the number of arias and accompanied recitatives assigned to individual characters, however, does not fully describe the proportional relationship between the musical material and a character's role. In this particular work, over one-third of the music is associated with the title character. Since he has but one aria and a brief accompanied recitative in Part I, this means that the remaining music associated with David dominates Part II. Not only is the length of this material far greater than that associated with any of the other characters, it is also more striking with respect to the scoring, for David sings two arias in which the theorbo and trombone are used as obbligato instruments respectively.

According to information on the title page of the score, the biblical story takes place in Jerusalem during the reign of Saul. David, who faithfully defended Saul's kingdom against the Philistines, brought honour and fame to his name. His victories in battle made him a very popular figure, but this popularity stirred feelings of jealous rage and fear in the king. Saul laid plans to have David killed, but each time his plans were thwarted, either through David's own actions or through those of Saul's children, Jonathan and Michal, who constantly protected him from their father's wicked schemes. Although David and Michal were allowed to marry, this did not put an end to Saul's desire to have his kingdom rid of this national hero.

Twice in the course of the biblical account the narrator describes David playing the lyre (*kinnôr*) to produce a calming effect on Saul when he is possessed with an evil spirit. The sound of the lyre was supposed to act as a healing balm for restoring one's mental state. And twice, spear in hand, Saul attempts to kill David while he is playing this instrument. After this second incident, David flees the kingdom, seeking the protection of Samuel in Ramah where he and others are given to prophesying. Saul sends messengers to find David, but when they come upon him in the company of Samuel, they are overwhelmed with 'the Spirit of God' and begin to prophesy. Finally, when all attempts to capture David fail, Saul himself undertakes the journey to Ramah, but he also gets caught up in the act of prophesying. The final words of I Samuel 19:24 are those of the final chorus of *David*: 'Is Saul also among the prophets?'.

The precise make-up of the orchestral forces needed to perform Conti's works is often open to interpretation, but internal evidence in the form of performance directives can offer valuable clues. With respect to *David*, those clues make clear that in addition to the upper strings (first and second violins and violas), the lowest part of the basic four-part scoring is to be played by one or more of the following: *cembalo, violoncelli, contrabassi, fagotti*. All four of these instruments are identified in the score solely on the basis of those passages where words such as *senza fagotti* or *senza cembalo* indicate that these instruments are momentarily to stop playing the continuo part. The only other instruments mentioned in the manuscript are the theorbo and the trombone which have obbligato roles in their respective numbers. There is, of course, the possibility that the theorbo also shared in the realization of the continuo throughout the oratorio.

The overture to *David*, entitled 'Sinfonia', is in C minor and scored for four instrumental parts. It consists of a sixteen-bar introductory *adagio* movement, an *allegro* fugue for the second movement, and a very brief (four bars) concluding section in an *adagio* tempo that recalls the initial bars of the overture. A similar design obtains in the overtures to *Naaman, Il David perseguitato, L'osservanza della divina legge*, and *Gioseffo, che interpreta i sogni*.[20] Two aspects of the overture to *David*, however, differ enough from the style of instrumental writing usually encountered in Conti's works for them to be singled out here for discussion. One concerns the rapid alternation of *forte* and *piano* (two or three changes in dynamics per bar) which overlays the chordal texture in the initial four bars of the introductory movement.[21] The relevance of these changing dynamic levels to the rest of the oratorio becomes clear as a similar pattern of dynamic changes is present in several of the arias, including Micol's 'Al Genitor mio Re' and Saul's 'Stringe Iddio'. The other has to do with the first of the two subjects of the *allegro* fugue (ex. 11.1). Its angular profile, involving a descending fourth, an ascending sixth, and an ascending leap of a seventh, suggests that Conti intended to convey something that went beyond the mere sound of the melodic line. Given the fact that the libretto takes up the story of David right after he has slain Goliath, could Conti possibly be using the exceptionally wide leaps here to call to mind the giant of a man that this Philistine was said to resemble? If such had been his intention, it would have been an ingenious means by which to place the libretto into its rightful context. Other melodic material remarkable for its angularity in the score is the vocal part sung by Saul in the aria 'Stringe Iddio' in Part I and in the final aria, 'A passo di gigante' of the oratorio.

Example 11.1. *David*: 'Sinfonia', bars 17-20

Also of interest in this second movement is the way the fugue comes to a close. Nine bars from the end, both fugue subjects are presented simultaneously for the final time, the initial subject by the first violins and the second subject by the violoncello, which at this point in the score has been separated from the continuo. This five-part texture, however is short lived, for as soon as the violoncello presents its subject, the texture reverts back to four parts. Sustaining the cello's separate thematic presentation is a pedal note on the dominant played by bassoons and contrabass (*'fagotti e contrab:'*), the only instruments indicated here for the continuo part.

In this particular oratorio, sections of *recitativo semplice* are considerably longer than in some of Conti's other oratorios, such as *Il David perseguitato*, a factor that can be directly attributed to the librettist. The decision to set certain sections of recitative with instrumental accompaniment to intensify passages of dramatic importance, however, rests with Conti. Those sung by Saul usually express anguish and therefore involve a very agitated style with alternating *allegro* and *adagio* sections with instrumental interjections occurring between vocal phrases. Some of the accompanied recitatives sung by David differ from the type of *stromentato recitativo* described above because the mood Conti wants to create is one of contemplation and supplication rather than anger or fear. For example, following his aria in Part I, David has a twelve-bar recitative (inserted between sections of *semplice* recitative involving other characters) in which he addresses his concerns to God. His vocal part is melodically very simple and individual phrases are expressed without any accompaniment or with just a sustained tone in the continuo. In between these phrases, however, the upper strings arpeggiate several chords, simulating a sound suggestive of various biblical references to David and his lyre. Other *stromentato* passages sung by David tend to be given a sustained accompaniment by the strings.

A variety of compositional styles is present among the sixteen arias of *David*. The initial aria 'Al Genitore' for Micol (soprano), marked *larghetto* and in F minor, begins with a ten-bar ritornello in a concerto style, its strongly rhythmic motifs indicative of the military theme that pervades this biblical story. When the voice enters, it takes up the theme as first presented by the second violin, the other instrumental parts accompanying with a restatement of that same portion of the ritornello. Whereas the upper parts employ rapid violin figuration and are consistently active, the bass line remains somewhat static, is primarily relegated to providing harmonic support, and in many passages is performed solely by the violoncello.

Other arias in this oratorio that have a similar style include David's 'Guisto prezzo a iniquità'(Part II) and Saul's 'Stringo Iddio'(Part I). David's aria recalls not only the dotted rhythms of Micol's aria, but also the fluctuation of tempos from *adagio* to *presto* that prevails in the overture. Of interest here are David's vocal melismas which are fairly extensive and tend to be accompanied solely by the continuo.

Saul's aria also recalls some of the same rhythmic figuration that was in Micol's aria, primarily because both numbers are expressing similar affections. There are, however, important differences between their two arias. Conti designed the role of Saul for a specific singer, Francesco Borosini, whose vocal agility he was ever eager to display. As has already been mentioned in earlier chapters, Borosini's vocal lines are frequently written in both the tenor and bass clefs to accommodate the wide range of his melodic material, and indeed that is exactly what occurs here. In order to insure that the instrumental parts do not detract from Borosini's part, Conti has created an accompaniment wherein the tutti passages are primarily reserved for interludes between the vocal phrases. He also has seized upon opportunities in the text to pair word-painting with vocal material that can draw attention to the singer's talent. Such is the case with his setting of 'ch'io cada' and 'caderò' where the image of falling is descriptively set with extensive downward leaps in the vocal part (ex. 11.2). The *B* section of this aria is typical

Example 11.2 *David* (Part I): aria, 'Stringo Iddio'

(a)

brac - cio   e vuol, ch'io ca - da,   e vuol ch'io ca - da

(b)

Ca - de - rò,   ca - de - rò,   ca - de - rò

of many in this oratorio. It is relatively short and places emphasis upon the singer and the text rather than on the instruments. Conti accomplishes this by limiting the tutti to one brief interlude between vocal phrases, by giving the continuo more of an active role, and by providing a fairly extensive melisma for the voice on the accented syllable of the word 'sdegnato'. The *A* and *B* sections conclude with a few chords in an *adagio* tempo, suggesting that the singer should embellish these cadential points with a vocal cadenza.

This oratorio's two *doppelfugato* arias are scored for the bass soloist and four instrumental parts. Each begins with a double fugue exposition in the ritornello, at the conclusion of which the voice takes up the initial subject while the instruments accompany with restatements of the second one. The contrapuntal texture of the opening section, however, is not always maintained throughout the entire aria, the harmonic or vertical dimension having a greater influence than the linear one on the overall structure. These arias tend to be well constructed, with most of the orchestral and vocal material derived principally from the material first presented in the ritornello; they are also among some of the most effective numbers in the oratorio.

Arias that exhibit dance-like qualities are commonly found in oratorios written for the court in Vienna, as Fux's contribution to the genre demonstrates. Some of these arias are light and gay; others, in slower tempos, relate more to the style of the saraband. *David* has relatively few arias that fall into this category, but there is 'Quale angellino al monte', the only aria sung by the title character in Part I. Elements in this aria, such as triple metre (3/8), symmetrical phrases, slow harmonic rhythm, repeated rhythmic patterns, and lightly orchestrated accompaniment in which the uppermost parts are emphasized, reflect a *galant* or pre-Classical style. Interjected between the dance-like motifs given to the violins in both the ritornello and the vocal portion of the aria are single bars of rapid figuration, which are sometimes in the form of runs that span the interval of a thirteenth. These interjections are presumably meant to convey in musical terms words derived from *fuggire* (meaning to flee) that repeatedly occur in the text (ex. 11.3).

Variations in the instrumental scoring is another means for delineating the characters within the drama. For example, in the first of the two arias for Abner (alto castrato), the scoring calls for a rearrangement of the strings indicated as follows: 'violini primi e viola prima; violini secondi e 2:da viola; due violi soli; [continuo part] senza cembalo'. The texture is contrapuntal, with the solo violas usually reinforcing the vocal part. For the second aria, in triple (3/8) metre and marked *andante*, the scoring is reduced to *violino solo* and continuo. The violin's obbligato part is extremely florid in the ritornello and was definitely meant to call attention to the performer. Since no other character in the oratorio is paired with an obbligato use of a violin or viola, it would seem that Conti intentionally employed this particular sonority to define Abner, who is Saul's general.

Occurring at the dramatic high point in Part II are several of this oratorio's most memorable numbers. First and foremost there appears a grouping of three numbers that in essence constitutes a separate unit within the context of the whole oratorio. This group begins with an instrumental 'Preludio', continues with an accompanied recitative, and concludes with an aria made distinctive by its

Example 11.3. *David* (Part I): aria, 'Quale angellino'

exceptionally long introductory ritornello. In all three of these numbers, the theorbo is featured as the obbligato instrument. [22]

The relatively short 'Preludio' is to be played *largo non troppo*; its four instrumental parts are marked '2 viol: piano piano; tiorba; [continuo] senza cembalo'.[23] Throughout most of this instrumental number, the theorbo and violins establish a dialogue with each other, the theorbo introducing a thematic idea and the violins restating it at the unison or octave above. Only in the final bars does the written-out melodic material of the theorbo give way to a series of chords that are to be arpeggiated in support of the violins. The sparsely notated continuo line merely serves to reinforce the harmonic structure. In the recitative, marked *adagio*, David's vocal part (alto clef) is accompanied by five instrumental parts consisting of sustained strings played by the basic four-part ensemble and by a series of chords (one per bar) which are to be arpeggiated by the theorbo.

The third number within this group, 'Quanto mirabile', is also sung by the title character and accompanied by unison violins, theorbo, and a continuo line that is to be played only by the violoncello and contrabass instruments. It is in D minor, the same key as the 'Preludio', has triple metre (3/4), and a tempo marked *andante*. The aria opens with a ritornello that is seventy-six bars long, providing ample opportunity to feature the instrumentalists. Although the theorbo has a very prominent part, the music it has been given does not draw undue attention to the instrument. In fact, the theorbo and violins work together in dialogue, sharing each other's thematic material, which here consists of several two-bar phrases supported by a very sparsely configured continuo. The first of these phrases is in bars 1-2; a second is in bars 5-6, and it is this latter one that is eventually restated by the singer as his opening theme. The nature of the theorbo's initial thematic material is such that it is easily subdivided into smaller motifs out of which the entire ritornello evolves (ex. 11.4a). As soon as the singer enters, the theorbo part becomes much more varied. At times it is less active and doubles the continuo. At other times, it has arpeggiated chords (one per bar) while the violins have the thematically interesting material. In the *B* portion of the aria, the theorbo regains much of its role as a presenter of the thematic material. Not only does this occur in dialogue with the violins during an interlude between vocal phrases; it also occurs in dialogue with the voice when the vocal part has an extended melismatic phrase (ex. 11.4b). Conti has indicated that a complete *da capo* of the aria is intended, even though the introductory and concluding ritornellos for *A* are exceptionally long. Could this be a case of the composer providing an opportunity to promote himself as a performer?

A similar use of the theorbo can be found in *La fede sacrilega nella morte del Precurso S. Giovanni Battista* by Fux, an oratorio performed in Vienna in 1714. At the dramatic high point of Part II, Fux has inserted an aria for Heriodas which is accompanied by the theorbo. Its exceptionally extensive ritornellos and brilliant solo accompaniment passages for the theorbo provide what one author has termed a concerto for the theorbist, who on this occasion was none other than Francesco Conti.[24]

David's final aria in Part II, 'Dì al mio Re', features the trombone, an instrument traditionally associated with sacred music for the imperial court. This aria, marked *largo,* is scored for unison violins (directed to play *piano piano*),

Example 11.4. *David* (Part II): aria, 'Quanto mirabile', (a) bars 1-6; (b) *B* section

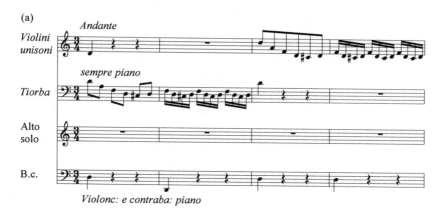

trombone (alto clef), and (continuo) *senza cembalo*. In the brief opening ritornello the trombone and violins work in dialogue with each other. When the voice enters, material similar to the opening bars of the ritornello are restated, only this time the voice is substituted for the trombone. Throughout the aria, the trombone tends to be silent during vocal passages because Conti prefers to use the instrument in alternation with phrases for the voice and/or violins rather than in an accompanying role.

David includes no vocal ensembles other than the three choral (SATB) numbers which were presumably sung by the 'Coro d'Israelite' mentioned in the cast list. It is not clear from the manuscript if this 'Coro' actually involved extra singers or if it was constituted from a grouping of the soloists. The choral numbers which conclude the two parts of the oratorio open directly with a short homophonic section for the chorus which, in turn, functions as an introduction to the choral fugue. These introductory sections in a slow tempo contrast with the faster tempos of the fugues. Throughout these two choruses the instruments play *col parte* and therefore there are no instrumental ritornellos or interludes. For the third chorus that opens Part II, Conti has chosen to set it as a through-composed number in a *concertato* style, with the instrumental ensemble playing a very important role.

Conti created oratorio scores over the course of his entire career, but unlike the operas which he composed and produced on a fairly regular basis year after year, his oratorios appeared in a somewhat more sporadic pattern. From 1703 to 1710, Conti wrote two oratorios for Vienna and contributed to two pasticcio oratorios performed in Florence. Between 1718 and 1725 there were performances of six new oratorios and the revival of two which had first been performed in 1710 and 1718. Two oratorios were performed at the court chapel in 1732 and 1736 respectively, and two more were reportedly commissioned for performances in Brno in 1736.

Il Gioseffo and *Il martirio di S. Lorenzo* were presented in the Hofkapelle long before Conti became an official composer for the emperor, but the very fact that he contributed to a *pasticcio* oratorio in Florence as early as 1703 suggests that he had had prior experience with the genre.[25] Giovanni Battista Neri's libretto for *Il Gioseffo* begins with a retelling of Genesis 39:6 of the Hebrew scriptures; it concerns the integrity of the title character when tempted by his master's wife. In the absence of both a libretto and a complete score, it is impossible to tell how much of the biblical account is incorporated into the oratorio. That it may encompass chapters 40 and 41 is suggested by the personages that make up the cast. Among them is one named Mascano, who is described as a cupbearer. He no doubt represents the Pharaoh's butler who was imprisoned with Joseph and who ultimately negotiated his release after Joseph correctly interpreted the Egyptian ruler's dreams.[26]

On the basis of the full score for Part I and the extant string parts for Part II, a reconstruction of the number of arias and ensembles in this oratorio has been attempted, the results of which show that *Il Gioseffo* has many more numbers than any of the other nine oratorios.[27] Conti takes full advantage of this by injecting considerable variety into the score, but he does so without detracting from the story itself. Part I contains sixteen numbers; of these, five arias and two duets are accompanied solely by the *basso continuo*. Two of these continuo arias are also concluded by a separate ritornello for four-part strings. That which follows the aria 'E gran pena' is only five bars long, the penultimate bar of which is given over to the first violin for a brief solo, much in the style of a cadenza.

In Part I, six arias use various combinations of strings and continuo for their accompaniments. Of these, three arias have the usual four-part string ensemble. The other three have either unison violins and continuo; violins, viola, and continuo; or four separate violin parts, viola, and continuo.[28] Part I also includes three arias which have instrumental accompaniments that are unique to each. The three-part accompaniment for Putiferre's 'Tergi pur l'umido' is scored for the bassoons (1 and 2) and continuo. Immediately following this aria there is an eighteen-bar ritornello scored for six parts in which the two bassoon parts and continuo are joined by violins (1 and 2) and viola. Gioseffo's 'Mi consolo col mio' is scored for seven parts: flutes 1 and 2, violins 1 and 2, viola, bassoon, and continuo. Flutes are used so seldom by Conti in any of his compositions that this aria takes on special significance. In the third aria, Noafa's 'Bramo un core', Conti introduces an obbligato instrument that he could have played, and probably did play, in the performance – the mandolin. The directions to the performer indicate that the mandolin is to be tuned a whole tone lower than its normal pitch. The part is written in the key of C major, whereas the other two instrumental parts involved in this accompaniment – unison violins and viola – are in the key of C minor. Throughout the aria, the viola is used very sparingly. In fact, the vocal part is often supported solely by the mandolin and violins. Conti's inclusion of a mandolin here is not unique to his score. Although this is his singular use of the mandolin in an oratorio, the instrument is featured in other oratorios of the period, such as Antonio Vivaldi's *Juditha triumphans* (1716).

Another feature that is of interest in this early work concerns the treatment of the voice. The duet 'Un ciglio sereno' shows Conti's ability to compose an ensemble wherein the distinction in emotions expressed by two characters is delineated musically. In the biblical account, Noafa is attracted to Gioseffo, but Gioseffo resists her advances because he owes his allegiance to the Pharaoh. To show that the two characters do not share a union of affections, Conti makes sure that in the passages where the two sing together, each character maintains his or her own thematic material. Only in the *B* portion of the duet do Noafa and David occasionally sing in thirds and share the same material. The manner in which Conti begins this duet is also unusual. There is no introductory ritornello. Instead, the duet opens with Noafa singing her first four-bar phrase in an *adagio* tempo.

Example 11.5. *Il Gioseffo*: (Part I): aria, 'Lo stupor con armi', (a) bars 7-9; (b) bars 34-8

(a)

(b)

Then the tempo shifts to *presto*; Gioseffo enters with a contrasting phrase, followed by Noafa, who repeats her initial phrase in the new tempo. Conti provides Noafa and Gioseffo with an equal number of arias (four) in Part I and writes both of the duets for them as well. The other three characters have but two arias each in Part I.

In the later oratorios, the bass soloist has some of the more complex arias to sing, the majority of them designed as *doppelfugato* arias.[29] Contrapuntal textures in *Il Gioseffo*, however, are almost entirely absent from Part I, but this does not preclude the bass soloist from having an aria that is a real *tour de force*. Such is Faraone's 'Lo stupor con armi', which could properly be called a bravura aria, owing to its extensive melismas and disjunct melodic lines with exceptionally wide leaps (ex. 11.5).[30]

A sizeable portion of the arias in *Il Gioseffo* have motto beginnings, often with substantial instrumental interludes between the first and second statement of the motto. There are, however, a few arias in this score that do not have any instrumental introductions and by the same token these same numbers tend to limit or even omit instrumental interludes. Although the *da capo* form for the arias prevails throughout, the ninth number (*largo* and in 3/2 metre) in Part II seems to depart from this norm. An analysis of the surviving string parts suggests that this aria may have had the following pattern: AABBAB-CC-AABBAB.

Only four years separate the performances of *Il Gioseffo* from *Il martirio di S. Lorenzo*, but within that short period of time Conti moved from an oratorio conceived more as a sacred opera to one that was aligned with a type of Viennese oratorio that had been evolving during the early decades of the eighteenth century. One major difference between the two scores concerns the number of arias and ensembles. *Il martirio di S. Lorenzo* has a total of eighteen numbers (including two choruses), nine in each of Parts I and II. That is just half the number of arias and ensembles in *Il Gioseffo*.

The distribution of arias as well as their instrumental accompaniments are often factors that can distinguish the principal from the supporting characters. Sacerdote (Borghi, tenor) and Prefetto (Praun, bass) each have three arias, but the accompaniments for Sacerdote's arias are confined either to the *basso continuo* or to violins that play *col parte* with the continuo. Prefetto's arias are accompanied by unison violins and continuo or by four-part strings. His first aria is a fugue, which foreshadows the more complex *doppelfugato* aria associated with the bass role in the later oratorios. Of the six arias sung by S. Lorenzo (Orsini, alto), three are scored for four-part strings, one for unison violins and continuo, and two involving five parts in which the fifth part in one of the arias is played by a solo violin and in the other, by chalumeaux. Obbligato instruments also appear in three of Angelo's (Schoonjans, soprano) four arias. They include theorbo, chalumeaux and basson chalumeaux, and prima and seconda baridon (baryton).

Conti's use of the bass (basson) chalumeau and baryton instruments is limited to a very few works composed between 1710 and 1715.[31] His use of the chalumeau is also primarily limited to these years, although this time-span could be somewhat extended if the cantatas are included in that count. Only the theorbo was to find a place in almost all of the oratorios he composed throughout his years at the Habsburg court. Using an obbligato instrument in Part II of an oratorio to emphasize the dramatic high point was a fairly common practice in the early decades of the eighteenth century and one that Conti regularly observed, except in this oratorio. Here he introduces the theorbo in Part I; it appears in the soprano (Angelo) aria 'D'odorosi eterni' and is joined by two other parts, one for violoncello and the other for continuo, the latter to be played *senza cembalo*.[32] The violoncello also has a very active role here and perhaps should be considered an obbligato instrument along with the theorbo. Within the opening ritornello are a number of thematic ideas which theorbo and violoncello share and this same material carries over into the vocal part. Conti does not go out of his way to feature the theorbo. In fact, the theorbo is relegated to a very secondary role, in a number of passages, especially where there are extended vocal melismas.

After *Il martirio di S. Lorenzo*, eight years passed before Conti brought forth *La colpa originale* in 1718. Although the earlier of these two works established a basic formula which Conti followed in subsequent settings of oratorio librettos, the later one reveals a considerable refinement of particular aspects of that formula. Most notable is the development of the theorbo aria as a sort of signature piece in Conti's oratorios. One such aria, 'Quanto mirabile', has already been discussed in connection with *David*. It is also the only theorbo aria that Conti wrote for an alto (castrato); all of the others are for sopranos (not castrati) who, with but one exception, are cast in female roles. That exception occurs in *Gioseffo, che interpreta i sogni* (1736), wherein the soprano (Barbara Pisani) is cast as the title character.

The theorbo arias in *La colpa orginale* (1718), *Dio sul Sinai* (1719), and *Mosè preservato* (1720) seem to have been fashioned from a common mould. They are in minor keys and, in addition to the theorbo, require four string parts.[33] Within the opening ritornello of these arias, the theorbo's thematic material is such that it allows the performer to demonstrate various styles of playing. The sequence in which this happens is similar in all three: exposition of melodic ideas in dialogue with the upper strings and of passages involving rapid figuration; restatement and/or development of thematic motifs, some of which are to be played in an arpeggiated manner; and finally, a series of arpeggiated chords designed to harmonically support the violins as they continue to present material derived from the initial theme or themes. The viola and the instrument or instruments assigned to the lowest part are confined for the most part to providing harmonic support, and sometimes not even that, for they are frequently silent whenever Conti wants attention focused on the obbligato part.

For the opening vocal phrase, the singer is provided with a new melodic phrase, but she is accompanied by a restatement of the opening bars of the ritornello. As the vocal section unfolds and the singer shares more and more of the instrumental material, it becomes clear that the entire ritornello is being restated. Although the theorbo part is often assigned to the singer, this does not mean the instrument is silent during the vocal sections. It sometimes doubles the continuo line, but more often it engages in a dialogue with the voice or violins, thereby retaining some of its original role. For the conclusion of *A*, Conti either repeats the entire ritornello *(Mosè preservato)* or limits the repeated material to the final bars of the ritornello *(La colpa originale* and *Dio sul Sinai)*. The *B* portion of these arias tends to be fairly short and thematically related to *A*. Although there is a definite attempt to focus attention on the vocal part, the theorbo as well as the violins continues to have a significant role. The theorbo is more likely to have a prominent role in those passages where melismas occur in the vocal part, alternating rapid figuration with sustained notes. Passages in which the theorbo and voice move together in parallel motion are fairly rare, but one does occur in 'Latti e pianto prendi intanto' in *Mosè preservato* wherein they move in parallel sixths.

The two remaining oratorios that feature the theorbo, *Il David perseguitato* (1723) and *Gioseffo, che interpreta i sogni* (1736), contain arias which represent entirely different approaches to the use of an obbligato instrument. That which appears in *Il David perseguitato* is very similar to other theorbo arias already discussed, most especially to the one in *David* (1724). The ritornello material is presented in a quasi-imitative style, the theorbo's motifs restated at the distance of a half bar by the violins. Also included are solo passages in rapid figuration for the theorbo which seem designed solely to display the performer's talent, since they are played without any accompaniment.

Example 11.6. *Dio sul Sinai* (Part II): aria, 'Al mirar il sol nascente',
(a) bars 1-5; (b) bars 26-9

(a)

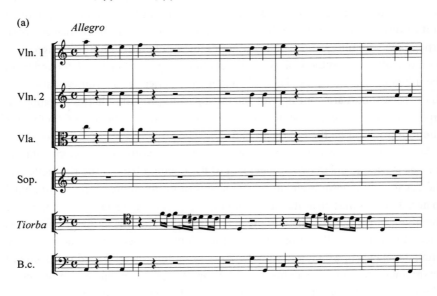

(b)

Example 11.6 (continued). *Dio sul Sinai* (Part II): aria, 'Al mirar il sol nascente', (c) bars 36-9

A far different use of the theorbo occurs in an aria sung by the title character in *Gioseffo, che interpreta i sogni*. 'Se Dio tutto può' is scored for soprano, theorbo, unison violins, and a continuo *senza cembalo*. At the outset of the fifteen-bar ritornello, the theorbo and violins play the opening theme in unison. These four bars are followed by a new motif, which is tossed back and forth between theorbo and violin until the violins, not the theorbo, set forth yet another motif derived from the opening theme. When the singer enters with the opening ritornello theme, the focus of the aria moves away from the theorbo. Apart from one or two brief bars of rapid figuration played unaccompanied, the theorbo is not given any solo passages. It is to the violins and voice that the attention is drawn throughout both the *A* and *B* portions of the *da capo*. That this aria is uncharacteristic of Conti's treatment of obbligato parts for the theorbo should be obvious. Why that should be so, however, is a question not easily answered.[34]

For the most part, Conti created theorbo parts which he would undoubtedly have taken delight in performing.[35] It is, therefore, all the more interesting to study these arias with theorbo accompaniment, for they offer an opportunity to view the dual careers of Conti within a single composition. Out of the seven arias cited here, there is one, 'Al mirar il sol nascente' in *Dio sul Sinai*, that presents a stellar example of Conti's writing for the theorbo as an obbligato instrument. It embraces more of a *concertato* style than the others and clearly shows the composer's move towards the pre-Classical style (ex. 11.6).

There are, in addition to *David,* three other oratorios – *La colpa originale, Dio sul Sinai,* and *Il David perseguitato* – that have arias which make use of the trombone as an obbligato instrument. These arias are in many ways similar to the one in *David* (described above): they are for the alto (castrato) voice, are marked with slow tempos, are positioned in Part II very close to the theorbo aria, and involve a string ensemble. The number of strings in these ensembles varies from violins and violas playing in unison (on a single staff using the alto clef or on two staves, both in the alto clef) and continuo *senza cembalo* to the basic four-part string group. What distinguishes one aria from another is the relationship of the trombone to the vocal and other instrumental parts. Throughout the *A* and *B* portions of Adamo's aria 'Mia compagna io la credea' in *La colpa originale,* the trombone and voice are accompanied by a constant pulsating semi-quaver motion of the strings played *sempre piano* (ex. 11.7). Here the trombone is ever present, even in the vocal passages. The ritornello opens with the trombone's nine-bar theme and from that point forward the trombone continues to have as much responsibility for presenting the thematic material as does the voice.

In Aronne's aria 'Or conosco il mio perfido errore' in *Dio sul Sinai,* a *concertato* style prevails. The ritornello begins with the trombone presenting its own theme independently of the upper strings and continues with the upper strings introducing an entirely different thematic idea that becomes the source from which the rest of the aria's accompaniment is derived. There are, however, no solo passages for the trombone other than that heard in the opening bars. In *Il David perseguitato,* David's aria 'Fuggo d'una in altra selva' begins with a very short ritornello in which the trombone and violins share in the exposition of thematic material. It also includes a significant passage of rapid figuration for the trombone in which to display the skill of the performer (ex. 11.8).[36]

The only other instruments used by Conti in an obbligato role are violas and violoncellos in unison, and the bassoon. The former combination occurs in Valore's aria 'Nò nel tuo sangue', sung as the penultimate number of *Il David perseguitato* by Borosini in the tenor role. The latter combination is in Part II of *L'osservanza della divina legge.* The bassoon is introduced at the same relative point in the oratorio where Conti would have used a theorbo or trombone: namely, in the aria 'Gia atroce il dolore', sung by the 'seventh son'. In this aria, Conti has provided an opportunity for the bassoon to play a cadenza in a place marked *ad libitum* that occurs just before the beginning of the *B* portion of the *da capo.* Aside

Example 11.7. *La colpa originale* (Part II): aria, 'Mia compagna io la credea', bars 1-10

Example 11.8. *Il David perseguitato da Saul* (Part II): aria, 'Fuggo d'una in altra selva'

from the choral numbers, there are very few vocal ensembles in Conti's oratorios.[37] Some are through-composed and most are limited to a *basso continuo* accompaniment. Three duets are in *Gioseffo, che interpreta i sogni*, the oratorio with the greatest number of vocal ensembles, and each one is accompanied by the orchestra. Moreover these duets are for the lower voices (AB, TB, and AT) whereas all of the other ensembles involve at least one soprano in combinations that range from SS, SA, SB, to SSA. This last grouping represents the only trio among the oratorios; it appears in Part II of *La colpa originale*.

Conti's ten extant oratorios reveal the work of a composer who took seriously the texts that he set to music. He carefully orchestrated the material to enliven the dramatic events being portrayed and never allowed the vocal parts to stray from the exposition of well-defined affections. Those works that appeared after 1710 have many numbers within them that are clearly representative of the pre-Classical style; they also have *doppelfugato* arias and choral fugues that give evidence Conti was well versed in the contrapuntal tradition. This Janus-faced approach to composition in which a balance is achieved between the older and newer styles can be most clearly observed in *L'osservanza della divina legge*, the last of Conti's oratorios performed at the court during his lifetime.

Notes

1   The twelve oratorios are: *Il Gioseffo* (1706; ?); *Il martirio di San Lorenzo* (1710/1724; G. D. Filippeschi); *La colpa originale* (1718/1721; P. Pariati); *Dio sul Sinai* (1719; G. Giardini); *Mosè preservato* (1720; ?); *Naaman* (1721; A. Zeno); *Il David perseguitato* (1723; A. Avanzo); *David* (1724; A. Zeno); *L'osservanza della divina legge nel martirio de' Maccabei* (1732; A. M. Lucchini); *Gioseffo, che interpreta i sogni* (1736; G. B. Neri); *Il martirio della madre de' Maccabei* (1736; A. M. Lucchini); *Sant'Elena al Calvario* (1736; A. M. Lucchini). *Il David perseguitato* is the title found on the manuscript (A/*Wn*: Mus.Hs. 18159), but the libretto is entitled *Il David perseguitato da Saul*. The title cited for Conti's oratorio *Gioseffo, che interpreta i sogni* is taken from the manuscript (A/*Wn*: Mus.Hs. 18165), but some secondary sources list the oratorio as either *Giuseppe, che interpreta i sogni* or *Gioseffo, che interpreta i segni*. Both *sogni* (dreams) and *segni* (signs) are applicable to the biblical story.

In a footnote to his discussion of two masses by Francesco Conti in the Dresden Sächische Landesbibliothek mistakenly attributed to a 'Jean Contini', Wolfgang Horn includes a quotation from the François-Joseph Fétis *Biographie universelle des musiciens* (II, 352) that mentions an oratorio by Jean Contini entitled *Il pescatore castigata* was performed in the church of the Dominicans in Prague in 1735. Although Horn discounts any connection of this oratorio with Francesco, further investigation might lead to a different conclusion. For more on these masses, see chapter twelve. See also Horn, *Die Dresdner Hofkirchenmusik 1720-1745* (Kassel, 1987), 166n1.

2   In his *I libretti italiani* (Cuneo, 1990, 1994), IV, 82 and V, 119, Claudio Sartori indicates that the librettos for *Il martirio della madre de' Maccabei* and *Sant'Elena al Calvario* were printed by Giacomo M. Swoboda in Bruna (Brno). He also indicates that a copy of the first named is in the Brna archives. That information now appears to be incorrect. According to Dr František Novák, director of the Archiv města Brna (who kindly responded to my inquiry), a libretto by Lucchini connected with a 1736 performance of *Il martirio della madre de' Maccabei* does not currently exist in that archive. It is therefore not possible to compare the 1732 libretto of *L'osservanza della divina legge nel martirio de' Maccabei* with the 1736 one to determine if the latter was an entirely new creation or simply a reworking of the former. Since the 1736 libretto involves six characters whereas the 1732 has but five, the two librettos obviously had to differ in some, if not all, respects.

Gottlieb Jacob Dlabačz, in his *Allgemein historisiches Künstlerlexicon für Böhmen*, I, 260, also lists a *Sant'Elena al Calvario* libretto by Lucchini representing a 1736 performance in Brno, but the libretto in question credits the music to Antonio Caldara. An oratorio with this same title was indeed set by Caldara, but his libretto was by Metastasio and the first performance was in 1731 in Vienna (repeated in 1737), followed by other performances in Jaromerič (1733), Prague (1736), and Brno (1736). Ursula Kirkendale, in her study of

Caldara's oratorios, contends that the attribution of the 1736 *Sant'Elena al Calvario* libretto to Lucchini rather than to Metastasio must be an error on the part of Dlabač. See her *Antonio Caldara* (Graz-Köln, 1966), 138.

3 *Naaman* is the only score that includes three *doppelfugato* arias: one each for soprano and bass in Part I and another for the bass in Part II.

4 The vocal score for Part II of *Il Gioseffo* has not survived nor has a copy of the libretto been located, making it impossible to know if this oratorio concluded with an ensemble. Although the cast of characters listed on the initial folios of Part I does not mention a chorus, this does not negate the possibility that individual characters joined together to sing a final number. *Gioseffo, che interpreta i sogni*, for example, does not list a chorus as part of the cast, but choral numbers nevertheless conclude Parts I and II.

5 One of the three choral numbers in *Mosè preservato* also has a middle section scored for a bass soloist.

6 The term *madrigale* was applied to the final chorus in oratorios composed as early as the second half of the seventeenth century. Limited use of the word for a similar designation continued through at least the first two decades of the eighteenth century in Vienna. See, for example, *La fede sacrilega* (1714) by Fux.

7 The seven oratorios are: *Il martirio di San Lorenzo*, *Il colpa originale*, *Dio sul Sinai*, *Mosè preservato*, *Il David perseguitato*, *David*, and *Gioseffo che interpreta i sogni*. Part II of *Il Gioseffo* (1706) might also have included the theorbo. The string parts for Part II of *Il Gioseffo* are extant. From them it is possible to determine that the second half of the oratorio had seventeen vocal numbers (one of which might have been a chorus) and a separate ritornello. On the basis of the continuo/bass part, the ninth aria (in 3/2 metre and a *largo* tempo) can be diagramed as AABBABCC (*da capo*). The parts for this particular aria also indicate that the voice was accompanied by the continuo, while the strings played only for the intervening ritornellos. In another aria, the violoncello is omitted and the upper strings are to play a pizzicato-type of accompaniment *sempre pianissimo*. Perhaps an obbligato instrument was involved here, but since the only orchestral parts that were preserved for this, as well as for all of Conti's other operas and oratorios, are for the strings, there is no way to determine what, if any, other instruments were involved in the scoring. It is this type of aria accompaniment, however, which would have invited the introduction of a theorbo or mandolin as an obbligato instrument.

8 Metastasio's libretto, *Sant'Elena al Calvario*, and Caldara's setting of the same indicate on their respective title pages that the oratorio was intended for performance at the holy sepulchre in the Hofkapelle. The published libretto for an oratorio with this same title by Lucchini lacks any information that would suggest Conti's setting of the text had a similar type of performance in Brno. For a study of the *sepolcro* type of oratorio, see Harry White, 'The *Sepolcro* Oratorios of Fux: an Assessment', in Harry White, ed., *Johann Joseph Fux and the Music of the Austro-Italian Baroque* (London, 1992), 164-230.

9 See Ruth Smith, *Handel's Oratorios and Eighteenth-Century Thought* (Cambridge, 1995) and a review of the same by Hermine W. Williams in *The European Legacy* 2 (December 1997):1437-8.

10 See chapter two. See also Hermine W. Williams, 'The Sacred Music of Francesco Bartolomeo Conti: Its Cultural and Religious Significance', in Edmond Strainchamps and

Maria Rika Maniates, eds, *Music and Civilization: Essays in Honor of Paul Henry Lang* (New York, 1984), 328-30.

11   The authors for the librettos of *Il Gioseffo* and *Mosè preservato* remain unidentified.

12   Note the spelling of Lucchini's name is not given here as it is found on the title page of the *L'osservanza della divina legge* score and in the *Wienerisches Diarium* report of this oratorio's performance. There the name is spelled Luchini and a similar spelling occurs on the title pages of the three librettos cited.

13   Pietro Pariati supplied Fux with at least six oratorio librettos. Claudio Pasquini also supplied a number of oratorio librettos for Vienna, although not one was ever set by Conti.

14   See, in particular, Zeno's letter to Giusto Fontanini of 6 November 1733 which appears as letter no. 810 in Apostolo Zeno, *Lettere* (Venice, 1785) IV, 382. See also Zeno's dedication addressed to Charles VI and Elisabeth Christina in his *Poesie sacre drammatiche di Apostolo Zeno* (Venice, 1744), unnumbered fols 6-8.

15   The biblical passages from which Zeno has fashioned each section of his oratorio texts are indicated in the margins of the printed edition of his librettos.

16   Source used for *Naaman* is A/*Wn*: Mus.Hs. 18155.

17   The exact wording of the *Diarium*'s announcement is given below:
    '[1724] Donnerstag / den 30 Martii. Nachmittag wurde bey Hof in der Kaiserl. Capellen ein Italiänish-gesungenes Oratorio (welches der David benahmset und von dem Herrn Apostolo Zeno, Kaiserl. Poeten und Historico, verfasset und die Music hierüber von Herrn Francesco Conti, Kaiserl. Tiorbisten und Cammer-Compositoren gemacht ware) wie auch die gewöhnliche Italienische Predig gehalten'.

18   Letter no. 739, dated 1 May 1728, is in Zeno, *Lettere*, 243.

19   The source used for *David* is A/*Wn*: Mus.Hs. 18161.

20   At first glance, a similar slow-fast pattern in its two-movement structure seems to be involved in the overture to *Il Gioseffo*. There are, however, two important differences: the second movement of the *Il Gioseffo* overture is not a fugue, although it does have a quasi-contrapuntal texture, and the words *da capo*, which appear at the end of the second movement, cause the design to be transformed into an ABA structure. For a more detailed discussion of this overture, see chapter seven. The overtures to *Il martirio di S. Lorenzo*, *La colpa originale*, and *Dio sul Sinai* have an *allegro-largo-allegro* pattern, while that for *Mosè preservato* reverses the pattern to *adagio-allegro-adagio*. These overtures are discussed in chapter seven.

21   In one of the manuscript sources for *Mosè preservato*, the overture opens with an alternation of *forte-piano* chords in the first two bars.

22   Although the librettos for Conti's *David* and Handel's *Saul* are based upon the same biblical account and Handel's score does include a theorbo for an aria positioned in relatively the same place as Conti's obbligato use of the same instrument, there is no direct evidence suggesting that Handel's setting of the libretto was influenced by Conti's. One, of course, cannot rule out the possibility that Handel knew *David*, since several years prior to the writing of *Saul*, he had made use of some of Conti's music in *Ormisda*.

23   The theorbo part is written in both the tenor and bass clefs to accommodate the wide range of notes (G' - g) in its part.

24   Egon Wellesz, *Fux* (London, 1965), 41.

25 Sources used for *Il Gioseffo* are A/*Wn*: Mus.Hs. 18148 (score) and Mus.Hs. 18149 (parts). Although the day and month when this oratorio was performed is not indicated, the year of its première seems to be well documented. See, for example, the entry in the *Tabulae Codicum Manu Scriptorum in Bibliotheca Palatina Vindobonensi Asservatorum*, X, 105. The title of this oratorio suggests it may have been written to honour Joseph I, who, according to the *Wienerisches Diarium,* was proclaimed emperor on Friday, 19 March 1706.

26 The names of the characters and singers who filled those roles are Gioseffo (Franzel – soprano), Putifarre (Lorenzino – alto), Noafa (La Cunigonda – soprano), Mascano (Barbaretti – tenor), and Faraone (Borrini – bass).

27 The overture to *Il Gioseffo* is discussed in connection with the London version of *Clotilde* and in chapter seven.

28 To learn how the surviving string parts can offer clues about the scoring for Part II of this oratorio, see note 7 above.

29 There are, of course, some bass arias in Conti's oratorios that are not written in a fugal style. Examples include one of the bass arias in *La colpa originale* and one in *Dio sul Sinai*, the single bass aria in *Mosè preservato*, and both of the bass arias in *Gioseffo, che interpreta i sogni.*

30 A similar type of bass aria is sung by Praun in the role of Sospetto in Part I of *Il David perseguitato*: 'Per trar l'altero a morte' has exceptionally wide leaps in the vocal part in the *B* section.

31 For the revival of *Il martirio di S. Lorenzo* in 1724, the 1710 orchestration appears to have been retained, even though Conti at that point in his career would not have included these instruments in his scoring for newly created works.

32 This same aria is printed in Karl Schnürl, ed., *Wiener Lautenmusik im 18. Jahrhundert*, vol. 84 of *Denkmäler der Tonkunst in Österreich* (Graz, 1966). The source from which this aria was taken is A/*Wn*: Mus.Hs. 18163. In this manuscript, the first obbligato instrument is indicated as *tiorba* and the second, as *violonc:*. The editor of the volume in which the aria appears misread the abbreviated designation for the cello, mistaking the ͞c for an ͞e and consequently believing the word to be *violone*. A second manuscript of this oratorio is in A/*Wgm*: III. 14.240 (Q 718) and the scoring for this same aria makes clear that both a *tiorba* and a *violoncello* (this word is spelled out in full) are to play the obbligato parts. The error made in the published edition has also misled others who have used this source. See, for example, Wolfgang Horn, in his *Die Dresdner Hofkirchenmusik 1720-1745*, 171n9.

33 In *Dio sul Sinai*, the instrumentation for the lowest of the four parts is not indicated, but in *La colpa originale*, the lowest part is to be played by the *contrabasso senza cembalo* and in *Mosè preservato*, by the *contrabasso e violoncello senza cembalo.*

34 In seeking to understand the rationale for Conti's departure from a type of aria that was a credit to his name, these questions might be relevant: Did he write the theorbo part with someone else in mind as the performer, possibly Ignazio? Did Francesco complete the score before his death or did someone else put the finishing touches to a rough draft of it?

35 In several of these theorbo arias, Conti was accompanying one of his wives. Maria Landini was the soloist for the theorbo arias in *Il colpa originale* (1718) and *Mosè preservato* (1720); Maria Anna Lorenzani sang the solo in the revival of *Il colpa originale* (1725).

36   Pietro Casati sang the roles of Adamo in both the première and revival of *La colpa originale* (1718 and 1725) and of David in *Il David perseguitato*. He also may have sung the role of Aronne in *Dio sul Sinai*, but the names of the singers are not provided in the manuscript.

37   Oratorios that lack vocal duets or trios are *Il martirio di S. Lorenzo*, *Naaman*, *David*, and *L'osservanza della divina legge*.

CHAPTER TWELVE

Sacred music

Long after Conti died, his music continued to hold a place in the cultural life of Vienna and its environs. Interestingly, his reputation as a composer was perpetuated primarily by works he had composed for services of worship. Evidence that some of these compositions formed part of the liturgical choral repertoire year after year comes from the covers of part books where later generations of musicians recorded the dates when his music was performed in the Hofkapelle and Schottenkirche on the Freyung. One work that was frequently performed was his *Sinfonia à 4*, listed as number 8 of the 'Hofcapelle musica opus 261'. Before this three-movement *Sinfonia* became associated with the repertoire for the imperial chapel, it had served as the overture to his *Pallade trionfante*. Whereas the opera seemed to bloom and fade all within the year of its creation, 1722, the overture, once placed in its new surroundings, continued to be performed at least until 1753, the last date entered on the folder containing the instrumental parts.[1]

It is difficult to assess the full range of Conti's liturgical works, for the number of manuscripts available for study is fairly limited. Some scores are lost; others are extant only in versions which have been modified by other individuals.[2] Among the manuscripts currently in the 'lost' category are those once housed in the archives of the Stift Herzogenburg in Austria. An inventory of this monastery's eighteenth-century holdings is available in two handwritten catalogues wherein a total of nine works by Conti are listed with title, incipit, and scoring for each. Six are vocal works with orchestral accompaniment and three are for instruments alone as shown in table 12.1.

Of particular interest is the *Offertorium de venerabili*, which opens with the words 'Languet anima mea'. Even though this work is no longer in the Herzogenburg archives, the music has nevertheless been preserved in a most unlikely source – a score entitled *Languet anima mea* in the hand of Johann Sebastian Bach. Circumstances surrounding Bach's encounter with Conti's music

Table 12.1

Works by Francesco Conti listed in the Stift Herzogenburg catalogues

Aria de venerabili à basso solo, 2 violins, 1 viola, organo e violone (6 parts)

Kyrie et Gloria à 6 voc. conc:, 2 violini, 1 viola, 2 tromboni, 2 clarini e tympano,
    organo e violone (16 parts)

Laudate pueri à capella: 4 voces, 2 soprani, organo e violone (7 parts)

Motetto de SS. Angelis à 4 voces, Canto, Alto, Ten., Basso concto, 2 violini, 1 viola,
    2 clarini e tympano, con org. e violone [number of parts not listed]

Offertorium de venerabili, à canto solo, 2 violini, viola, organo e violine (6 parts)

Stabat mater à 7 voc. conc:, 2 violini, 2 tromboni, 1 viola, organo e violone (14 parts)

Sinfonia à 2 violini, e basso (3 parts)

Sinfonia à 2 violini, viola oblig., basso (4 parts)

Sonata à 2 violini, viola, e basso (4 parts).[3]

---

remain a mystery, but at least one fact can be established with some certainty. Bach created his copy of Conti's 'Languet anima mea' while he was still in Weimar, as indicated by 'Fine / an[no] 1716' written on the final page of music in his own hand.[4] The title page, also in Bach's hand, credits 'Signor Francesco Conti' with the composition and lists the scoring in this order: '2 Violini Concertati, 2 Violini Ripieni, 1 Viola, Violoncello, Soprano Solo, and Continuo'. Centred at the top of the page is the word 'Motetta', but it is not in Bach's hand.[5] Sometime after the score was prepared, Bach added '2 Oboi' to the list of instruments on the title page, inserting the words in a space above the '1 Viola'. Was Bach's decision to augment the scoring prompted by an initial performance of the work and, if so, where might this performance have taken place?

Bach's 1716 score of Conti's *Offertorium de venerabili* consists of five movements: recitative (accompanied by four parts of which only the uppermost part has an instrumental indication, 'Violini P. Concerti é Ripeni', written above it), *da capo* aria (accompanied by four parts with no instrumental indication), recitative (accompanied by continuo), *da capo* aria (accompanied by two parts with the upper one indicated for 'Violino P. Concerto solo'), and a through-composed aria which sets a single word, 'alleluja' (accompanied by four parts with no instrumental indications). The source from which Bach copied Conti's music has yet to be discovered. There is reason to believe he had access to a set of parts such as those listed in the Herzogenburg catalogues, for in the fifth movement he has positioned the music for the first and second violins on two separate staves even though the parts are identical.[6] In the Herzogenburg catalogue description of Conti's *Offertorium*, it is made clear that the manuscript did not require *concertato* and *ripieno* violins.[7] That leaves open the question of whether or not Bach was responsible for adding the *ripeno* notes to the violin parts, signalled by downward stems. They are to be found in the initial aria, the only place in the score that calls for this particular division of the violins.

Another difference between Bach's score and the catalogue incipit of Conti's *Offertorium* concerns the opening measures of the first recitative. The incipit reproduces the first seven bars of the continuo line with a semibreve D reiterated in each of the first six bars followed by a semibreve G♯ in the seventh. At the comparable place in the 1716 score, Bach has the same number of notes, but he has tied the semibreve D in the first bar across the next five bars, sustaining the pitch in the manner of a pedal note.

After Bach left Weimar, he and several of his copyists prepared a set of parts for *Languet anima mea*. Judging from the paper on which they are written and the copyists involved, these parts seem to date from a time when Bach was living and working in Köthen (1717-23). He retained the instrumentation as was listed on the title page of the 1716 score except for the violoncello, which he replaced with the violone. He also included parts for two oboes and one viola da gamba. The continuo part in this set has been transposed a whole tone lower than the rest of the score and is written on paper that differs in size from the original. The hand of a copyist has been identified as Christian Gottllieb Meissner, whose association with Bach dates from February 1723. The presence of this particular transposed part may indicate that a performance of the work took place in Leipzig, because the pitch of the organ in that city was a whole tone lower than that of organs in Weimar and Köthen.[8]

In the preface to a published score of *Languet anima mea*, the editor claims that 'the present edition . . . reproduces Bach's version with oboes and not the composer's original. Those who wish to perform the work in its original form need only leave out the oboe parts'.[9] Unfortunately, this suggestion is in error. The edition represents a collation of the 1716 score (D/*Bds*: Mus.Ms. 30098) and the eleven extant parts (D/*B*: Mus.Ms. 4081) and therefore more than an omission of the oboes would have to be undertaken to recreate Conti's scoring of two violins, one viola, and a continuo line for only organ and violone. In fact, omitting the oboes will not even reproduce the score as notated by Bach in 1716, for that score did not have the dynamic mark for *piano* in bar 23 of aria no. 1, the word 'Solo' in bar 31 of the same aria, nor the array of instruments suggested for the continuo line – all of which are to be found in the modern edition.

Languet anima mea holds many features in common with Conti's secular cantatas that have orchestral accompaniment. They include the rhythmically defined cadence of the opening recitative, the extensive instrumental sections with well-defined thematic motifs, and the elaborate obbligato part for the violin in the second aria. That having been said, there is also much in this work that falls far short of the level of craftsmanship exhibited in the majority of Conti's other compositions.[10]

Another of Conti's compositions which no longer survives in the music archives of the Stift Herzogenburg, 'Kyrie et Gloria', can be studied from what is probably its original source. The monastery catalogues suggest, by way of the incipit and scoring accompanying the entry for this composition, that it is part of a larger work by Conti entitled *Missa Sancti Petri et Pauli*, the vocal and instrumental parts of which are extant in the archives of the Schottenstift on the Freyung in Vienna. On the front cover of the folder containing the parts for this concerted work in C major is written 'Kyrie, Gloria, Credo, sine Sctus et Agnus', indicating that the work is complete in the form in which it has been preserved. On the back cover (upper left-hand corner) is a date which Georg Reichert has interpreted to be 20 April 1721, but which could also be read as 20 April 1751, a date that might have some significance relative to posthumous performances of another mass by Conti discussed below.[11]

Both the Kyrie and Gloria of the *Missa Sancti Petri et Pauli* are scored for a *concertato* (SSATBB) and *ripieno* (SATB) group of singers, clarini 1 and 2 (in C), tympano, violini 1 and 2, 'viola obligata', trombone 1 (alto clef) and 2 (tenor clef), fagotto, violoncello, violone, and organo, with the last four instruments assigned to the continuo part in the tutti sections.[12] Differences between this scoring and that given in the Herzogenburg catologues for the 'Kyrie et Gloria' include a reduction in the number of singers ('6 voci conct.', but no *ripieno* voices), the removal of the word 'obligata' from the viola part, and the elimination of parts for the bassoon and violoncello, leaving only the 'organo e violone' to play the *basso continuo*.[13]

The title, *Missa Sancti Petri et Pauli*, and the presence of clarini and timpani in both versions of the mass indicate that the music was intended for a solemn

Example 12.1. *Missa Sancti Petri et Pauli*:
      (a) Kyrie I ; (b) Kyrie I; (c) Christe eleison; (d) Kyrie II

service of worship. According to imperial custom, clarini (also *trombe*) and timpani were expected to be included in the scoring of music designed for performance at services of worship or at other events in Vienna that were deemed to be of considerable importance. Confirmation that this custom obtained over a significant number of years can be found in the *Wienerisches Diarium*, which contains numerous reports of performances of sacred works with 'Trompeten und Paucken' (trumpets and timpani). Some were services of worship related to feast days in the regular liturgical calendar; others were commemorative events, such as a New Year's Day service or a service of thanksgiving for victory in a military campaign. Kilian Reinhardt, in his *Rubriche Generali per le Funzioni Ecclesiastiche Musicali* of 1727, assigned masses with clarini and timpani to a separate category, as did some of the eighteenth-century catalogues of sacred music in monastic and church archives. Although performances of this festive music could take place in a variety of venues, sacred works elevated to this status were heard most often in the court chapel, St Stephen's Cathedral, or in one of the old parish churches (Pfarrkirche) such as the Schottenkirche, where Johann Josef Fux served as organist for a number of years.

The *Missa Sancti Petri et Pauli* opens with a festive setting of 'Kyrie eleison' for the full ensemble in an *allegro* tempo (ex. 12.1a, b), followed by the 'Christe eleison' scored for two *concertato* bass voices with orchestral accompaniment (ex. 12.1c).[14] Instead of repeating the opening 'Kyrie' section in the manner of a *da capo*, Conti provides a different musical setting for the second statement of the text, giving special emphasis to an alternation of *concertato* and *ripieno* vocal parts (ex. 12.1d).

Example 12.2. *Missa Sancti Petri et Pauli*: 'Gloria in excelsis'
(opening bars of the soprano solo)

A substantial instrumental ritornello introduces the next section of the mass before the opening words 'Gloria in excelsis Deo' are sung by the soprano soloist(ex. 12.2). Here, as in the previous sections, the melodic material is conceived tonally in well-defined phrases and is enlivened rhythmically in a manner that places the style of composition in a sphere that is closer to the masses of the early Classic period than to those of the Baroque.

It was Conti's setting of the Credo, however, that attracted the attention of Georg Reichert for his history of musical settings of the mass in Vienna during the first half of the eighteenth century. He found two different elements worthy of investigation: the use of ostinato motifs in the accompaniment (ex. 12.3a, b) for a large portion of the Credo and the unrelenting repetition of the word 'Credo' set to a distinctive four-note motif in the opening section of the movement (ex. 12.3c, d).[15] Conti was not alone in introducing these elements into a setting of the Credo, as Reichert's survey of the repertoire makes clear. Rather, it was the manner in which Conti incorporated these elements into his composition that set his Credo apart from those of his colleagues.

Example 12.3. *Missa Sancti Petri et Pauli*: Credo,
(a) violin ostinato; (b) clarino variant of the violin ostinato

The multiple repetitions of the word 'Credo' places the *Missa Sancti Petri et Pauli* in the category of the so-called 'Credo-Mass', a type of setting that can be found in Viennese masses from the 1720s (if not earlier) until the latter part of the eighteenth century.[16] In this setting, the initial bars of the instrumental introduction present the four-note motif to which the word 'Credo' will be wed at bar 13. This motif is restated twice at the same pitch (bars 5-6 and 11-12), each time accompanied by the ostinato figure (ex. 12.3a) with which it was paired in bar 1, before the full chorus (which for this movement is reduced to SSATB) enters at bar 13. The 'Credo' motif is given to the soprano part and from that point forward is tossed from one vocal part to another, its longer note values allowing

Example 12.3 (continued). *Missa Sancti Petri et Pauli*: Credo,

(c) opening choral exposition of the word 'Credo';

(d) juxtaposition of the 'Credo' motif with other portions of the Credo text

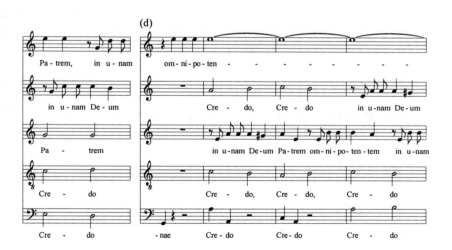

it to maintain a recognizable identity against the musical material to which the words 'in unum Deum Patrem omnipotentem factorum coeli et terra' have been set.

Conti's *Missa Sancti Pauli* in G minor has also been preserved at the Schottenstift. Although the date of composition is not known, information found on the folder containing the individual parts for the Kyrie and Gloria suggests that this particular setting of the mass continued to be a part of the standard repertoire at the Schottenkirche long after Conti's death. Seven dates which presumably reflect occasions when the mass was performed are on the back cover of the folder. The earliest date is 14 February 1746; the latest, 8 May 1857. This folder includes parts for SATB *concertato*, SATB *ripieno*, violins 1 and 2, viola, viola da gamba, fagotto, violoncello, violone, organo, and one for the *maestro di capella* ('MDC'). The performance parts for the remaining sections of the mass are contained in a second folder, but only those for the Credo are in the same hand that copied the parts for the Kyrie and Gloria.

The *tempo giusto* setting of the first 'Kyrie' involves the full complement of singers, with an occasional brief passage or two reserved for the four (SATB) soloists (ex. 12.4a). Both instruments and voices derive their thematic material from the initial motif (bar 1), subjecting it to various transformations within homophonic and imitative textures. The 'Christe eleison' section is sung by three of the four soloists (SAB) in an *andante* tempo, followed by a lively fugue for second 'Kyrie' in which the instruments are asked to play 'col parte'(ex. 12.4b).

Example 12.4. *Missa Sancti Pauli*: (a) Kyrie I; (b) fugue subject for Kyrie II.

The Gloria for the *Missa Sancti Pauli* is similar to the multi-sectional (cantata-type) settings that are typical of other Viennese masses by Conti's contemporaries. Of the two options available for the initial phrase of text – 'Gloria in excelsis Deo' or 'Et in terra pax' – Conti chose the intonation text. It is sung by a soprano soloist, her colouratura phrases punctuated by orchestral interjections of the repeated-note motif first presented in the instrumental introduction.[17] When the chorus enters (bar 13), it too takes up this same motif for its syllabic rendition of the same text. That an overall harmonic plan is operative here becomes evident when the soprano's opening phrase is reintroduced by the alto soloist (bar 22) in the key of the dominant instead of the tonic.

A dramatic change occurs at the start of the next section. The tempo shifts abruptly from *allegro* to *adagio* as basses and tenors use an arpeggiated seventh chord to introduce the second phrase, 'Et in terra pax'. Chromaticism, a favourite element in Conti's compositional palette, also makes its presence felt here. Of particular interest is the violoncello obbligato used throughout the 'Laudamus' section. It mimics the motivic figuration in the first violin part, sometimes doubling what the violins are playing and at other times playing in alternation with the tutti ensemble. With the 'propter magnam gloriam' section comes another change in style and tempo, as Conti creates a fugal exposition with subject and countersubject for the chorus, the instruments playing 'col parte'.

Each of the three brief verses of text beginning with the word 'Domine' features one or more vocal soloists. The first verse, 'Domine Deus, Rex coelestis, Deus Pater omnipotens' is sung by the alto and accompanied by violin solo, viola da gamba, and continuo ('senza bassi'). In order for the obbligato instruments to have sufficient opportunity to be featured, Conti includes a fairly substantial ritornello in which the violin's melody is restated a fifth below by the viola da gamba at the distance of one bar. When the voice enters, the obbligato parts assume independent roles in order to compliment the melismatic vocal line. No sooner does this portion of the text end than the next is introduced by the soprano, accompanied only by the continuo. A brief instrumental interlude separates her presentation of the 'Domine Filii, Jesu Christe' verse from the third one, which Conti has scored for soprano and bass (duet) and the full string ensemble. A lengthening of the text in these three verses is made possible by the extensive melismas placed on 'Pater', 'Patris', and 'Jesu'.

The first of the 'Qui tollis peccata mundi' phrases is set in an *adagio* tempo for the tutti ensemble; the second one, in an *andante* tempo, is for tenor soloist with orchestral accompaniment. The tempo increases yet again with a return to an *allegro* for the final two segments of the Gloria text. The first of these, 'Quoniam tu solus', is for soprano soloist and orchestra. The second, 'Cum Sancto Spiritu', begins as a fugue for chorus (ex. 12.5) with the orchestra playing 'col parte', but the contrapuntal texture quickly dissolves as both chorus and orchestra go their separate ways in presenting their respective thematic material (ex. 12.5). For the violins, this involves the reiteration of a motif similar to one previously used to accompany the soloist in the 'Quoniam' segment. By recalling this motif, Conti is able to unify the final section of the Gloria, bringing it to a resounding close with the customary repetitions of the word 'amen'.

Example 12.5. *Missa Sancti Pauli*: Gloria, 'Cum sancto spiritu' (fugue subject).

Tenor

Cum Sanc - tu   Spi - ri - tu   in glo -ri- a De -i   Pa -tris a   -   men

Conti's setting of the Credo for this mass is similar to the one he created for the *Missa Sancti Petri et Pauli*, for it once again has multiple repetitions of the initial word 'Credo'. Each of these acclamations of faith are sung by the full chorus (expanded to SATBB) to a hammer-stroke motif heard initially in bar 1 of the instrumental ritornello. Unlike the 'Credo' motif in the *Missa Sancti Petri et Pauli*, which had a distinctive melodic profile and could therefore be woven into the linear design of the musical material, this motif is strictly chordal and is used accordingly. Each interjection of the 'Credo' motif is self-contained and therefore does not cause a telescoping of the text. Syllabic choral passages alternate with those of a more melodic nature which are sung by either a solo voice or a single choral part (ex. 12.6). Here the orchestra does more than merely accompany; it acts as an equal partner, providing melodic interest with the restating and developing of thematic material from the introductory ritornello.

Also worthy of note, both here as well as in other sections, are the number of times Conti inserts whole bar rests between vocal phrases so that the orchestra's themes can be heard without any distraction. Given the clear-cut organization, tonally and melodically, of this entire opening section, which extends up to the 'Crucifixus' portion of the text, Conti's style of writing unmistakably foreshadows that found in masses of the classic period.

Conti offers a very moving setting of the 'Crucifixus etiam pro nobis' phrase in which the first word is sung by the bass voices of the chorus, followed by the

Example 12.6. *Missa Sancti Pauli*: Credo (opening bars for the SATB chorus).

whole ensemble giving forth the rest of the text in a descending sequential pattern of unresolved seventh chords. Upon repetition of the same segment of text, Conti has the sopranos instead of the basses sing the word 'Crucifixus'.

Certain passages of the Credo text – 'passus et sepultus est' and 'ascendit'– invite word-painting. Conti sometimes resorts to predictable solutions, such as an ascending arpeggio for 'ascendit'; at other times he offers a more creative approach, as in his setting of 'passus et sepultus est'. Repetition of certain words and phrases for the sake of emphasis is yet another technique Conti uses effectively, as exemplified by the 'non erit' and 'non sedet' passages.

For the 'Et resurrexit' section, Conti relies upon the tutti-solo *concertante* style to generate a lively setting. Of special interest is the inclusion of a substantial violoncello obbligato part, used primarily, but not exclusively, to accompany the soloists. Beginning with the words 'Et in Spiritum Sanctum', all four soloists take over the exposition of text. The soprano and alto are heard first, followed by the tenor and bass. As is customary in such passages, the soloists' phrases include melismas designed to highlight specific words while simultaneously providing the singer with a vehicle for a small measure of virtuoso display. The extensive melisma given to the bass on the word 'peccatorum', however, definitely seems designed to show off the skill of the performer rather than to convey any emotional content of the text. The fourteen-note range covered in this melisma suggests that the part may have been intended for Borosini who regularly performed opera and oratorio roles in both the tenor and bass range. Predictably, the setting of 'mortuorum' and the 'Et vitam' section adheres to well-established patterns of other concerted masses of the period, with the former consisting of an *adagio* section sung solely by the basses and the latter consisting of a fugue for the chorus supported by the instruments playing 'col parte'.

As mentioned earlier, the hand that copied the Sanctus and Agnus Dei parts that are extant at the Schottenstift differs from that which copied the first three movements. Some might argue that this indicates that these two movements represent a later addition to Conti's original composition. Perhaps they do, but to date no other manuscripts have been located in Vienna to prove the case one way or the other. Although the Sanctus and Agnus Dei movements are relatively short, they nevertheless conform to expected structural divisions for their settings. Throughout both movements, but especially in the Sanctus, the continuo line is extremely active, its melodic material somewhat reminiscent of the dotted rhythm patterns of the orchestral themes in Kyrie I. The *concertato* element is still operative here as soprano and alto soloists introduce the opening phrase of the Sanctus and the chorus concludes with the 'Osanna in excelsis', all in an *andante* tempo. For the 'Benedictus', the scoring is limited to two soloists (soprano, alto) and continuo. To further accentuate the contrast with the foregoing section, the metre shifts from duple to triple, and the tempo from *andante* to *largo*. A restatement of the 'Osanna' text by the chorus involves musical material that is similar to, but not identical with, that found in the first 'Osanna' section.

The last movement of the mass is divided into two sections. The first, in an *adagio* tempo and duple metre, observes the tripartite form of the 'Agnus Dei' text. Each of the three phrases is scored differently: the first is for chorus (SATB), 'col parte' instruments, and continuo; the second is for tenor and alto soloists with only continuo accompaniment; the third (only four bars long) is scored for the full ensemble. For the 'Dona nobis pacem', Conti changes the metre (3/8) but retains the *adagio* tempo. A considerable portion of this section is devoted to the reiteration of the word 'pacem' set to a simple motif fashioned from the three notes of the tonic chord. Especially effective is the manner in which this motif is incorporated into the orchestral parts for the final thirteen bars of the entire movement. Against the sustained notes of the tonic chord in both the continuo and vocal parts, each of the upper strings individually takes a turn in playing this same motif which by this point in the score has become so firmly associated with the word 'pacem' that there is no mistaking the meaning that Conti wishes the instruments to convey. In fact, unlike the final bar of the Sanctus where both vocal and orchestral parts end together, the final two bars of this movement are for the instruments alone as they repeat the 'pacem' motif once more before coming to rest on the tonic note G (ex. 12.7).[18]

Example 12.7. *Missa Sancti Pauli*: Agnus Dei, 'Dona nobis pacem' (concluding bars)

A catalogue of the music manuscript holdings of the Benediktiner-Abtei in Lambach indicates a *Missa in G minor* by Conti was once housed in this monastery's archives. That the mass was none other than the *Missa Sancti Pauli* is confirmed by the incipit supplied with the catalogue entry; the opening bars of the continuo are identical for both compositions. Unfortunately, the Lambach manuscript seems to have disappeared.[19] There is, however, at least one other manuscript of the *Missa Sancti Pauli*. It is in Dresden's Sächische Landesbibliothek, listed under the title *Missa mirabilium Dei*. This manuscript

(Mus. 2367-D-2) appears to be in the hand of Philipp Troyer, a Dresden court musician who also served as one of Jan Dismas Zelenka's principal copyists.

Zelenka (1679-1745), a double-bass player, was appointed in 1710 to the Dresden court where he served not only as a performer but also as a composer, receiving the title 'Kirchen-Compositeur' in 1735. He spent most of his career in Dresden, but there were occasions when he was absent for an extended period of time. For example, in November 1715 he and three other Dresden musicians were dispatched to Venice to serve the Crown Prince of Saxony, Friedrich August, whose duties required him to take up temporary residence in that Italian city. During this time abroad, Zelenka was expected not only to improve his skills as a composer, but also to acquire liturgical music by other composers that could bolster the repertoire at the Dresden court chapel. The need to augment the repertoire was prompted by a shift in the court's religious preference from Protestantism to Roman Catholicism that occurred in 1697. Whether or not Zelenka fulfilled his obligations in Venice has not been substantiated. What is known is that he sojourned for a period of time in Vienna, a fact which he himself notes in his 'Studienband', a volume of compositions collected in the imperial city and brought back to Dresden in 1719.[20]

Under the guidance of Johann David Heinichen, who was appointed Kapellmeister in 1717, many liturgical works originally composed for services of worship in Vienna made their way into the repertoire of Dresden's Hofkapelle.[21] Some were performed in their original versions; the majority of works, however, were transformed by Zelenka to suit the tastes of the Dresden court. These changes could be as minor as adding oboes to the violin parts or transposing the clarino parts from C to D (the preferred pitch for the clarino in Dresden); they could be as major as revising and expanding the original scores. Included among the masses listed in Zelenka's 1726 inventory of music in his private possession is Conti's *Missa mirabilium Dei*, which survives in a full score format.[22] A fragment of the same mass (D/*Dl*:Mus. 2367-D-3) also is extant. Zelenka's hand differs noticeably from his two major copyists, making it relatively easy to see at a glance any changes he might have superimposed upon manuscripts prepared for his use. In the case of the *Missa mirabilium Dei*, Zelenka altered the score, adding oboes to the tutti ensemble, producing a thoroughly figured continuo part, and expanding the choral texture of the 'Dona nobis pacem'.[23]

The Dresden archives once held two masses by Conti, *Missa con Trombe* (Mus. 2367-D-1) and *Missa S. Caroli Borromei*, but the latter is no longer extant. Surviving information indicates the *Missa S. Caroli Borromei* was in C major and scored for six voices (SSATBB), *trombe* 1 and 2, timpani, violins 1 and 2, viola, and continuo. On the basis of the title alone, it is probably safe to assume this work originated in Vienna before becoming a part of Zelenka's inventory.[24] The other mass, also in C major, is scored for SATB, clarini 1 and 2, timpani, violins 1 and 2, trombone 1 (alto clef) and 2 (tenor clef), tromba 1 and 2, violoncello or bassoon, and organ. Obviously both masses were intended for solemn occasions, but since neither mass is dated, it is impossible to tell when they were composed or first performed.[25]

The *Missa con Trombe* is part of the Heinichen collection. It was once thought that this mass was in the hand of Girolamo Personè (d. July 1728), a Dresden copyist, but that interpretation has recently been questioned.[26] The manuscript presents a clean copy with no additions by other hands and appears to have been hastily prepared, given the number of wrong notes and some crossed-out bars at the beginning of the 'Cum Sancto Spiritu'. The instrumentation is a bit puzzling, for it contains no part for a viola. A partial explanation of its omission may be provided by yet another mass in C major by Conti, the *Missa Assumptionis de B. M. Virginis* which is in Berlin. This version lacks parts for brass and timpani; the scoring is for SATB, violins 1 and 2, viola, organ and obbligato parts for oboe, bassoon, and violoncello. Unlike the Dresden manuscript, this one is extremely neat and may date from the latter part of the eighteenth century or later. Of particular interest is the viola part in the introductory section of Kyrie I. In six of the first thirteen bars, smaller-sized notes occur in addition to the regular notes. Presumably the copyist had before him a manuscript with an extra instrumental part which he attempted to incorporate into his score by providing an optional 'divisi' part for the viola.

A comparison of these six bars with the Dresden score indicates that the viola part of the Berlin score represents a composite of material assigned to the two trombone parts, with its secondary part (i.e. the smaller-sized notes) being closely related to the second trombone part. This comparison also makes clear that the Dresden score did not serve as a source for the Berlin copyist, for the latter produced a score that does not replicate notational errors of the former. The question that remains unanswered is this: did the primary source from which both the Dresden and Berlin scores were fashioned originally contain a part for the viola? An error in bar 3 of the Dresden's second violin part may provide a clue. In addition to the two notes (B♭, B♮) that constitute the material for that bar, two other extraneous notes also appear there. They occupy the same position on the staff as notes for the viola in bar 3 of the Berlin score (but lacking, of course, the alto clef). Since bars 1 and 2 of the first trombone part are identical to the viola part, it would appear that the Dresden copyist was copying from a part notated in the alto clef and that he mistakenly placed the notes for bar 3 on the wrong staff. What is even more curious is that instead of correcting the problem by placing those same 'viola' notes in the trombone part, the copyist simply has the trombone double the alto vocal part instead. A slightly different reading of the first violin part as well as the scoring in the final three bars of the introductory portion of the Kyrie should also be mentioned. The Berlin score concludes with all four instrumental parts, the viola doubling at the octave what is assigned to the continuo; the Dresden score uses only three, omitting the part in the alto clef (which in the Dresden score is assigned to the first trombone).

Although neither the Dresden nor Berlin score brings us any closer to knowing what Conti originally composed, that seems quite beside the point when judging this mass from the standpoint of its contribution to the eighteenth-century repertoire, for both versions are extremely effective. The overall structure of the *Missa con Trombe* differs somewhat from the other two masses in the Schottenstifte discussed above. Most noticeable is the fact that Conti does not set the intonation texts for either the Gloria or Credo movements, thereby removing any possibility of this work being considered a 'Credo-Mass'. He varies the tripartite form of the Kyrie by having an *adagio* section for the full choral and instrumental ensemble serve as an introduction to Kyrie I. Repetition of material also plays a role in his organization of this mass. For example, at the conclusion of the 'Christe eleison', scored for soprano and alto soloists and continuo, there follows an abbreviated repetition of Kyrie I, formed from the first fourteen and the last nine bars of the seventy-nine bar Kyrie I. A true *da capo* scheme obtains in the Sanctus, where the entire 'Osanna' section is repeated after the 'Benedictus'.

Obbligato parts for three different instruments – violin, violoncello or bassoon, and clarino – appear in the 'Domine' verses of the Gloria assigned to alto, bass, and soprano solo voices respectively. The 'Domine Deus, Rex celestis' features the violin, the 'Domine Fili' calls for either the violoncello or bassoon, and the 'Domine Deus, Agnus Dei' uses the clarino (ex. 12.8). In the Berlin version of this mass, the bassoon is chosen instead of the cello for the second verse and an oboe is substituted for the clarino in the third.[27] The use of the clarino in an obbligato capacity in masses designed for special liturgical functions in Vienna was a fairly common practice among Conti's contemporaries, provided the clarini were already included in the tutti ensemble. In this setting of the 'Domine Deus, Agnus Dei' text, Conti uses a fourteen-bar ritornello to introduce the clarino, its obbligato part designed to display the virtuoso capabilities of the instrument. The soprano's initial phrase is a restatement of the first five bars of the clarino theme, but before she can continue with bars 6-14 which would have provided her with an opportunity for a bravura display, Conti reintroduces the clarino for this same purpose. A concluding ritornello follows the completion of the textual portion in which both soprano and clarino participate.

Example 12.8. *Missa con Trombe*: Gloria, (a) 'Domine Fili'; (b) 'Domine Deus, Agnus Dei'

(a)

(b)

Both before and after these 'Domine' verses, Conti features the tenor soloist, first in the 'Laudamus te' section (tenor and continuo) and then in the 'Qui tollis' (tenor, violins unisoni, and continuo). It is to the latter section that Wolfgang Horn has drawn special attention in his description of the *Missa con Trombe*. He finds Conti's simplistic, yet emotionally dramatic, depiction of a person imploring God for forgiveness to be unparalleled in the masses of the Dresden repertoire which he has studied.[28] What Horn is referring to is Conti's setting of one word, 'suscipe'. There are two phrases of text in this section of the Gloria: 'Qui tollis peccata mundi, miserere nobis' and 'suscipe deprecationem nostram'. The first, set to a *siciliano* (6/8) rhythm, is treated as a self-contained unit, beginning and ending in G minor. For the first word of the subsequent phrase, the flow of the *siciliano* is abruptly interrupted for one bar wherein 'suscipe' is set to a single D minor chord in an *adagio* tempo. The *siciliano* rhythm and related thematic material is then resumed for the remainder of the phrase, with the whole section seemingly completed by a ten-bar instrumental ritornello that cadences in D minor. Then the unexpected happens. The mood abruptly changes yet again as Conti repeats the word 'suscipe', using the same one-bar *adagio* setting as before (except the chord is G minor, not D minor). A three-bar instrumental cadence similar to that found in the introduction to Kyrie I concludes the aria.

The clarini, *trombe*, and timpani in this mass are used primarily to articulate the structure. Their majestic sound, when added to the rest of the ensemble, undergirds the opening and/or closing bars of most of the choral sections of each movement, such as the final six bars of the 'Et vitam' chorus. An exception occurs in the Sanctus where the only brass required for the choral 'Sanctus' and 'Ossana' sections are the trombones. There are, of course, a few passages where the clarini do more than reinforce the tutti ensemble. One occurs in the final chorus of the Gloria, where the clarini–timpani group acts independently in presenting melodic material in dialogue with the other instrumental parts. Another can be found in the final two bars of the entire mass. Instead of having all parts conclude the lively dance-like setting of the 'Dona nobis pacem' simultaneously, the Dresden score continues the parts for the two clarini for an additional bar where, unaccompanied and in parallel thirds and sixths, they provide one last arpeggiated chord. Interestingly, since the Berlin score does not have parts for the clarini, all instrumental parts in that version of the mass conclude with the chorus as the final 'pacem' is sung.

Two sections of the Credo that deserve to be highlighted because of their exceptionally expressive renditions of the text are the 'Et incarnatus est' and 'Crucifixus'. Both are in an *adagio* tempo and triple (3/4) metre, with the first in C minor and the second in G minor. The 'Et incarnatus est' is scored for soprano and alto soloists, accompanied by violin 1 solo, trombone 1 solo, violoncello or bassoon, and continuo.[29] In the opening instrumental ritornello, the trombone and violin imitatively present a flowing melodic line that seventeen bars later is repeated in a similar fashion by the singers. Juxtaposed to this pastoral setting is the 'Crucifixus', scored for tenor and bass soloists, violins 1 and 2, and continuo.

A simple rhythmic motif established in bar 1 of the accompaniment is repeated unrelentingly throughout the entire section. Against this pulsating pattern of the so-called 'lamento-bass' in which the second of the three beats per bar is a rest, the vocal parts sustain melodic phrases that are six or more bars long.

All three masses have characteristics that continued to be present in Viennese masses composed as late as the 1780s. First and foremost is the degree of tonal unity Conti maintains in both individual movements and an entire work. The *Missa con Trombe* exemplies well this principle of organization, for not only does the mass begin and end in the tonic key of C major, but so also do each of the five movements. The pace of harmonic rhythm is fairly slow especially in the choral segments, with whole phrases anchored on a single chord. The presence of the timpani can account for a partial slowing of the harmonic pace, for the limitations of that instrument often caused Conti to anchor phrase upon phrase in a tonic-dominant sequence. Thematic unity within separate sections is achieved by the interdependence of instrumental and vocal material. More often than not, the instrumental ritornello preceding either a choral or a solo section introduces thematic material that is restated by the vocal parts. The prominent position given the trombone is also another element that persisted for many years in masses and other sacred works composed for performance in Vienna. Of greater significance, however, is the degree of independence given to the viola. Conti's writing for this instrument is often forward looking and that is why the absence of a viola part in the *Missa con Trombe* seemed unusual for his style of composition. Whether or not Conti's masses influenced succeeding generations of Viennese composers is a matter of conjecture, but the mere fact that all three extant masses seemed to be of interest long after they were composed suggests that they may have provided worthwhile models for others to imitate.

Some of Conti's other extant offerings in the sacred music category are his four-part *a cappella* settings of ten Latin hymns, *Hymni sacri per tutto l'anno*, and a *da capo* aria entitled *Pie Jesu* for tenor, violins 1 and 2, viola, and continuo.[30] This aria at one time belonged to Zelenka (D/*Dl*: Mus. 2190-E-1), although it was not listed among the items in his 'Inventarium'. It offers a glimpse into Conti's ability to weave multiple thematic ideas into a seamless polyphonic fabric, all the while creating a supportive framework for the expressive vocal part. Some unusual harmonic progressions, unprepared dissonances, and a fair amount of chromaticism are in evidence here which seem to result more from the contrapuntal texture than from any effort to convey a particular mood. The Italian text does not appear to be related to the Roman Catholic liturgy and therefore it is not possible to suggest an occasion when the music would have been performed.[31]

Conti's setting of the antiphon *Alma redemptoris mater* is also in the form of an aria. It is in 6/8 metre and scored for tenor, violins 1 and 2, viola, and organ (continuo). A manuscript copy of this work was originally held in a private collection but earlier in this century the aria was made available in a published ediiton of sacred solo motets from the eighteenth century.[32] This aria offers the singer a much more florid vocal part than the one in *Pie Jesu*, with some of the melismatic figuration recalling similar passages in the vocal parts of *Il trionfo della fama*. Although a single arpeggiated motif pervades the accompanying parts for the entire antiphon, there is nonetheless much more sharing of thematic ideas between the voice and instruments than in *Pie Jesu*. For example, the first violin's introductory phrase of the ritornello becomes the initial phrase sung by the voice. Conti style of writing allows the instruments and voice to weave together threads of melodic material to create a work that is dramatic, yet respectful of the sacredness of the text.

Liturgical compositions on a grander scale include the *Motetto per ogni festivita* in the archives of the Benediktiner-Abtei Lambach. It is composed for four voices (SATB), two violins, three clarini, timpani, organ, and violone.[33] Another is his Te Deum scored for a ten-voice double choir (SSATB), solo singers, and a double orchestra with each scored for two clarini, timpani, two violins, viola, and organ (continuo). No date is indicated on the sole surviving manuscript in Vienna's Gesellschaft der Musikfreunde, but given the substantial proportions of this Te Deum, it would seem reasonable to conclude that it was composed to commemorate an important event in the imperial city. From its triumphal homophonic statements to its introspective *a cappella* sections, from its antiphonal exchanges between choirs and instruments to its majestic multivoiced fugal writing, this is indeed a majestic work, a glorious tribute to God and to the emperor.[34]

Notes

1   When preparing material for *The Symphony 1720-1840*, Series B, vol. II: *Italians in Vienna* (New York, 1983), the author discovered that the overture to *Pallade trionfante* and the *Sinfonia à 4* were one and the same composition. The archival listing (A/*Wn*: Sm 3623 / M 543-79) in the Österreichische Nationalbibliothek has since been changed to reflect this information. There are twelve orchestral parts extant for the *Sinfonia*. They include violins

1 and 2, viola, and 'basso', 'violone', 'fagotto', and 'organo'. The dates of performance noted on the folder containing the parts are: 18 August 1748, 7 July 1749, 27 September 1750, 24 April 1753 (only the first movement performed), 7 January 1757, 24 December 1757.

2 According to Josef Schneider, the 'Luigi Cherubini' Conservatorio Statale di Musica Biblioteca in Florence, Italy has a setting of the *Salve Regina* by Conti. Unfortunately this information could not be verified by the author because the library is closed to scholars during the building's restoration. See Schneider, 'Francesco Conti als dramatischer Componist' (diss., University of Vienna, 1902), 90 (169, new pagination).

3 These works are discussed in chapter seven. The author wishes to thank Wolfgang Payrich for his help in collating information from the two Herzogenburg catalogues and for confirming that the manuscripts by Conti are no longer in the monastery archives.

4 This 1716 manuscript is in Berlin's Deutsche Staatsbibliothek and carries the shelfmark of Mus.Ms. 30098, the same shelfmark under which the Bach manuscript is given in the Breitkopf list of so-called 'house' manuscripts. See George B. Stauffer, ed., *J. S. Bach, the Breitkopfs, and Eighteenth-Century Music Trade* (Lincoln, NE, 1996), 118. Robert Eitner listed this score under Francesco Conti's name in his *Quellenlexicon*, III, 36, and indicated its location was in the Könglich Bibliothek (now known as the Deutsche Staatsbibliothek) with a shelfmark of Ms. 1516. He listed the parts (D/*B*: Mus.Ms. 4081), however, under Ignazio Conti's name.

5 Yoshitake Kobayashi's edition of Conti's *Offertorium de venerabili* ('Languet anima mea') with Bach's revised scoring has been published in the *Stuttgarter Bach-Ausgaben*, Serie C, Supplement (Stuttgart, 1982). In the preface (translated by Anthony Pringsheim) to the edition, Kobayashi states that although Bach's 'autograph manuscript carries the description of this work as *Motetta*, according to modern usage this composition is a solo cantata'. It should be pointed out, however, that the category *Offertorium de venerabili* under which Conti's work appears in the Herzogenburg catalogues includes other works which use 'Motetto' (not 'Motetta') for a title.

6 A similar conclusion was reached by Yoshitake Kobayashi. See the preface to her edition of *Languet anima mea*.

7 It is entirely possible that Conti originally scored the opening movement with *concertato* and *ripieno* violins, but that his division of the violins was not retained when the Herzogenburg parts were prepared. This is, in fact, what happened when the Herzogenburg parts were prepared from Conti's *Missa Sancti Petri et Pauli*, as is noted below.

8 Kobayashi provides information about the copyist of the continuo part and the pitch of the Leipzig organ in the preface to the edition cited above. The eleven instrumental parts which Bach and two of his copyists prepared are in the Staatsbibliothek Preussischer Kulturbesitz in Berlin with a shelfmark of Mus.Ms. 4081, the same source formerly attributed to Ignazio Conti by Eitner. See note 4 above.

9 See the preface to *Languet anima mea*.

10 See, for example, the excessive repetition of a motif in the violins in the first aria and the overall melodic and harmonic style of the final movement.

11 A comparison of the clefs drawn by the copyist for the Kyrie and Gloria sections are similar to those of other works by Conti dating from 1721 and 1722. See, in particular, *Alessandro in Sidone* and folios 1-40 of *Pallade trionfante*.

12   There are twenty-eight separate parts in the folder, with an extra part included for alto *ripieno* and tenor *ripieno* and two extra parts for both *violino primo* and *violino secondo*. These extra parts may indicate the actual number of persons required for the performance.

13   See *Catalogus Selectiorum Musicalium . . . Conscripti Anno 1751* (Stift Herzogenburg). There are actually two catalogues in the Herzogenburg archives; the contents (but not the numbering or foliation) of each are almost identical. Only *Catalogus II*, however, lists all of the works by Conti originally housed in these archives. See also Barry Brook and Richard Viano, eds, *Thematic Catalogues in Music: An Annotated Bibliography*, 2nd edn. (Stuyvesant, NY, 1997), 194-5.

14   It is quite common to find the 'Christe eleison' set as a separate movement in Viennese masses. What is not so common is to have it sung by two basses. Most composers preferred to write the movement for two upper voices (soprano and alto or two sopranos).

15   Georg Reichert, 'Zur Geschichte der Wiener Messenkomposition in der ersten Häfte des 18. Jahrhunderts' (diss., University of Vienna, 1935), 16-18, 32. His study continues to provide invaluable information.

16   Whether or not this constitutes the earliest extant example of a Viennese 'Credo-Mass', as suggested by Reichert in his study cited above, is contingent on verification of the date when Conti composed this mass.

17   In traditional settings of the mass, the words 'Gloria in excelsis Deo' were usually reserved for the celebrant to intone using one of the prescribed chants. This meant the choir would begin with the second phrase 'et in terra pax'. A similar situation obtains with the opening words of the Credo, which the celebrant also intoned. In the concerted mass settings, the intonation texts for both the Gloria and the Credo are treated according to each composer's preference. They can be left for the celebrant to intone or they can be set as part of the whole composition. Examples of both procedures can be seen in Conti's masses.

18   For a similar treatment of the concluding bars of the 'Dona nobis pacem', see Conti's *Missa con Trombe* discussed below.

19   This catalogue is also reproduced in vol. 2 of Gerda Lang, 'Zur Geschichte und Pflege der Musik in der Benediktiner-Abtei zu Lambach mit einem Katalog zu den Beständen des Musikarchivs', 3 vols. (diss., University of Salzburg, 1978).

20   It has been suggested that during his stay in Vienna he studied composition with Johann Josef Fux. See Brian Pritchard's introductory essay to a facsimile edition of Antonio Caldara's *Missa a 4 voci D-Dur* (Leipzig, 1987), xi. For a summary of the contents of Zelenka's 'Studienband', see Moritz Fürstenau, *Zur Geschichte der Musik und des Theaters am Hofe zu Dresden* (Dresden, 1862), II, 73-4.

21   For a discussion of Zelenka's role at the Dresden court chapel, see Brian Pritchard's introductory essay cited above and Wolfgang Horn, *Die Dresdner Hofkirchenmusik 1720-1745* (Kassel, 1987). Since most European churches and court chapels were supplied with a repertoire composed by persons in their employ, the decision taken by the Dresden Hofkirche to import musical compositions no doubt generated considerable discussion.

22   This mass is listed as 'Nr. 32; Inv. 85'. It remained part of Zelenka's private library until his death, at which time his entire collection of sacred music was donated to the Hofkapelle in Dresden.

23   Other portions of the mass also show Zelenka's hand, such as fol. 59 of the Agnus Dei.

24 This mass is listed as 'Nr. 25, Inv. 84'. Antonio Caldara also composed a mass with this same title; it is listed in Zelenka's 'Inventarium rerum musicarum ecclesia servientium' but has since disappeared from the Dresden archives. The feast-day for commemoration of St Charles Borromeo was 4 November, the name-day for Charles VI.

25 Brian Pritchard believes most of Antonio Caldara's sacred works listed in the Heinichen and Zelenka collections were brought from Vienna to Dresden in 1719 and thus this date becomes an important 'aid in establishing a chronology' for that composer's liturgical music which seldom is extant in datable sources. If a similar line of reasoning can be applied to Conti's Dresden manuscripts, then some of his extant liturgical works may also have been written prior to 1719. See p. xi of Pritchard's essay in the facsimile edition of Antonio Caldara's *Missa a 4 voci D-Dur* cited above.

26 The author is grateful to Urte Härtig of the Sächsische Landesbibliothek (Musikabteilung), Dresden for this information. See also Wolfgang, 'J. D. Zelenka und seine Dresdner Kopisten', *Zelenka-Studien* I (Kassel, 1993).

27 In late eighteenth- and early nineteenth-century editions of Viennese masses composed prior to 1750, an oboe was frequently substituted for the original obbligato clarino part.

28 Horn, *Die Dresdner Hofkirchenmusik*, 171.

29 The Berlin score substitutes a bassoon (notated an octave lower) for the trombone and then chooses the violoncello instead of the bassoon to compensate for that choice.

30 Both manuscripts (undated) are now located at the Sächsische Landesbibliothek in Dresden. The hymns (D/*Dl*: Mus. A 63a) that were set include: *Lucis creator optime*; *Ad regias agni*; *Salutis humana*; *Veni creator spiritus*; *Sum sol recidit*; *Tantum ergo sacramentum*; *Ut queant laxis*; *Ave maris stella*; *Exultat orbis gaudiis*; *Sanctorum miritis indita*; and *Sanctorum meritis inclita.*

31 The only other work by Conti with which this aria may bear a relationship is his *Aria de venerabili* for bass soloist, violins 1 and 2, viola, organ, and violone. It is listed in the catalogue of the Stift Herzogenburg but is no longer extant in that archive.

32 This antiphon is extant in two handwritten copies that originally belonged to Raphael Georg Kiesewetter. One copy presents the work in full score; the other provides a reduction for keyboard and voice. These copies are now preserved at the Österreichische Naitonalbibliothek. For the published version, see Camillo Schoenbaum, ed., *Geistliche Solomotetten des 18. Jahrhundert*, vol. 101/102 in *Denkmäler der Tonkunst in Österreich* (Graz, 1962).

33 The scoring for this motet is similar to that for Conti's *Motetto de SS. Angelis*. See the list of works formerly located at the Stift Herzogenburg cited above in table 12.1.

34 Another more modest Te Deum for four voices is said to be in the archives of the Stift Heiligenkreuz , but the author was unable to view that manuscript.

Conclusion

When Francesco Conti died in 1732, there was little notice taken in contemporary publications that this musician's talents would no longer enrich the cultural life of the Habsburg court. As important as his roles had been, both as performer and composer, there was never any question that other musicians would be available and eager to fill them. The emperor lost no time commissioning composers to provide entertainment for the Carnival season, which had been the coveted event for showcasing Conti's full-length operas. A theorbist was also secured to carry forth that aspect of the musical performances, for Ignazio was not skilled enough to assume his father's position. In short, life at the court continued under Charles VI with a certain sameness that had held sway during the whole of Conti's tenure in Vienna.

The number of works Conti is known to have composed is relatively small when compared with those by his colleagues, Fux and Caldara. Nevertheless, the significance of his musical contributions was considerable, a fact that did not go unnoticed by some contemporaries. Conti's style of composition is as varied as the works he composed. Since he was ever eager to explore the whole gamut of the compositional palette, it is difficult to discern specific elements that adequately characterize his personal manner of composing. What is consistent throughout his works is the element of experimentation. Even when he achieved what for him must have been a milestone in organizing thematic and harmonic materials to create a structure that would later be termed sonata forms, he did not codify that design and reuse it over and over again in subsequent overtures. Instead, he sought new dimensions for overture construction, not the least of them the introduction of a lyrical middle movement.

Conti's achievement as a contrapuntist has generated few comments from scholars, yet his writing of instrumental and choral fugues with single and double subjects is worthy of comparison with compositions by his colleagues. He may have gained his contrapuntal skills directly from Fux, either by studying with him or by hearing and performing Fux's music. Along with this skill came an even more important one, the ability to compose melodic material that was not only memorable but adaptable to thematic repetition and transformation.

For more than a century after his death, Conti's name was kept before the public with occasional performances of his masses, cantatas, and selected arias from his secular dramatic works. As live performances of these compositions dwindled, attention among those interested in discovering the foundations of late eighteenth-century Viennese opera shifted to an investigation of his full-length secular dramatic works. One who conducted research in this area was Gustav Schmidt and he came to the conclusion that no German composer before Mozart could excel Conti's mastery of the comic style.[1] Indeed, much has been made of Conti's skilful handling of comic episodes, but discussions of this aspect of his style tend to focus on only one work, his *Don Chisciotte in Sierra Morena*. Important as this opera is, it is not wholly representative of his comic style. To fully comprehend the scope of his involvement with comedy, one has to consider both the comic episodes that form an integral part of his serious operas and the intermezzos. His achievement in this sphere of composition is one that definitely deserves more recognition.

Conti was associated with some of the same personnel throughout his entire career at the court and no doubt he was as much influenced by their talents as they were by his. His close association with the librettist Pariati, the scene designers of the Galli-Bibiena family, and the musicians and choreographers engaged by the Kapellmeister obviously caused him to create his material to suit the abilities and tastes of these people. The closeness of such relationships is especially evident in the arias composed for Francesco Borosini which he designed specifically to display this singer's abilities.

Conti's music should be as appealing to modern audiences today as it was to the court audiences in the eighteenth century, yet few have had the opportunity to hear it. With the exception of the oratorio *David* and several cantatas which have been given performances in Austria within the past decade, Conti's music is known principally from the published editions of an antiphon, a cantata, nine of his *sinfonie*, the facsimile edition of *Don Chisciotte in Sierra Morena*, and the Bach transcription of the motet 'Languet anima mea'. Until more music is made available in print, there is no possibility of arranging performances of his music, even though the masses and Te Deum, and the theorbo-accompanied arias would make for excellent concert material. With the rediscovery of the music of several of his contemporaries (Caldara, Telemann, and Albinioni, among others), perhaps the time is ripe for a rediscovery of Conti's music. For those who make the effort to become acquainted with this composer's repertoire, they will be richly rewarded with music that is as beautiful as it is elegantly crafted.

Notes

1   Gustav Schmidt, 'Zur Geschichte, Dramaturgie und Statistik der frühdeutschen Oper (1627-1750)', *Zeitschrift für Musikwissenschaft* VI (1923-24): 524.

Appendix

The *Hofprotokollbuch: 1700-1709* (fols 201v-202v) contains the official recommendation and appointment of Francesco Conti as theorbist to serve Emperor Leopold I at the imperial court, together with a confirmation that his initial stipend would be 100 gülden (florins) per month:

Mensis Iulius Anno
1701
Den 12 Julÿ 1701

Relatio ad Casarem
Allergnädigster Kaÿsser

Conti   francesco Bartholomeo Conti musicus Supplicirt umb die besoldung vorgebend ewer Kaÿl: Maÿtt: hetten Ihn alss Theorbisten in diesnt aufgenohmen.

Bericht

Indem Supposito, dass ewer Kaÿl: Maÿtt: den Supplicanten alss Theorbisten mit Hundert güleden Monnathlicher besoldung, Von 1sten Aprilis disses Jahrs aufgenohmen, weiss der Capellmaister nichts anders darzur zu sagen, alss dass er disse besoldung wegen seiner sonderbahren Virtù und guetter wissenschafft meritire.

Res:^e Cas:^e

für den Conti und Siglin   Der Teorbist Conti solle mit Hund.^t gülden, und die Cunigunda Siglin ie zo verheÿrathete Sutterin mit Neünzig gülden Monnathlicher besoldung von ersten Merz disses Jahrs aufgenohmen werden.

Besheid

Ihre Kaÿl: Maÿtt: haben den Supplicanten mit 100 fl. Monnathlicher besoldung alss Theorbisten in dienst aufgenohmen, vorüber Ihme die ordinanz von anfang Aprilis ohne abbruch des ersten quarthals ausgefertigt werden solle.

Wienn den 23. Aug. 1701

Bibliography

Unpublished sources

Florence. Archivio di Stato. Collazione Mediceo, filza 5599; filza 5655; filza 5781.

Molitor, Simon von. 'Materialen zur Musikgeschichte'. Vienna: Österreichische Nationalbibliothek, Musiksammlung No. 19239, vol. A-D, fasc. xviii.

Vienna. Finanz- und Hofkammerarchiv. *Gedenkbücher (1707-1713)*.

———. *Hofrechnungsbücher (1702-1713)*.

———. *Kameral-Zahlamts-Bücher (1714-1723)*.

———. *Nieder-österreichische Herrschaftsakten*. W/Wien, 61/A.32, Nr. 164, 817-29.

———. *Österreichische Hoffinanz* rote Nr. 830 (4 January 1720); Nr. 860 (9 April 1723); Nr. 930 (22 January 1731).

———. [Bericht]. Report to Emperor Charles VI concerning payment of stipends to Francesco Bartolomeo Conti.

Vienna. Staatsarchiv. *Hofprotokollbücher (1700-1734)*.

Vienna. Stadtarchiv. *Kirchenbuch von St. Stephan:1704-1707*, XXXVI, 361.

———. 'Testament / Francesco Bartolomeo Conti', Nr. 6881/1732.

———. 'Testament / Maria Landini Conti', Nr. 21693/1722.

———. *Totenprotokoll (1700-1735)*.

Published sources

Adler, Guido. *Handbuch der Musikgeschichte*. Frankfurt am Main: Frankfurter Verlagsanstalt, 1924.

Albinoni, Tomaso. *Pimpinone*. Michael Talbot, ed. Madison, WI: A-R Editions, 1983.

Allacci, Lione. *Drammaturgia*. Venice, 1755.

[Anonymous, trans.] *A Comparison between the French and Italian Musick and Opera's. Translated from the French; With Some Remarks. To which is added A Critical Discourse upon Opera's in England, and a Means proposed for Their Improvement.* London: 1709. New edn with introduction by Charles Cudworth. London: Gregg International Publishers Ltd., 1968.

Arlt, Wulf. 'Zur Deutung der Barockoper: *Il trionfo dell'amicizia e dell'amore Wien, 1711*'. In *Musik und Geschichte: Leo Schrade zum sechzigsten Geburtstag.* Cologne: Arno Volk, 1963, 96-145.

Beare, Mary. *The German Popular Play 'Atis' and the Venetian Opera.* Cambridge: Cambridge University Press, 1938.

Bennett, Lawrence E. 'The Italian Cantata in Vienna, ca. 1700-1711'. Ph.D. diss., New York University, 1980.

Bennett, Lawrence E. 'The Italian Cantata in Vienna, 1700-1711: An Overview of Stylistic Traits'. In Brian W. Pritchard, ed. *Antonio Caldara: Essay on His Life and Times.* Aldershot: Scolar Press, 1987, 185-211.

Bertolotti, Antonino. *La musica in Mantova.* Milan: G. Ricordi, 1891.

Boetticher, Wolfgang. *Handschriftlichen Überlieferte Lauten- und Gitarrentabulaturen des 15. und 18. Jahrhunderts.* Munich: G. Henle, 1978.

Bologna. Civico Museo Bibliografico Musicale. Biblioteca. *Catalogo del Regio Conservatorio di Musica 'G. B. Martini'.* Florence, 1942.

Botstiber, Hugo. *Geschichte der Ouverture und der freien Orchesterformen.* Leipzig: Breitkopf & Härtel, 1913.

Boyd, Malcolm. 'Form and Style in Alessandro Scarlatti's Chamber Cantatas'. *The Music Review* (1964):17-26.

Breitkopf, Johann G. I. *Catalogo delle sinfonie, partitie, . . . in manuscritto nella officina musica di Giovanni Gottlob Breitkopf, in Lipsia.* Leipzig, 1762-65. Reprint, Barry Brook, ed. *Breitkopf Catalogo.* New York: Dover, 1966.

Brook, Barry, ed. *Breitkopf Catalogo delle sinfonie . . . che si trovano in manuscritto nella officina musica di Giovanno Gottlob Immanuel Breitkopf, in Lipsia. Parte I-VI (1762-1765).* New York: Dover, 1966.

——. *The Symphony 1720-1840.* Series B, vol. II: *Italians in Vienna.* New York: Garland, 1983.

Brook, Barry S. and Richard Viano. *Thematic Catalogues in Music.* 2nd edn. Stuyvesant, NY: Pendragon Press, 1997.

Buelow, George J. *The Late Baroque Era From the 1680s to 1740.* Englewood Cliffs, NJ: Prentice Hall, 1994

——. 'A Lesson in Operatic Performance by Madame Faustina Bordoni'. In *A Musical Offering: Essays for Martin Bernstein*. New York: Pendragon, 1977, 79-96.

Burney, Charles. *A General History of Music*. 4 vols. London, 1776-89.

Burney, Charles. *A General History of Music*. Frank Mercer, ed. 2 vols. New York: Dover Publications, [1957].

——. *Memoirs of the Life and Writings of the Abate Metastasio, Including Translations of His Principal Letters*. 3 vols. London, 1796; New York: Da Capo Reprint, 1971.

Burt, Nathaniel. 'Opera in Arcadia'. *The Musical Quarterly* (April 1955): 145-71.

Caldara, Antonio. *Missa a 4 voci D-Dur*. Brian W. Pritchard, ed. Leipzig: Zentral Antiquariat, 1987.

Campanini, Naborre. *Un precursore del Metastasio*. Florence: Sansoni, 1904.

Carreras y Bulbena, Joseph Rafel. *Carlos d'Austria y Elisabeth de Brunswich Wolfenbüttel a Barcelona y Girona*. Barcelona: L'Avenc, 1902.

Chischolm, Joseph. 'New Sources for the Libretto of Handel's *Joseph*'. In Stanley Sade and Anthony Hicks, eds. *Handel Tercentenary Collection*. Ann Arbor, MI: UMI Research Press, 1987, 182-208.

Clausen, Hans Dieter. *Händels Direktionspartituren*. Hamburg: Karl Dieter Wagner, 1972.

——. 'The Hamburg Collection'. In Terence Best, ed. *Handel Collections and Their History*. Oxford: Clarendon Press, 1993, 10-28.

Collins, Michael and Elise K. Kirk. *Opera & Vivaldi*. Austin: University of Texas Press, 1984.

Conti, Francesco Bartolomeo. *Don Chisciotte in Sierra Morena*. Howard Mayer Brown, ed. Vol. 69 in *Italian Opera 1640-1770*. New York: Garland, 1982.

——. *Languet anima mea*. Yoshitake Kobayaski, ed. *Stuttgarter Bach-Ausgaben*. Series C. Supplement: Durch Johann Sebastian Bach überlieferte Werke. Stuttgart: Hänssler, 1982.

Cummings, Graham. 'Handel's Compositional Methods in His London Operas of the 1730s, and the Unusual Case of *Poro, rè dell'Indie* (1731)'. *Music and Letters* 79 (August 1998): 341-67.

Dahms, Saibylle. '*Gregorio Lambranzi di Venetia* e il ballo d'azione a Vienna'. In Maria Teresa Muraro, ed. *L'opera italiana a Vienna prima di Metatasio*. Florence: Olschki, 1990, 251-69.

Dean, Winton. *Handel's Dramatic Oratorios and Masques*. London: Oxford University Press, 1959.

Dean, Winton and John Merrill Knapp. *Handel's Operas 1704-1726*. Oxford: Clarendon Press, 1987.

Deutsch, Otto Eric. *Handel: A Documentary Biography*. New York: W. W. Norton, 1979.

Dlabačz, Gottlieb Jacob. *Allgemein historisches Künstlerlexicon für Böhmen*. Prague, 1815.

Dooley, Brendan. 'Pietro Pariati a Venezia'. In Giovanna Gronda, ed. *La carriera di un librettista*. Bologna: Il Mulino, 1990, 15-44.

Edler, Arnfried and Friedrich W. Riedel, ed. *Johann Joseph Fux und seine Zeit: Kultur, Kunst, und Musik im Spätbarock*. Laaber: Laaber, 1996.

Einstein, Alfred. 'Italienische Musiker am Hofe der Neuburger Wittelsbacher'. *Studien für Musikwissenschaft* 9 (1907-1908): 402.

Eitner, Robert. *Biographisch-bibliographisches Quellenlexicon*. 10 vols. Leipzig: Breitkopf & Härtel, 1898-1904.

Fabbri, Mario. *Alessandro Scarlatti e il principe Ferdinando de' Medici*. Florence: L. S. Olschki, 1961.

Fehr, Max. *Apostolo Zeno (1668-1750) und seine Reform des Operntextes*. Zurich: Tschopp, 1912.

Fétis, François Joseph. *Biographie universelle des musiciens*. 8 vols. 2nd edn revised. Paris: 1875-78.

Flemming, Willi. *Das Schauspiel der Wanderbühne*. Leipzig: P. Reclam Jr, 1931.

Frischauer, Paul. *Prince Eugene*. New York: W. Morrow, 1934.

Fruchtman, Efrim, and Caroline Fruchtman. 'Instrumental Scoring in the Chamber Cantatas of Francesco Conti'. In James W. Pruett, ed. *Studies in Musicology: Essays in History, Style, and Bibliography of Music in Memory of Glen Hayden*. Westport, CT: Greenwood Press, 1976, 245-59.

Frylund, Daniel. 'Viola di Bardone'. *Svensk Tidskrift för Musikforskning* IV (1922): 129-52.

Fürstenau, Moritz. *Zur Geschichte der Musik und des Theaters am Hof zu Dresden*. 2 vols. Dresden: Rudolf Kuntze, 1862; reprint, 1971.

Gregor, Joseph. *Geschichte des Österreichischen Theaters*. Vienna: Donau, 1948.

Gronda, Giovanna. 'Il mestiere del librettista'. In Giovanna Gronda, ed. *La carriera di un librettista*. Bologna: Società Editrice Il Mulino, 1990, 113-65.

——. 'Per una ricognizione dei libretti di Pietro Pariati'. In Susi Davoli, ed. *Civiltà teatrale e Settecento emiliano*. Bologna: Società Editrice Il Mulino, 1986, 15-36.

Gronda, Giovanna, ed. *La carriera di un librettista: Pietro Pariati da Reggio Lombardia*. Bologna: Società Editrice Il Mulino, 1990.

Haas, Robert. *Gluck und Durazzo im Burgtheater*. Zurich: Amalthea, 1925.
———. 'Die Musik in der Wiener deutschen Stegreifkomödie'. *Studien zur Musikwissenschaft* 12 (1925): 3-64.
Hadamowsky, Franz. 'Barocktheater am Wiener Kaiserhof. Mit einem Spielplan (1625-1740)'. In *Jahrbuch der Gesellschaft für Wiener Theaterforschung 1951/52*. Vienna: A. Sexl, 1955, 7-117.
Händel-Handbuch. 4 vols. Leipzig and Kassel: Bärenreiter, 1978.
Hawkins, John. *A General History of the Science and Practice of Music*. London: Novello, Ewer, 1875.
Heyde, Herbert. 'Blasinstrumente und Bläer der Dresdener Hofkapelle in der Zeit des Fux-Schülers Johann Dismas Zelenka (1715-1745)'. *Alta musica* 9 (1987): 39-65.
Horn, Wolfgang. *Die Dresdner Hofkirchenmusik 1720-1745*. Kassel: Bärenreiter, 1987.
Kanduth, Erika. 'Silvio Stampiglia, poeta cesareo'. In Maria Teresa Muraro, ed. *L'opera italiana a Vienna prima di Metastasio*. Florence: Olschki, 1990, 43-63.
Kantner, Leopold. 'L'oratorio tra Venezia e Vienna: un confronto'. In Maria Teresa Muraro, ed. *L'opera italiana a Vienna prima di Metastasio*. Florence: Olschki, 1990, 207-16.
Kennard, Joseph. *The Italian Theater from the Close of the Seventeenth Century*. New York: Rudge, 1932.
Keÿssler, John George. *Travels through Germany, Bohemia, Hungary, Switzerland, Italy, and Lorrain*. 3rd edn. 4 vols. London: G. Keith, 1760.
Kier, Herfrid. *Raphael Georg Kiesewetter (1773-1850), Wegbereiter des musikalischen Historismus*. Regensburg: Gustav Bosse, 1968.
King, Richard G. 'The Fondo Schoelcher: History and Contents'. *MLA Notes* 53 (1997): 697-721.
———. 'New Light on Handel's Musical Library'. *Musical Quarterly* 81 (December 1997): 109-38.
Kirkendale, Ursula. *Antonio Caldara*. Graz-Köln: Herman Böhlaus, 1966.
Kirkendale, Warren. *Fugue and Fugato in Rococo and Classical Chamber Music*. 2nd edn Margaret Bent, trans. Durham: Duke University Press, 1979.
Köchel, Ludwig Ritter von. *Die Kaiserliche Hof-Musikkapelle in Wien von 1543 bis 1867*. Vienna: Beck, 1869. Reprint, Hildesheim: Georg Olms, 1976.
———. *Johann Josef Fux*. Vienna: A. Hölder, 1872. Reprint, Hildesheim: Georg Olms, 1974.
Kohlhase, Thomas von. 'Der Dresdener Hofkirchenkomponist Jan Dismas Zelenka'. In *Musik Des Ostens*. Kassel: Bärenreiter, 1992, 168-212.

Kunze, Stefan. 'Die Entstehung eines Buffo-Librettos: Don-Quijote-Bearbeitungen'. *Deutsches Jahrbuch der Musikwissenschaft* 12 (1968): 75-95.

Lang, Gerda. 'Zur Geschichte und Pflege der Musik in der Benediktiner-Abtei zu Lambach mit einem Katalog zu den Beständen des Musikarchivs'. 3 vols. Ph.D. diss., University of Salzburg, 1978.

LaRue, C. Steven. *Handel and His Singers: The Creation of the Royal Academy Operas, 1720-1728.* Oxford: Clarendon Press, 1995.

Lawson, Colin. 'The Chalumeau in the works of Fux'. In Harry White, ed. *Johann Joseph Fux and the Music of the Austro-Italian Baroque.* Aldershot: Scolar Press, 1992.

The London Stage 1660-1800. Parts 1-5 in 11 vols. Carbondale, IL: Southern Illinois University Press, 1960-68.

The London Stage 1660-1800, Index to. Ben Ross Schneider, ed. Carbondale, IL: Southern Illinois University Press, 1979.

Lustig, Renzo. 'Saggio bibliografico degli oratorii stampati a Firenze dal 1690 al 1725'. *Note d'archivio per la storia musicale* (1937).

MacIntyre, Bruce C. *The Viennese Concerted Mass of the Early Classic Period.* Ann Arbor, MI: UMI Research Press, 1986.

Marcello, Benedetto. *Estro poetico-armonico.* Venice, 1724-26. Reprint, London: Gregg Press, 1967.

Marpurg, Friedrich Wilhelm. *Historisch-kritische Beiträrge zur Aufnahme der Musik.* Vol. 1. Berlin: G. A. Lange, 1755.

Marx, Hans Joachim, and Dorothea Schröder. *Die Hamburger Gänsemarkt-Oper. Katalog der Textbücher (1678-1748).* Laaber: Laaber, 1995.

Mattheson, Johann. *Critica Musica.* Hamburg, 1722-25.

——. *Grundlage einer Ehren-Pforte.* Hamburg, 1740.

——. *Der musicalische Patriot.* Hamburg, 1728.

——. *Der vollkommene Capellmeister.* Hamburg: Christian Herold, 1739.

——. *Der vollkommene Capellmeister.* Ernest C. Harris, trans. Ann Arbor, MI: UMI Research Press, 1981.

McCredie, Andrew D. 'Nicola Matteis, the younger: Caldara's collaborator and ballet composer in the service of the Emperor Charles VI'. In Brian W. Pritchard, ed. *Antonio Caldara.* Aldershot: Scolar Press, 1987, 154-82.

Mengozzi, Stefano, ed. *La cantata barocca.* Vols 28/29. *Archivum musicum.* Florence: Studio per edizioni scelte, 1990-91.

Merbach, Paul Alfred. 'Das Repertoire der Hamburger Oper von 1718 bis 1750'. *Archiv für Musikwissenschaft* VI (1924): 354-72.

Metastasio, Pietro. *Tutte le opere di Pietro Metastasio.* 4 vols. Florence: Tipografia Borghi, 1832.

——. *The Works of Pietro Metastasio.* John Hoole, trans. Vol. I. London: T. Davies, 1767.

Milan. *Annali della fabbrica del Duomo.* Vol. II. Milan, 1885.

Milan. *La Cappella musicale del Suomo di Milano. Catalogo della musiche dell'Archivio.* Milan, 1957.

Milhous, Judith and Robert D. Hume, eds. *A Register of English Theatrical Documents 1660-1737.* 2 vols. Carbondale, IL: Southern Illinois University Press, 1991.

Molitor, Simon von. 'Ehrenrettung des weilands kaiserlichen Hofkompositeurs in Wien Francesco Conti gegen eine in Matthesons *Vollkommene Kapellmeister* überlieferte ehrenruhrige Anedote'. *Allgemeine Musikalische Zeitung* (7 March 1838): 153-8.

Müller, Erich H. 'Zum Repertoir der Hamburger Oper von 1718 bis 1750'. *Archiv für Musikwissenschaft* 7 (1925): 329-33.

Muraro, Maria Teresa. *L'opera italiana a Vienna prima di Metastasio.* Florence: L. S. Olschki, 1990.

Nettl, Paul. 'An English Musician at the Court of Charles VI in Vienna'. *The Musical Quarterly* 28 (July 1942): 323ff.

Neville, Don J., ed. *Studies in Music: Opera I.* 4 vols. London (Canada): University of Western Ontario, 1979. S.v. 'Conti', no. 50.

The New Grove Dictionary of Music and Musicians. Stanley Sadie, ed. 20 vols. London: Macmillan, 1980.

The New Grove Dictionary of Musical Instruments. Stanley Sadie, ed. 3 vols. London: Macmillan, 1984.

The New Grove Dictionary of Opera. Stanley Sadie, ed. 4 vols. London: Macmillan, 1992.

North, Nigel. *Continuo Playing on the Lute, Archlute, and Theorbo.* Bloomington, ID: Indiana University Press, 1987.

The Norton / Grove Dictionary of Women Composers. Julie Anne Sadie and Rhian Samuel, eds. New York: W. W. Norton, 1994.

The Oxford Dictionary of the Christian Church. Oxford and New York: Oxford University Press, 1997.

Pastor, Ludwig, Freiherr von. *The History of the Popes.* Vol. 33. London: Kegan Paul, 1941.

Paumgartner, Bernhard. S.v. 'Conti'. In *Die Musik in der Geschichte und Gegenwart*. Friedrich Blume, ed. Vol. II, Kassel: Bärenreiter, 1952.

Petzoldt, Richard. *Telemann*. Horace Fitzpatrick, trans. New York: Oxford University Press, 1973.

Pichta, Alois. 'Johann Sebastian Bach und Johann Adam Graf von Questenberg'. *Bach-Jahrbuch* (1981): 23-8.

Pöllnitz, Karl Ludwig. *The Memoirs of Charles Lewis*. Stephen Whatley, trans. Vol. I, Dublin: S. Powell, 1737-38.

Pritchard, Brian W., ed. *Antonio Caldara: Essays on his life and times*. Aldershot: Scolar Press, 1987.

Quadrio, Francesco Saverio. *Della storia e della ragione d'ogni poesia*. 7 vols. Bologna: F. Pisarri, 1739-52.

Raccolta copiosa d'intermedj, parte da rappresentarsi col canto, alcuni senza musica, con altri in fine in lingua milanese. 2 vols. Amsterdam [Milan], 1723.

Raguenet, François. (See Anonymous, trans.)

Reich, Wolfgang. 'J. D. Zelenka und seine Dresdner Kopisten'. *Zelenka-Studien*. Vol. I. Kassel: Bärenreiter, 1993.

Reichert, Georg Nikolaus. 'Zur Geschichte der Wiener Messenkomposition in der esten Hälfte des 18. Jahrhunderts'. Ph.D. diss., University of Vienna, 1935.

Riedel, Friedrich W. 'Die Kaiserkrönung Karls VI. (1711) als musik-geschichtliches Ereignis'. In *Mainzer Zeitschrift, Mittelrheinisches Jahrbuch für Archäologie, Kunst und Geschichte. Jahrgang 1960/61*. Mainz: 1966, 34-40.

———. *Kirchenmusik am Hofe Karls VI (1711-1740)*. Munich-Salzburg: Emil Katzbichler, 1977.

———. 'Die Musik bei der Erbhuldigungsreise Kaiser Karl VI nach Innerösterreich 1728'. In Christopher-Hellmut Mahling, ed., *Florilegicum Musicologicum – Hellmut Federhofer zum 75 Geburtstag*. Tutzing: H. Schneider, 1988, 275-86.

Rosen, Charles. *Sonata Forms*. New York: W. W. Norton, 1980.

Ryom, Peter. *Verzeichnis der Werke Antonio Vivaldi*. Leipzig: VEB, 1974.

Sartori, Claudio. *I libretti italiani a stampa dalle origini al 1800*. 6 vols. Cuneo: Bertola & Locatelli, 1990, 1994.

Scheibe, Johann Adolph. *Critischer Musikus*. Leipzig: B. C. Breitkopf, 1745; reprint, Hildesheim: G. Olms and Wiesbaden: Breitkopf & Härtel, 1970.

Schmidl, Carlo, ed. *Dizionario universale dei musicisti*. Milan: Sonzogno, 1938.

Schmidt, Gustav Friedrich. *Georg Caspar Schürmann*. 2 vols. Regensburg: 1933.

———. *Neue Beiträge zur Geschichte der Musik und des Theaters am Herzoglichen Hofe zu Braunschweig-Wolfenbüttel.* Munich: W. Berntheisel, 1929.

———. 'Zur Geschichte, Dramaturgie und Statistik der frühdeutschen Oper (1627-1750)', *Zeitschrift für Musikwissenschaft* V (1922-23): 582-97, 642-65; VI (1923-24): 129-57, 496-530.

Schneider, Josef. 'Francesco Conti als dramatischer Componist'. Ph.D. diss., University of Vienna, 1902.

Schnitzler, Rudolph. 'The Viennese Oratorio and the Work of L. O. Burnacini'. In Maria Teresa Muraro, ed. *L'opera italiana a Vienna prima di Metatasio.* Florence: Olschki, 1990, 217-37.

Schnürl, Karl, ed. *Wiener Lautenmusik im 18, Jahrhundert.* Vol. 84. *Denkmäler der Tonkunst in Österreich.* Graz: Akademische Druck- und Verlagsanstalt, 1966.

Schoelcher, Victor. *The Life of Handel.* James Lowe, trans. London: R. Cocks, 1857; reprint, 1979.

Schoenbaum, Camillo, ed. *Geistliche Solomotetten des 18. Jahrhundert.* Vols. 101/102. *Denkmäler der Tonkunst in Österreich.* Graz: Akademische Druck- und Verlagsanstalt, 1962.

Schulze, Walter. *Die Quellen der Hamburger Oper (1678-1738).* In Gustav Wahl, ed. *Mitleilungen aus der Bibliothek der Hansestadt Hamburg.* Vol. 4. Hamburg: Oldenburg, 1938.

Sehnal, Jiří. 'Das mährische Musikleben in der Zeit Antonio Caldaras'. In Brian W. Pritchard, ed. *Antonio Caldara.* Aldershot: Scolar Press, 1987.

Seifert, Herbert. 'Pietro Pariati poeta cesareo'. In Giovanna Gronda, ed. *La carriera di un librettista.* Bologna: Il Mulino, 1990, 45-72.

Selfridge-Field, Eleanor. 'The Viennese Court Orchestra.' In Brian W. Pritchard, ed. *Antonio Caldara.* Aldershot: Scolar Press, 1987.

Smith, Ruth. *Handel's Oratorios And Eighteenth-Century Thought.* Cambridge: Cambridge University Press, 1995.

Smith, William C. *A Bibliography of the Musical Works Published by John Walsh During the Years 1695-1720.* London: Bibliographical Society, 1948.

———. *A Catalogue of Vocal and Instrumental Musick Published by John Walsh and His Successors 1706-90.* London: First Edition Bookshop, 1953.

———. *Handel: A Descriptive Catalogue of the Early Editions.* London: Cassell, 1960.

Smith, William C. and Charles Humphries. *A Bibliography of Musical Works Published by John Walsh 1695-1766*. 2 vols. London: Bibliographical Society, 1968.

Smither, Howard E. *A History of the Oratorio*. Vol. 1: *The Oratorio in the Baroque Era*: *Italy, Vienna, Paris*. Chapel Hill, NC: University of North Carolina Press, 1977.

Smithers, Don L. *The Music and History of the Baroque Trumpet before 1721*. Syracuse, NY: Syracuse University Press, 1973.

Sonneck, Oscar G. T., ed. *Catalogue of Opera Librettos Printed before 1800*. 2 vols. Washington, DC: Government Printing Office, 1914.

Stauffer, George B., ed. *J. S. Bach, the Breitkopfs, and Eighteenth-Century Music Trade*. Vol. 2 of *Bach Perspectives*. Lincoln, NE: University of Nebraska Press, 1996.

Strohm, Reinhard. 'Pietro Pariati librettista comico'. In Giovanna Gronda, ed. *La carriera di un librettista*. Bologna: Il Mulino, 1990, 73-112.

——. 'Scarlattiana at Yale'. In Nino Pirrotta and Agostino Ziino, eds, *Händel e gli Scarlatti a Roma. Atti del convegno internazionale di studi (1985)*. Florence: Leo S. Olschki, 1987, 113-52.

Talbot, Michael. 'Albinoni's *Pimpinone* and the Comic Intermezzo'. In Iain Fenlon and Tim Carter, eds, *Con che soavità: Studies in Italian Opera, Song, and Dance, 1580-1740*. Oxford: Clarendon Press, 1995, 229-48.

——. *Tomaso Albinoni, The Venetian Composer and His World*. Oxford: Clarendon Press, 1990.

Telemann, Georg Philipp. *Pimpinone*. Th[eodore] W. Werner, ed. Mainz: B. Schott's Söhne, 1936.

Troy, Charles. *The Comic Intermezzo*. Ann Arbor, MI: UMI Research Press, 1979.

Tyler, James, and Paul Sparks. *The Early Mandolin*. Los Angeles: University of Southern California, 1989.

Van der Meer, John Henry. *Johann Josef Fux als Opernkomponist*. 3 vols. Bilthoven: Creyghton, 1961.

Vehse, E. *Memoirs of the Court: Aristocracy and Diplomacy of Austria*. Franz Demmler, trans. 2 vols. London: Longman, Brown, Green, 1856.

Vlaardingerbrock, K. 'Faustina Bordoni Applauds John Alensoon'. *Music and Letters* (1991): 536-51.

La Voce. (Fall, 1997):2 [newsletter of Glaire Givens Violins, Inc., Vermillion, SD.]

Ward, Glennys. 'Caldara, Borosini and the One Hundred Cantici, or some Viennese canons abroad'. In Brian Pritchard, ed., *Antonio Caldara*. London: Scolar Press, 1987, 302-42.

Weilen, Alexander von. *Geschichte des Wiener Theaterwesens von den ältesten Zeiten bis zu den Anfängen der Hof-Theater*. Vienna: Gesellschaft für vervielfaltigende Kunst, 1899.

——. *Zur Wiener Theatergeschichte*. Vienna: A. Hölder, 1901.

Wellesz, Egon. *Essays on Opera*. Patricia Kean, trans. New York: Dennis Dobson, 1950.

——. *Fux*. London and New York: Oxford University Press, 1965.

White, Harry. 'The Sepolcro Oratorios of Fux: an Assessment'. In Harry White, ed. *Johann Joseph Fux and the Music of the Austro-Italian Baroque*. Aldershot: Scolar Press, 1992.

White, Harry, ed. *Johann Josef Fux and the Music of the Austro-Italian Baroque*. Aldershot: Scolar Press, 1992.

Wienerisches Diarium. Vienna: Joh. Peter v. Ghelen, 1703-1740.

Williams, Hermine Weigel. 'Francesco Bartolomeo Conti: His Life and Operas'. Ph.D. diss., Columbia University, 1964.

——. 'Francesco Bartolomeo Conti: Nine Sinfonie'. In Barry Brook, ed. *The Symphony 1720-1840*. Series B, vol. II: *Italians in Vienna*. New York: Garland, 1983, xiii-xxxvi, 1-96.

——. 'The Sacred Music of Francesco Bartolomeo Conti: Its Cultural and Religious Significance'. In Edmund Strainchamps and Maria Rika Maniates, eds, *Music and Civilization: Essays in Honor of Paul Henry Lang*. New York: W. W. Norton, 1984, 326-34.

Wolff, Hellmuth Christian. *Die Barockoper in Hamburg 1678-1738.* 2 vols. Wolfenbüttel: Moseler, 1957.

——.'The Neapolitan Tradition in Opera'. *Report of the Eighth Congress of the International Musicological Society: New York 1961*. Kassel, 1962.

——. *'Pimpinone* von Albinoni und Telemann – ein Vergleich'. *Hamburger Jahrbuch für Musikwissenschaft* 5 (1981): 29-36.

Zeno, Apostolo. *Lettere di Apostolo Zeno*. 6 vols. 2nd edn. Venice: Francesco Sansoni, 1785.

——. *Poesie drammatiche*. Gasparo Gozzi, ed. 10 vols. Venice, 1744.

——. *Poesie sacre drammatiche di Apostolo Zeno, Istorico e Poeta Cesareo, cantata nella imperial cappella di Vienna*. Venice: Cristoforo Zane, 1735.

Zuth. Josef. 'Die Mandolinhandschriftern in der Bibliothek der Gesellschaft der Musikfreunde in Wien'. *Zeitschrift für Musikwissenschaft* 14 (1931): 89-99.

Index of works by Conti

General index